False Confessions

The True Story of Doug Williams and
His Crusade Against the Polygraph Industry

JACK STRAW

with Doug Williams

Table of Contents

CHAPTER THIRTY-THREE

CHAPTER THIRTY-FOUR

AUTHOR'S NOTE

On May 29, 1969, Doug Williams walked out of the White House. He wasn't leaving after a guided tour or a rare chance to complain to a top official or anything of such a mundane nature. No. Doug Williams was leaving the White House after three years of successful service in the Situation Room, the hub of world activities. As a member of the United States Air Force, Doug had attained the highest security clearance possible. His job had been to gather and to read intensely classified teletypes, documents, and information coming into the Situation Room and to, personally, deliver these classified items directly into the hands of the President of the United States.

As you might guess, the selection process for such a position as Doug held is painstakingly long and detailed. It requires that a candidate pass the independent investigations of several agencies - agencies such as the CIA, the DOD, the FBI, the Secret Service, the State Department. The list goes on and on, and any one of these agencies can blackball a candidate at any time during the background investigation, removing him from consideration. A candidate doesn't apply for a position like this; he is sought out and approached. His entire life is scrutinized to an extent that most individuals would not care to have done. Ultimately, from the many hundreds of elite candidates that were investigated and interviewed at that time, Doug Williams was the man selected.

While performing his highly sensitive duties in the Situation Room, Doug became associated with - and, even, friendly with - a number of important people with whom he interacted on a daily basis. These people had names like Alexander Haig and Henry Kissinger. When Doug eventually decided to leave his duties in 1969, many of these people attended his going-away party and signed a card wishing him good luck in the future. Because of his valuable services and impeccable record, a number of people - primarily Henry Kissinger - repeatedly asked Doug to stay on in his position in the White House. Even after he left the Situation Room staff, he was asked to return on numerous occasions. But, Doug had tired of the fishbowl life of Washington and wanted to pursue a career in law enforcement. Ironically, the "fishbowl" he longed to escape would follow him throughout the rest of his life in ways he could never have imagined at the time.

I met Doug - my friend and co-author of this book - while we were both serving sentences in the Federal Prison Camp at Florence, Colorado. I had already served seven-plus years by the time we became acquainted in 2015, and during that time, I had met several hundred inmates. In talking with them, I had long determined that, without exception, they all had one thing in common: they were all guilty. Perhaps some of them were not guilty of everything they had been charged with, but they were all guilty of something. I came to this conclusion based upon the fact that, beyond all other things that I may be, I am a realist. Things have to be proven to me. I do not believe in UFO's. I have never experienced an apparition - floating, or otherwise. Nessy does not swim in the Loch. There was no one on the grassy knoll. Big Foot stories make me chuckle, and absolutely every inmate I have ever met was guilty of a crime. That is, until I met Doug Williams. Doug is what I call a "freak" - an anomaly - an innocent person in prison. How the hell does that happen? How does a man with an impeccable record and a security clearance beyond most people in the government end up in prison? And, how did this happen to an innocent man?

I'm not a conspiracy theorist...okay, well, I wasn't. Actually, I'm still not a conspiracy believer, except in Doug Williams' complicated case. Once I began researching what had happened to him, it almost made me wonder whether I shouldn't consider dragging a net through the Scottish Loch and take one more look at the Zapruder film. The fact is that the case against Doug Williams is a travesty. He was put on trial for three counts of witness tampering and two counts of mail fraud - none of which was true. Although his attorney counseled him to make a deal, none of these counts represented the real reason that some people in authority wanted Doug in prison. Ultimately, he was behind bars because he had challenged a long-abused procedure that has been utilized for almost one hundred years in this country to manipulate, misrepresent, and malign millions of people. Doug doesn't whine about what happened to him, and that's not what this book is about. But, I will tell you before I move on: read the transcript of the testimony that was used to convict him, and then explain to me or to anyone else of reasonable intelligence how he was convicted of anything. I dare you.

This is the story of the world of "Lie Detection" - the world of the Polygraph. It's a complicated and bizarre story with one, very simple and obvious outcome. The polygraph does not work. It never has. However, instead of admitting that there are issues with the process and ceasing to use the polygraph machine, people in authority have continued to abuse millions of people with an instrument and procedure that has kept those same people from getting jobs, removed them from their careers, or convicted them of crimes they did not commit. The results from polygraph testing are not allowed in a court of law in this country, with certain extraordinary exceptions, because the results can be manipulated and are inconclusive. However, the polygraph is still freely used in order to scare people into giving false confessions with the hope that the legal system will "go easy" on them.

After leaving his position at the White House, Doug moved to Oklahoma City where he became a police officer; subsequently, a detective sergeant; and ultimately, a polygraph operator. He gave, literally, thousands of polygraph examinations, and became an expert interrogator. He was at the pinnacle of the polygraph world, top of the heap, a big dog. And, then, his conscience came to the forefront and he had to come to grips with the truth. Over time, Doug had discovered what a horribly corrupt system the lie detection process had become. Daily, he could see innocent peoples' lives being trashed, while liars walked away unscathed. But, it wasn't the polygraph equipment that was to blame. As the old saying goes, "Guns don't kill people; people kill people." Well, the polygraph machine, itself, doesn't keep you from getting a job. It doesn't call you a liar all by itself. It is, in reality, the polygraph operator who does that. He is the one who reads the results and decides if you are truthful, or not. It is he who will decide the outcome of your test. The polygraph operator is a god, and there's no use in questioning his opinion, because there is no appealing a god's decision. Truth has very little to do with anything. Doug eventually realized the real truth:

The Lie Detector, itself, was all a lie - because Doug Williams knew just how to beat that machine every single time. And, if he could, so could anyone else.

Following the call of his conscience, Doug Williams embarked upon a crusade spanning forty years of mostly solitary work in order to right a terrible, misery-producing wrong. Yet, he does not claim to be without blame, himself. Doug openly admits that, for a time during his years as a polygraph operator, he was a willing participant. He openly states that he was guilty of what he calls "crimes against humanity." That's a hell of an admission...a hell of a burden, and one fiery, driving force in his life.

The main issue involved here is Money. Lots of it. Polygraph operators make a lot of money, while Mr. and Mrs. Taxpayer foot the bill. And, what is their contention? They contend that, were it not for polygraph testing, national security would be at risk because vast numbers of spies could freely roam the streets of America without detection. Really? Let's name one - just one terrorist, spy, or anti-American insurrectionist that has been deterred by this system. There aren't any. However, there are many who were tested and passed easily while actively betraying their country. Aldridge Ames, CIA agent actively working as a spy, passed. Ana Belen Montes, spy for sixteen years while working for U.S. Military Intelligence, passed. Nicholas Sirgando, Cuban double agent against the CIA for ten years, passed. Larry Chin, intelligence analyst for twenty years who spied for Beijing until he was arrested in 1985, passed. Edward Snowden, NSA employee planning to make top secret information public, passed. At the same time, some young lady in North Carolina, or father in Texas, or mother in Iowa was being denied employment with some government agency because the polygraph operator decided that was the patriotic thing to do - and, all to keep from losing his own job and to keep the money he made from doing that job.

As Doug Williams continued his crusade fighting against this heartlessly corrupt system, he was described by the polygraph fraternity as a renegade and a crazy man. Rather than to refute Doug's message and offer proof in support of their faulty lie detection system, their reaction was to "shoot the messenger." Instead of giving solid and substantial data, they called Doug unpatriotic. Polygraph proponents ignored Doug's countermeasures - the tricks he can teach anyone in order to pass a polygraph test. Quite simply, these tricks consist of shallow breathing on some questions, and tightening the anal sphincter muscle on others. Yep, that's it. They denied the fact that foreign and home-grown spies could utilize such simple tactics as slowing down your breathing or tightening up your ass to beat their machine. Yet, as I sit here in this highly technical world where we are concerned about teenage computer geeks hacking into national security defense systems and defeating firewalls to steal your credit card and social security numbers...a world where computer hackers are constantly engaged in a cyber war with American companies...I have to wonder how it is that the polygraph industry would have us believe that a foreign intelligence agency would not be able to teach their operatives to follow Doug's simple physical techniques to pass a test allowing them to infiltrate our country.

Inside the covers of this book, you will read the proof. Evidence will be given; experts will be quoted; tests will be conducted. Not one person or test will be able to offer any evidence - scientific, or even, imaginary - as to the viability of the polygraph. And, we promise that the story will not be boring. Doug Williams takes us on an incredible journey as he lays out the past, present, and future of the polygraph industry. His journey is fascinating. It is a story of threats and intrigue, of coercion and sacrifice. It's the story of one man's lone fight against not only an institution of gigantic proportion, but against his own conscience and fear. As his strength and determination grow, so do the numbers of his supporters and believers. I am one of them.

INTRODUCTION

In 1982, the "Green River Killer" defied capture as his murderous rampage left numerous victims in his wake. The small community of King County near Seattle, Washington demanded capture of the predator in their midst, and the police responded by forming a special task force to ensure his capture, asking for assistance from anyone in the area who had possible information.

Melvin Wayne Foster, a 43-year-old cab driver, responded to the police request with suspicions he had about some of his fellow cab drivers. But, it was Mr. Foster, himself, who caught the attention of the police and seemed to fit their 'profile'. Their evidence? Without a doubt, the most damning evidence against him came from the results of a lie detector test administered by police to Foster. He failed. Bingo. They had their man.

Although he denied any involvement in the murders, Foster became the prime suspect in the Green River case. Twice, the police searched his home. They collected hair and blood samples from him, but no physical evidence was found. They had an undercover officer purchase a car Foster had advertised for sale. They dissected it and sent it off for testing, but this quest for evidence, too, provided nothing. The police placed Foster under twenty-four-hour surveillance for several months. Nothing. But, the polygraph test results upon which they relied so heavily provided everything - absolutely everything - *for Mr. Gary Ridgeway...*

...Ample time, unfettered opportunity, and unobstructed movement as he continued his horrific labors as the Green River Killer. Ridgeway would kill at least nineteen women and young girls during the specific time that police officials intently focused their attention upon an innocent man, Melvin Foster. And, why? Because a simple polygraph test had told them that he had lied.

Finally, in 1985, forensic science completely ruled out Melvin Foster as a suspect or person of interest with any connection to the Green River killings. Gary Ridgeway was ultimately convicted not only of those crimes, but of having committed forty-nine murders. Sadly, the delay in his capture and his subsequent conviction offered no consolation for the victims. Their lives were over.

This incredible incident is not so much about Melvin Foster failing the polygraph as it is about the failure of the polygraph, itself. A fallible machine failed nineteen young women in Green River...all the way to their graves.

CHAPTER ONE

A Time for Confession

Capitol Hill, Washington, D.C.
Tuesday, July 30, 1985

"Mr. Williams?"

"Good job. Got me on the first try," I respond.

The young blonde woman in the dark business suit smiles and holds out a perfectly manicured hand for me to clasp briefly. She gives her name and position as the Chairman's top aide.

"Your seat will be over there," she says, nodding to an area just left of the center of the room. "The Chairman will call for you when they need you to give testimony. In the meantime, you will be able to listen to the other speakers."

"Let the good times roll," I answer with my twice-brushed smile.

She stands and stares at me momentarily. Maybe she's taken with my rugged Oklahoma swagger, or maybe she's entranced by my country-boy charm. Maybe, it's my Clint Eastwood walk or my Steve McQueen eyes that she can't resist. She turns and walks away. Maybe, not.

My first heartbreak of the day complete, she disappears into the crowd and I walk to my seat. I pass a table of people with two guys wearing identical blue suits with red ties, identical watches and briefcases. Haircuts are combed in tandem. Only difference is their hair color. I give them a wave. Very friendly like, all at the table wave back but the two. One writes something quickly on a piece of paper and shows it to the other. They both look at me, then nod grimly. I stop, grab the paper, pull the pen from the one's hand, write something on it and give it back. They look at it with mild shock. I blow them a kiss and walk to my assigned seat. They're still staring at the paper, open-mouthed. When I reach my table and pull out my expensive wooden chair to sit down, I can't help but to notice that my table is the only one with just a single seat. The rest of the tables have two, three, four, or more seats that are already filled. Maybe, my antiperspirant has broken down...or, maybe this is the solo flight table.

A gavel strikes, a name is called, and the parade begins. Testimony. I listen intently. Then, I listen politely. Then, I listen casually. Then, I listen to the Jesse Colter song playing in my head. It makes more sense. Jessie is an incredible singer, and it helps me to mentally duck all the flying bullshit in this arena. About the second or third time Jessie tells me she's not Lisa, I take a closer look at the front of the room. While we in the public are seated at floor level, the desks in front are substantially elevated. The men seated up there are looking down at us, literally. The grand gurus of the day's event are mounted atop a platform in order to show their authority, disdain, or the regalia of their positions. They are the Congress; we are not.

Seated in the general admission seats behind me are the staffers, attorneys, and media, media, media. Most of them seem to be looking my way - until I look back at them. When I look away, they look back at me again. Whispers. Lots of whispers.

"Is that the guy?"

"He's all by himself?"

"It must be him."

Whispers.

"What's the guy at the table going to say?"

"He can't say much, can he?"

Whispers.

Then, a voice. A commanding voice.

"Mr. Williams, would you proceed with your testimony, please?"

I pull the microphone closer. I wait for a moment.

My name is Douglas Gene Williams, and I plead guilty to crimes against humanity...

CHAPTER TWO

When Washington Calls, You Answer

Back in the mid-60's, I'd enlisted in the United States Air Force, and it was during that time when my evaluation as a possible candidate for an elite White House position began. Mind you, I didn't know any of this at the time. I had no idea that an intense, detailed background investigation into the secret life of Doug Williams was in full swing. And, what did they discover during this top-level investigation? They discovered that Doug Williams didn't have a secret life. He was the adoring son of faithful, loving Methodist parents in Oklahoma, and was now a dedicated member of the U.S. Air Force. There were no skeletons in the closet, no monsters under the bed, nothing. Ultimately, I was selected for a top-secret communication position in Washington, D.C. I hadn't applied for this position. I don't even think you can apply for a position like that. *They* pick *you*. Although I had a lot of fascinating experiences serving our country during my time with that strategic organization, I find it ironic that it was during the final qualifying stage for the job when I first encountered the polygraph.

My journey into the world of the polygraph was a bit bizarre from the very beginning, but, what happened one night during the hiring process for my job in the White House was even more so. Dark suited men with sunglasses, a long drive late at night to an undisclosed location, no one speaking - even all that didn't compare with the actual test, itself. After we had arrived - wherever the hell they'd taken me - the aforementioned men motioned me through a door into a long hallway. The hall was poorly lit - depressingly dim would be the best description for it. As they closed the door behind me, I looked to the opposite end of the hallway and saw another door. This door was slightly ajar with light shining out. I presumed that this was where I was supposed to go, so I went. After about thirty steps, I stopped and opened the door.

The square room was small, with no windows. The walls were the color of beige, or off-white. There was a desk with two chairs. One was a comfortable looking office chair; the other, a butt-breaking wooden seat. On top of the desk was a black metal box with some wires and a couple of tubes sticking out of it. Behind the desk in the good chair sat a stocky man in a white short-sleeved sport shirt. He was smoking a cigarette. He had a military-type haircut and his body language did not say, "Welcome, friend."

"Sit," he said, nodding toward the wooden chair.

I'm military. We follow orders. So, I sat. For a moment, no one spoke. Apparently, he didn't care to start, and I didn't know where to start. Then, he tapped the black box on his desk.

"This is a lie detector," he said. I nodded. I'd never seen one before, and up to that moment, I'm not sure that I'd ever really even heard much about a lie detector.

"I'm going to ask you some questions," he said, crushing his cigarette into a round copper-colored ashtray. I nodded again.

"So, what we're going to do here is this. I'm going to hook you up to this machine. Then, I'm going to ask you some questions. If the machine says you're telling me the truth, you leave. If the machine tells me you're lying, even once," he said, reaching behind the black box and pulling out a .45 caliber military-style handgun and laying it on the desk in front of him, "I'm gonna blow your fucking head off."

We sat there, again, for a moment in silence. I felt the urge to say something, so I did.

"May I ask, Sir, who are you?"

He stared me directly in the eyes for a few, very long seconds and then lifted the weapon - not directly aiming but positioning it to point at me.

"As far as you're concerned, I'm God."

I don't recall much about the test, but, apparently, I passed - or, at least, satisfied whatever standards had been set by whoever had set them. It was quite a night. And, although the Polygraph Machine and I wouldn't meet again for quite some time, my first encounter was one I would never forget.

Eventually, after all the background checks, I was plucked from the bush of unknown candidates and sent to the Capitol, where I began my new career in what is called the "Situation Room." The Situation Room is the highly secured communication center in the White House for U.S. Military and Intelligence services around the world

Information that comes through the Sit Room has a direct affect upon what is going on and will go on around the globe. Quite often, messages and information came in that were directed to our Commander-in-Chief. My job was to take those messages directly to the President, and no one else was to put eyes on them except the man, himself. This never varied. It was etched in stone, and I was to follow that standing order at all costs. Pretty heady job for a young man from Oklahoma.

Hand-delivering messages to the President and having him address you by your first name is almost surreal - until you get used to it. When you get to know a lot of the people in those lofty positions in government, you realize that they're not a whole lot different from other people. A lot of them are okay. Of course, you've got a big portion of self-important, ass-kissing staffers and vote-vulture politicians running around, but when it comes to "smarts," they're no different from the rest of us. Except for one person. President

Johnson was a distinct personality. He was an in-charge guy, and no one doubted it. When you faced him, you knew exactly who was on the throne. The Vietnam War was in high gear at that time, so you can imagine that nearly all of the communications I received and read and delivered to the President were about the War. As tense as the world situation had become, the Johnson White House remained fairly open and, mostly, professional. I felt pretty much at ease handling my daily duties, despite the ever-growing pressure that the administration was receiving over the American involvement in Southeast Asia. With all the activity at my duty station, those years passed very quickly. Eventually, as we all know, Johnson left office and Richard Nixon entered the White House. As with all changes in any administration in business or government, there is an evolutionary shift in policy. Sometimes, it's a slow progression, and other times, it's very quick. With Nixon, it was quick.

During my three years with LBJ, my orders had always been to deliver any received messages to the POTUS (President of the United States), and to him, alone. I was under direct orders to obey that rule without exception. That's what I did with President Johnson, and I was never questioned about entering the Oval Office when I had something for the 'Old Man,' as we all called him. With President Nixon, however, there were barriers - lots of them. His subordinates began to intervene without what I perceived to be any kind of authority and attempted to take the intelligence messages from me before I had a chance to give them to the President.

In one very early exchange, John Ehrlichman and H.R. Bob Haldeman attempted to take a message from me as I was on the way to Nixon's office to deliver it. I refused; they demanded. I politely told them to go to hell. They got more demanding and became less polite. When I would not acquiesce, they headed to the Oval Office, apparently, to "tell on me." I, in turn, retreated to the Situation Room and contacted my Commander, prepared to defend the message I had for the President. My Commanding Officer showed up almost immediately and advised me to stand my ground while he tried to find out what was going on. He returned a short time later.

"Listen, Williams," he said. "Things apparently have changed."

"How so, Sir?" I asked.

"Well, President Nixon has said that you can give the messages to his staff if he is not available."

"So, does that include Mr. Haldeman and Mr. Ehrlichman?"

"Well, those two assholes are the only two mentioned, so far."

At that moment, Haldeman showed up with Ehrlichman in tow to get the message.

As he held out his hand to retrieve the message from me, I addressed my Commander.

"All due respect, Sir, but the order you relayed to me can only be given to me by the President, himself. I'm sure you are aware of that."

He smiled at me, knowing that I was jerking the two staffers' chains a little, but doing it with policy on my side.

"Oh, yes, absolutely. You're absolutely correct. Excuse us, Gentlemen," he said.

We walked past them and directly into the Oval Office. Once we arrived, closely trailed by the barking bobble-heads, we were admitted entry and found the President at his desk talking to a man I didn't know and to a female staffer. My Commander told the President that, due to protocol, I would need to hear directly from him that messages from the Sit Room could be handed off to the staff.

"Oh, okay," Nixon said. He looked at me as if I were going to present a statement. I didn't say anything, though, because there was nothing to say.

"Uh, Williams? It is Williams, am I right there?"

"Yes, Sir," I answered.

I was expecting an ass-chewing. Haldeman and Ehrlichman were hoping for one, and my supervisor was just standing there, enjoying the moment.

"Okay, Williams. It's okay in the future to give messages to these gentlemen right here when I'm not available," Nixon said.

"Yes, Sir," I answered.

"So, is that clear?" Haldeman said with a smile of victory.

"Very clear," I answered.

Haldeman held out his hand. I smiled back, then walked past him and handed the message to the President at his desk. Haldeman gave me a look of astonishment and contempt.

"Did you hear the order the President just gave to you?"

"Yes, Sir," I answered.

"Then, why didn't you follow it?" Ehrlichman yipped.

"I did. I was instructed by the President to give messages to you gentlemen if he's not available. He is sitting right here. I am standing right here. I believe that constitutes 'available,' Sir."

Realizing it was a good time to end the meeting, my Commander jumped in.

"Will there be anything else, Mr. President?"

"No, I believe that's all," Nixon answered. And, we left.

This situation was indicative of a White House organization that had a lot of internal turmoil, control battles, and egos-run-amok. There was also a growing paranoia that started with Nixon and worked its way through a lot of the staff. At one point, the President decided to have all the staffers periodically take polygraph tests, apparently to prove their loyalty. When someone made the comment to him that they didn't think the polygraph actually worked, he responded, "I don't give a damn if it works. All I know is it scares the hell out of people. That's what I like about it." That's a very telling endorsement, if ever there was one.

Despite all the strangeness of that administration, I did become friends with many of the people involved with the day-to-day business of government. Henry Kissinger and Al Haig were good guys who, in my opinion, were trying to do legitimate work for the country. At times, I'm sure it had to be difficult for them to avoid politics, but they took their jobs and duties seriously.

Regrettably, my position at the White House caused my personal life to suffer after a while. This certainly was not because of President Nixon, but because of the total scrutiny all of us were under due to our positions in the highly secure world of the White House staff. Our telephones were tapped, and we were being watched or, at the very least, monitored by unknown people every minute of every day. A social life was restricted to make certain you didn't hang out with the "wrong" kind of people. And, even when you hung out with the "right" kind of people, you couldn't talk shop because of all the security restrictions surrounding you. After a while, this all starts to wear on you, especially if you're a young fella, as I certainly was at the time.

Ultimately, it wasn't long under Nixon's administration when I decided that living in a bubble no longer appealed to me. I still didn't feel at ease with some of the staff members, and I'm sure some of them didn't care for me. In the end, though, it was the lack of a private life that pushed me to resign. So, I gave my notice at the end of my tour of duty, and after a couple of sessions with Mr. Kissinger and Mr. Haig who both encouraged me to stay, I stuck with my gut feeling to leave. Word of my pending departure flew around quickly, and the staff - like me, or not - gave a big going away party for me. I'll admit that I was surprised to see all the people from different departments that showed up. Everyone from custodians to high-level operators were there. Maybe, they just liked cake. Well, whether they liked me or the cake, it made no difference because in 1969, I said goodbye to Washington - for the moment.

CHAPTER THREE

Ambition of Lies

Home. Oklahoma City. A nice, middle income home to live in. A police department position as a patrolman. No one to choose my friends, hangouts, or monitor my phone calls and conversations - a simpler life from my years in Washington, D.C. Sounds fundamentally mid-American, doesn't it? It was supposed to be, but most everything - and, sometimes, not anything - is what it's supposed to be.

For a while, my law enforcement career had been rewarding and pretty damn good. Going in, I hadn't been just some pimple-pocked kid that made it through puberty by a hair - no pun intended - or had watched too many episodes of *Gunsmoke* and *The FBI* and decided it was time to polish the badge, strap on a sidearm, and save the world. Of course, I had planned on doing all that, too. But, the fact of the matter was that I hadn't just wandered into my new career empty-handed and vacant-headed. I'd held a very impressive portfolio of various degrees in psychology and criminology. I'd had a solid professional history in the Air Force, where I'd spent over three years in the White House Situation Room, handling TOP SECRET, EYES ONLY messages for the President of the United States. I'd held the highest security clearance available and served three years with President Johnson and six months with President Nixon during the tumultuous Vietnam era. I'd held a job that allowed me to peruse the continuous flow of classified messages that crossed my desk on a daily basis. I'd spent over three years inside the most secure and important decision-making hub in the world, reading messages that were intended for the eyes of the most powerful man in the world, and for his eyes only. Okay, so my White House years may not seem like qualifiers for a cop job, but, anyway, at least I was home again.

"Chief wants to see you," she says.

"Is there a problem?"

"As soon as he gets off the phone, he'll speak to you," she answers without looking up from her typing. Efficiency at its best.

As the Chief's secretary, she has three main functions: type; screen the man's calls; and, most important of all, guard the man's door. No one, absolutely no one enters the realm of the Chief of Police without three references, a medical screening, and the approval of the woman sitting at the wooden desk. Okay, so I made up the first two things, but, make no mistake, this conservatively dressed, slightly gray-haired woman is the defender of the door. Her phone flashes.

"Certainly, right away." She continues typing. "Go in."

This order is apparently for me, as there is no one else in the room.

"Thanks," I say, then add, "Have you done something different with your hair?"

No response. Just typing.

I open the door, walk into the inner sanctum, and observe the Chief sitting behind an expensive desk. On top of the desk are a few sheets of department letterhead papers, some pink phone message slips, a black telephone, and a white coffee cup.

"Close the door," he says, pointing to the chair. Subliminal message: "Sit." I take a seat; he stands up. Another subliminal message: "I am looking *down* at you." Our positions are now established.

"Son, just who the hell are you?" His voice is flat, but curious.

His face is crinkled slightly with the import of the question.

"Uh, well, I'm Doug Williams," I answer, because I really can't think of anything else to say.

"No," he says. "I asked who you are."

"Police Officer Doug Williams?"

He sits back down.

"Is there a problem, Sir?" I ask.

He reaches over to the corner of his desk, picks up the pink phone messages.

"You see these?" he says, holding them up.

"Yes, Sir."

"Well, these are my daily messages about the department. The public's always calling or complaining about something. Here's one about one of the traffic guys falling asleep in his car. Here's one about a slow response by one of our guys to a loud party call. Then, there's this one about Officer Doug Williams."

"A complaint about me, Sir?"

"No, no, not a complaint. Just a call from Henry Kissinger wanting to speak to you. Here's a second one where he called back and left a number. Here's a note from Alexander Haig wanting to speak with you."

He's holding the messages up one at a time as he speaks. "Here's one...oh, hell, it's just from some General - he goes to the bottom of the pile."

I just nod.

"I've got Cabinet members and White House people calling to talk to one of my third shift patrolmen, and when I ask him about it, all he does is nod...?"

"Well, Sir, all my prior employment information is on my application - at least, all of it that can be released."

"Williams, I get that," he says, tapping a file on his desk. "But, is there some issue of national security going on here?"

"In Oklahoma City?"

"Well, where the hell else would I be talking about?"

"Well, I don't think..."

"It's not about that little issue we had last summer with the bars downtown, is it?"

"Sir, I don't think Mr. Kissinger is concerned about the bar owner's complaints."

"So, what is it, then?"

"We're just friends, Sir. He's asked me to reconsider my situation and return to Washington, that's all."

"You're sure?"

"I'm sure, Sir."

"Well, if you're sure..."

"I am, Sir."

He leans back in his chair.

"May I go, Sir?" I ask.

"Huh, oh, yeah, go ahead." I stand and walk to the door.

"Hey, Williams," the Chief says.

"Yes, Sir?"

"When you were up there in Washington, did you ever meet old LBJ?"

"Well, yes, I met him, Sir."

"What was he like?"

"Pretty straight forward. An in-charge kind of guy."

"Huh. What about Nixon? What was he like?"

"Actually, Sir, he was a lot like you in some ways."

Chief breaks a smile, "Really...?" then stops smiling, squinting slightly as I walk out.

One evening, as I was walking through the squad room, I took a moment to glance at the bulletin board. Usually, the announcements and promotional listing dates didn't hold much interest for me, and I really wasn't expecting that night to be any different. I gave it a quick once-over and was about to walk away when I noticed a department memo asking for volunteers to enroll in a polygraph school. I read it over a couple of times and thought, "What the hell, why not?" The next day, I went to the person who had put up the memo, and a week or so later, I was registered for school. I was certain that this would be a good career move, or at the very least, something different to do. Besides, technology and law enforcement together sounded like a step into the future. Personally, I was tired of wrestling drunks while on patrol, and my recent move to investigations wasn't as exhilarating as I'd hoped it would be. The polygraph guys all had their own offices and pretty much their own schedules, plus they seemed to be in the middle of all the major goings-on in the department - so, why not me?

A short time later, I was sent to the National Training Center of Lie Detection in New York City. Very impressive title for a school, wouldn't you agree? This was the place where I was destined to become an expert polygraph operator...or "polygrapher"...or "polygraphist," depending upon the title you preferred. So, for fourteen weeks of daily instructional sessions, I learned everything that I could about the polygraph and the scientific world of lie detection. So, what did I learn? You're dying to know, right? Well, what I learned was a great deal about interrogation techniques - from the setting up of the room, to the questioning, itself - right down to the confession.

So, what about the polygraph machine, itself? Oddly, we didn't spend all that much time on it. We did learn what its function was in detecting bodily reactions to different stimuli, but that was about it. The main focus of the school was to "get the confession." In fact, we were told, regardless of the polygraph test, "tear off the chart and get the confession." As far as I could tell, the polygraph was just a prop, and the test was a scene - a well-choreographed, well-acted, thoroughly rehearsed scene. And, to accomplish what? To get "the confession." That phrase was repeated so many times, it literally became the school mantra. But, obviously, we were doing it for the right reasons, weren't we? Well, weren't we? And, that was the aching question that would later come to haunt me.

When I returned to Oklahoma City after my time in New York, I went right to work. It wasn't long before I discovered that I was pretty damn good at this "lie detection" game. I arranged my poly-graph suite to be as menacing as possible. Basically, it consisted of two chairs, a desk, and the center of the room's universe: the polygraph machine, strategically positioned on the desktop. Right out of the gate, so-to-speak, I tested people who were either sus-pected of or knowledgeable about crimes such as homicide, theft, and every category in between. You name it. Every type of suspect eventually planted their butt in my hot seat. I garnered confession after confession in that room, a fact that made me very popular in the department. Then, I began testing for the Internal Affairs boys. They're the guys who police the police, looking for officers who have stepped over the line. And, that made me very *unpopular* with a lot of the department.

But, regardless of which side of the street someone had come from, if they were unfortunate enough to wander into my cham-ber of torment, they were in for the most tortuous ride of their life. A person would enter the room confidently, maybe even a bit nervously, or even a little skeptical, but still walking upright. Hours later, that same person would drag himself out of the room, abused mentally, exhausted physically, and not quite sure what had just happened or why. I was the master. I held the whip. It may not have been a cowhide whip, but don't ever doubt that it was, indeed, a whip. In my hand was the polygraph - a real-life, mind-reading, lie-detecting machine, capable of ripping the inner-most personal thoughts from the mind of anyone I chose. There is no possible way to avoid the genius of the polygraph operator and his all-powerful lie detecting machine.

BULLSHIT. Every word of it - BULLSHIT.

But, people believed it! They believed it because we preached it. And, every day, here they'd come, walking in, oblivious as to what was about to happen. Some polygraph sessions would be easy - a quick breakdown, rapid confession, and out the door. However, most would not be so quick. Some would get loud; some would border on violent. Fear was to be struck into the heart of the person being interrogated and screaming at them was allowed. Getting right up in their face was allowed. Kicking chairs was allowed. Get the confession! That's all there was. Give me a confession and what's left of you can leave. Innocence? What if confessing would not be the truth? Truth? What the hell did innocence or truth have to do with it? The confession was the end-game. I was relentless. In order to get a confession, I was willing to go to great extremes. I made one man come back to my testing room seventeen times before he finally confessed. He probably gave up out of sheer exhaustion, or maybe he was just tired of looking at me.

After a long day of harsh, unrelenting polygraph sessions, I would retire to a session of my own - a daily drinking session. It was a ritual. A ritual that would last into the late night or early hours of the next morning. At first, I didn't realize it, but, the boozing was a symptom of something bigger going on in my head. A grim reality was setting in. At first, I was able to avoid it, bury it, casually disregard it without a look back. Over time, my wall of resistance began to crumble. A mental erosion began from the flow of non-stop adversarial meetings with people - people I didn't even know before that one polygraph encounter...people that I would never meet again...so many people that I couldn't even remember them at all.

Consider this: A person has had the experience of being interrogated, of being forced into a confession of something. They have had the experience of a life-changing event, and because of that event, they've suffered the loss of a job, prosecution, jail, or public humiliation. This one person, this human being, has been subjected to all of this, and all because of YOU. And, the man who has done all of this to you - well, he's done so many sessions like yours that he doesn't even remember you. You think that your life is important to the polygraph people? Think, again.

That's where I was: too many days of ripping the intellectual hearts out of people, followed by too many nights of drinking in search of justification. Sometimes, I drank alone. Sometimes, I drank with my co-workers, partaking in the jocular bragging about the day's journey into the land of the frayed souls, laughing at the poor bastard or nervous little broad who'd coughed up an admission because of our ammo belts of trickery and the simple box and chart graph on our interrogation room desks. Lots of beer. Lots of booze. Lots of bragging. You don't realize how funny destruction can be until you sit with a group of lounging lie detector pros.

CHAPTER FOUR

Facing the Truth

The next day, it would be back to work, bright and early, hungover and hellbent on bringing down the next person who walked through my door. I was always in search of one more confession...a never-ending cycle of senseless idiocy and persecution. I'd always considered myself to be a pragmatic person. If you look up the word "pragmatic" in the Oklahoma dictionary, you'll see the definition is "cut through the crap." So, it was time for just that - a little self-evaluation and some truth-detection.

I knew two things for absolute certain. First of all, the polygraph could *not* detect lies. It couldn't even evaluate the simplest of minds and tell the operator whether that person was being truthful, or not. I'd come to the conclusion that the machine was really only a stage prop used to scare people. And, in that sense, it worked really well. The second thing I knew was that, because of the cruel and agonizing testing sessions that we were putting people through, they were confessing to things they hadn't done, or that they were not even a party to. Pre-test allegations made about them that were subsequently confirmed by the polygraph operator were, quite often, one big lie. And, while so many confused or innocent people were being damned, countless cool-headed criminals were walking away unscathed.

All of this led me to one final bit of knowledge. If both of these things were true, and it was quite obvious to me that they were, then, the polygraph could be manipulated. Not only could it be manipulated but could be manipulated easily and under stressful conditions. But, how? Well, part of the answer was evident. We polygraph operators were manipulating polygraph test results by our questions, our actions, our test interpretations, and our own opinions.

However, what concerned me most was not that the polygraph operator was manipulating the test, but that the subject of the test was actually taking control and manipulating the test, itself, and its results. I was certain that this could be done, and I was just as certain that it WAS being done. So, again, I was back to *how?*

One of the basic reactions during a test was a direct response to the change in a person's breathing pattern. A person who could exercise control over the natural process of breathing could, in turn, change test results. This simple fact would be the initial offering of proof that the polygraph test did not work as a lie detector. After all, any test would be considered to be flawed if the person being tested could tamper with the testing procedure and change the results. And, that is exactly what controlled breathing would be: test tampering. So, the test, itself, was already without merit. The polygraph not only monitored breathing patterns, but also differences in blood pressure during the test. A person who could somehow control their blood pressure in a testing environment and cause what polygraph operators called a "spike," could undoubtedly dictate the results of the polygraph examination. The question was how to accomplish a spike and do it as naturally as possible. The answer came a short time later in a very surprising setting.

One night, I was having a beer (or, several) with some patrol cops when some stories about high speed chases started flowing back and forth. There was a lot of bragging, laughing, and story-stretching going on.

Suddenly, the guy next to me said, "Man, I remember the night I almost rolled my car chasing this guy. Talk about a close one! It made my asshole pucker up so tight that it almost took chunks out of my shorts! Just about shot my blood pressure through the top of my head!"

Everyone laughed. Everyone, except me. The pucker-factor! All cops knew what that was. It was the automatic surge reaction to a high stress situation - a violent fight...a gun pointed at you...a high-speed chase. *The pucker-factor.* Was it that simple? Could it be?? I threw some money onto the bar to buy the boys a round and said I had to go.

I went back to the office, hooked myself up to the polygraph, tightened my anal sphincter muscle - and, there it was. *A blood pressure spike!* I tried it again, and again, then again, and again. Same results each time. Very normal; very real. *Blood pressure chart movement on command.* With this discovery, I went back to work now, knowing more than ever that what I was doing was a FRAUD. It had to change, and I guessed it was up to me to change it. But, how? Just walk away?

Up until that point, it had seemed that everyone - my friends, supervisors, even I, myself - all believed that I was on a fast track to the FBI, the CIA, or any one of a number of the elite "alphabet" agencies. But, it 1979, all thoughts of an almost certain career ascension ceased. A cold, hard self-evaluation, combined with a mental collision between who I thought I was and who I had become, conspired to make me begin to hate myself and what I was doing so much that I had to stop. My hatred for the job had killed my career. The reasons may be, and probably are, numerous: part burn out; part disgust; but, mostly, just the suffering from the pain of a guilty conscience. I've heard people say that they're tired of living a lie. But, I wasn't just living a lie, *I was making a living from living a lie.* And, the biggest lie of all was the lie behind the lie detector.

Now, all this knowledge led to the spawning of guilt. A lot of it. Guilt is a hell of a thing to walk around with all day long. My guilt started out small, but, over time, it grew like a well-fertilized weed. Think about it. You start out every morning at the office with a cup of coffee, a cigarette, and a casual conversation with a co-worker.

Then, you step into a room with a person you have never met before, hook them up to a machine, mentally drum them into submission, tear out their soul to the point that they are convinced they are on a par just below serial killers and rapists, and that all they deserve is to be flushed with the rest of the human waste into a sewage drain. Once this has been accomplished, you push their remains out the door and smile at your next victim. Did I say, victim? I meant, "subject"...one more unsuspecting person who is soon to endure the most traumatic experience they will ever have, short of the loss of a loved one. I guess "victim" *is* the appropriate word.

In the beginning, you might be able to convince yourself that you're doing the right thing by sifting through the human psyche in your search for truth; but, as in my case, this delusion can't last forever. Some things you cannot justify; some things you cannot rationalize. You eventually come to realize that the ends do not always justify the means, and this is especially true of the polygraph test and interrogation. True, you may be able to get a confession or an admission, but at what cost? And, then, there is the nagging question: is the confession real? Is it right? So, the guilt starts growing within you. First, it's like a small tumor in the front of your brain. It's always there and it's always troubling you. But, before long, this small tumor of guilt grows to enormous proportions, and it, literally, starts to eat away at your very soul until your self-loathing becomes unbearable.

I wasn't the only one floating on this hate-filled barge of personal dejection. Lots of other polygraphists - at least, those who had retained some remnant of their principles - also suffered from the same disease of a guilty conscience. A lot of us attempted to anesthetize our pain with some form of self-medication, primarily booze or drugs or both. Despite the ill-advised efforts of sedation, thoughts of polygraph sessions would flow through my mind, projected onto the brain's movie screen of memories, appearing as vivid and as real as the moment they had occurred. A particularly haunting memory of a woman seated in my office, sobbing while I railed on her for a confession, returned to my mind almost daily. I had been pushing her for a confession.

"The polygraph says you're lying!" I shouted...

"I didn't do it," she'd cried...

I screamed back, "The machine is not wrong. You are lying. The machine is never wrong!"

After hours of mental pummeling, she'd balled up into a near-fetal position, almost convulsing in anguish. Suddenly, this woman turned her face to look squarely at me and cried out, "I did not do it! What are you trying to do? My God, what is wrong with you?"

There it was. Very plain, and corrosive as acid. What WAS wrong with me? And, that question led to more questions, bigger questions. What was wrong with all of this lie-detection trickery and the massive cult of operators who held so much power? Where had it started? How had it grown? How had it lasted all this time? I knew I needed answers to these questions.

CHAPTER FIVE

Research and Reveal

1979 had been quite a year for me. At the beginning of that twelve-month cycle, I was a well-known officer and polygraph operator for the Oklahoma City Police Department. At the end of the year, I was not. So, you might say that this marked both the beginning and the end - the end of what nearly everyone believed had been a promising and successful career in law enforcement, and a fruitful endeavor as a polygraph operator. I use the term fruitful because I don't believe "promising" and "successful" are realistic descriptions for a polygraphist. But, becoming a polygraph operator was fruitful for me in the sense that I was able to coerce many people into confessing to me during their exams; therefore, I had gained a lot of prestige and some pretty decent money along the way. But, it was certainly not fruitful for the many thousands of human beings who had become my victims. After all, there wasn't much prestige in confessing, and even less money. So, I began the year, 1979, gainfully employed and ended it as an unemployed vagrant, embarking upon a quixotic quest to destroy the massive and ever-growing lie detection industry. Oh, yes - that had been the same industry that was paying my light bill, feeding my cat, and buying my whiskey. Talk about biting the hand that feeds you...I was chewing on the gristle.

I began to research the sources and springboards that had brought this bizarre system into being. The polygraph had a long, dark history of destroying lives...the lives of those forced to bow to it...the lives of those with a conscience who worked with it...even the lives of those who cultivated it. The history of the polygraph dated from the early Twentieth Century and was begun by two pioneers named John Larson and Leonarde Keeler.

Dr. John Larson was a serious scholar. A medical student, he ultimately earned his Ph. D. in Science and is credited with being the inventor of the Lie Detector. Because he was a scientist, Larson tried desperately to prove that his theory was founded in sound, scientific fact. However, try as he might, he was unable to present any scientific data that would support his basic premise that the polygraph could, in fact, detect deception. It could not. But, due to his deeply held convictions, he persevered. Unfortunately for Larson, his quest to prove the validity and reliability of the polygraph collided head-on with the reality that he was wrong. He conducted test after test, and all his data-collecting produced the same results. He could not validate his theory. Much to his dismay, Larson finally had to conclude that there was no device that could tell if a human being was telling the truth. Despite this realization, his original concept of a lie detector, albeit disproven, had taken root elsewhere - somewhere, where truth meant little, and money meant everything.

Enter Leonarde Keeler, con man par excellence. Oddly enough, Keeler became a promoter of the polygraph at the same time that Larson, the idealist, became its chief detractor. Larson cautioned Keeler not to promote the polygraph as a "lie detector" because he knew that there was no scientific evidence to support such a claim. But, Keeler was an ambitious huckster who could not resist the pull of fame and fortune by touting the next "new thing" in police work. Keeler became a street-corner pseudo-scientist and marketer of epic proportions.

Despite the absolute lack of scientific data to prove the theory that the polygraph was capable of lie detection, Keeler continued with his preposterous claims. He had a plan. He was going to claim the idea of the world's first "lie detector" as his own in order to secure his place in history and, in the process, line his pockets with ill-gotten gains from all the people he could dupe into believing in his magic box. And, that is exactly what he did. In fact, Keeler's salesmanship was so good that the first commercial polygraph instrument bore his name, and Keeler turned into the very embodiment of Larson's fears. While Larson struggled in earnest to continue his search for scientific data to support his theory, Keeler became a shameless self-promoter.

Things became so distorted with Keeler's cheesecake-type interviews and carnival-like sideshows about his magical lie box that Larson knew he had to do something to stop the insanity. He began writing a book, which he intended to use to debunk the so-called magic of the polygraph and to expose Keeler as a fraud and a common crook. But, due to Keeler's incessant promotion and the mass consumption of the propaganda he spewed, Larson found his task overwhelming. Keeler would do anything to promote himself, even starring as himself in the movie, *CALL NORTHSIDE 777*. Larson found that his one-time protege was much better than he at propaganda and promotion, as well as the Hollywood movie publicity machine. Larson, the scholarly Ph. D., the thoughtful inventor, was being beaten by a connoisseur of an ancient shell game. Sadly, it turned out to be more than he could handle.

Larson's book was never completed, and he fell into a state of deep despair. Toward the end of his life, he is quoted as saying, "Beyond my expectation, through uncontrollable factors, this scientific investigation became, for all practical purposes, a Frankenstein's Monster which I have spent over forty years combatting." Larson had become completely consumed by his crusade to destroy the myth of the polygraph as a lie detector. He died despondent and deranged, his dream unfulfilled. His fervent hopes of exposing the fraud of lie detection died with him.

In the end, Keeler didn't fare much better. Under the pressure and demands he had brought upon himself through his zealous search for publicity, he found himself unravelling. His personal life suffered due to his instability. He consumed copious amounts of alcohol, became insanely jealous of his wife, began acting irrationally, and finally, drank himself to death.

I knew that a fate similar to what had befallen Larson and Keeler also awaited me if I did not make a drastic and immediate change. Proof of this became glaringly evident as I began developing mental problems of my own. The erosion of my physical and mental health was brought on by the knowledge I shared with John Larson, that the elaborate system of lie detection was just a myth. It had grown over time like a locust swarm or some terrible epidemic that moved like a malignant, unstoppable force, damaging everyone in its path. Some may consider me too zealous in my quest to destroy what I believed to be an evil industry. However, if you or anyone you know or care about has ever been on the receiving end of a polygraph examination, then you, too, have come face-to-face with the stark reality of just how evil it really is.

At the same time, my personal life was in a downward spiral and my self-destructive behavior was escalating. Drinking, lack of sleep, depression - you name it. It all had to stop, and the solution to the problem was obvious to me. First, I had to openly and publicly admit that I was part of the problem. And, once I had taken that step, I would also have to take the next stride: taking on the polygraph industry, itself. Taking responsibility for my own actions was easy compared to doing battle with the world of lie detection. That seemed like an insurmountable task, roughly akin to pole vaulting over Pikes Peak. But, what the hell? I didn't see anyone on the horizon capable of doing it as well as I could. I had the facts. I had worked extensively in the field, done extensive research, and owned the necessary knowledge. And so, armed with my background, the truth, and a boatload of determination, I declared war against the evil polygraph empire. Like Larson before me, I found myself becoming obsessed with exposing the fraud perpetrated by polygraphists. But, like Larson, I had no way of knowing that I was about to begin a forty-year crusade battling "Frankenstein's Monster." Larson had had one thing in his favor. His war had begun in the 1920's and was, basically, a debate with his one nemesis, Leonarde Keeler. By the time I declared my war, several decades had passed since the Larson/Keeler battle that had ended with the deaths of both combatants. Things had changed in a rather drastic fashion.

In today's world, the status of the polygraph industry had blossomed. Law enforcement agencies and numerous government agencies had embraced it. And, the use of the polygraph in private industry had grown to mammoth proportions. This had occurred largely because the polygraph scam was a way for unprincipled men and women to become very rich, very quickly. So, while Larson had done battle with one single foe, I would be facing a multitude of opponents with deep pockets to help support them financially and legally. Money doesn't make you right; and, just because something is deemed legal by the government, doesn't necessarily make it right, either. Be that as it may, having lawyers and money would benefit my opponents. All I had was the guy looking back at me from the bathroom mirror - and, right at the moment, he wasn't looking all that good.

Nearly one hundred years after Keeler was unable to bring any reliable scientific data to the table, there is still no proof that the polygraph can detect truth from lies. However, the lie detection industry (and, that's what it is - an industry, not a science) attempts to hang its hat of mendacity upon the sophistry of propaganda and the work of polygraph pioneers who, they claim, are above reproach.

One such grandly quoted pioneer is William Marston. In 1930, sometime after Larson and Keeler had begun their battle, Marston announced to the world that not only did the lie detector work, but that he had perfected a system whereby he could determine whether or not a person was lying simply by measuring their blood pressure during questioning. And, there you have it. Marston claimed irrefutable proof that liars could be unmasked. And, Mr. Marston claimed that his evidence was purely scientific and unimpeachable. To illustrate his astonishing hypothesis, he decided to have it tested by the one person he knew he could trust - the one person he was certain to be fair and objective. And, who would that person be? No other than the comic book character, Wonder Woman. "Wonder Woman" was the invention of Marston, and her Lasso of Truth was his representation of a lie detector. The more I researched, the more certain I became that the polygraph was never considered an actual lie detector by any serious scholars of science, or even by rational human beings.

CHAPTER SIX

Conspiracy

I now knew that quitting the department's polygraph squad was not enough. I had given thousands of polygraph exams, and I owed something to the people I had abused and deceived so badly during many of those tests. So, I decided to get the word out and, if possible, to go public. Late one night, as I sat at my dining room table with most of the lights off except for a small lamp nearby, my books and research material scattered all around, a cold realization struck me. This was more than a question of ethics, or even a disagreement on policy. It was even more than an oversight that had somehow slipped through the aged cracks of the law enforcement world. This machine and the fallacy of its authority had survived, nearly unscathed, for over half a century. Along the way, it had gathered support – strong support – from powerful protagonists all across the country, from big business to government enforcement agencies to the White House, itself. The question was how all this could have been possible considering the fact that the polygraph didn't work, and that so many of these same supporters of the "box" knew that it didn't.

Personally, I don't like the term "conspiracy," but you have to look behind the bush, sometimes – and, this bush was looking pretty thorny. The larger question became why. Why maintain this fraud and use it openly in such an invasive manner? Looking at the business of lie detection, the number of people involved with its use, the revenue derived from its use, and the hierarchy of its protection, the answer was simple: power and money. Or, money and power. The words are interchangeable. Their meanings are clear. Their abuses are as old as time.

Realizing how big this business was with all of the assets it possessed, if I were going to become a negative influence, I needed to closely examine my own arsenal. It didn't take long because my arsenal contained just one thing: TRUTH. But, the truth told me two very important things: honest people giving honest answers were being called liars, and dishonest people giving untruthful answers were being called truthful. Yet, there was a third thing that truth told me, and it was probably the most important thing of all. Everything about lie detection was controlled at the whim of the polygraph operator, and his decisions about a person's truthfulness, or lack, thereof, were entirely subjective.

Breaking down the polygraph is simple. Polygraph responses are recorded as tracings by ink pens on the polygraph chart. These are called "chart tracings," and, they track the subject's breathing pattern, heartbeat, and the increase and/or decrease of the sweat activity on their fingers. I, as a previous member of the brethren of charlatans who had claimed to be modern-day versions of Demosthenes, knew how to control every single one of these tracings, and so did most of my cohorts. Taking all of this a step further, I knew that I could teach anyone how to control his tracings on the polygraph chart at will, and how to always produce a "truthful" chart, regardless of whether or not they were telling the truth or lying. So, to summarize, I could prove beyond a doubt that referring to the polygraph as a "lie detector" was ridiculous. If I could teach any person to control tracings on his chart, that was *prima facie* evidence that the polygraph was NOT a lie detector.

As I've stated, the polygraph is just a machine that allows the operator to monitor a person's heart rate, sweat activity, and breathing while the operator asks them questions. As far as technological advances go, this crude machine has not changed significantly since it was invented in the 1920's. The box may look prettier, but the guts are the same. And, in case you don't remember the 1920's, those were the days of black-and-white movies. Black-and-white SILENT movies. When I explained this to people, they were astonished, their eyes widened with disbelief. Most everyone presumed that the polygraph was much more complicated, updated, scientific, and sophisticated. Some even believed that it could actually read their minds. Understandable, because that's what people are meant to believe. The unfortunate fact is that the polygraph is an antiquated instrument that is only capable of recording basic physiological reactions to questions. In other words, by monitoring the tracings on the chart, I could watch breathing patterns, heartbeats, sweat activity on the hands. A change in any of these tracings was labeled as a "reaction". If this reaction happened to occur after a subject answered a relevant question, he would be called a liar. Polygraph operators would, then, classify this event as a "lying reaction".

We all know that reality is far different. I knew that there was no such thing as a "lying reaction;" therefore, it followed that there was no such thing as a lie detector. I knew that the notion of a machine that could detect lies was based upon a false premise – the premise being that when you lie, you produce a physical reaction that indicates deception. But, the problem with the premise is that, in order for you to call a reaction indicative of deception, that same reaction must *always* indicate deception. And, that is simply not the case. The polygraph machine was only capable of recording a nervous reaction, or what is commonly referred to as the "fight-or-flight" response. This response is simply a person's reaction to a threatening stimulus that prepares them to either flee from or to fight whatever is frightening or threatening them.

However, I also knew from experience that the same reactions were often caused by simple nervousness that had nothing to do with deception. As a matter of fact, they very seldom indicated deception. As often as not, the reactions that the polygraph would brand as a lie were caused by many other innocent stimuli such as fear, embarrassment, rage at having been asked the question, or, just simple nervousness caused by the accusatory nature of the question. So, you can see why I had a real problem with labeling a subject a liar just because they experienced the symptoms of the fight-or-flight response when they answered a threatening or accusatory question. Think about it. If you were walking through a wooded area and ran into an angry bear, you would have the same reaction. This reaction is your natural decision to run away or to stand and fight. If you run away, are you a liar? If you stand and fight, are you a liar? Unwise, maybe...but, a liar?

So, if the polygraph is a false god, why do so many people in positions of authority within the government fight to keep it? Why is it so valuable to them? Why is it so important and held in such high regard? It is very simple. The polygraph is an interrogation tool of unparalleled stature. It is the world's greatest "confession-getter." It allows the operator to decide what is and what is not truth. The polygraph operator can call a person a liar without having to offer any evidence, whatsoever, to support his accusation, and there is no way to appeal his completely subjective opinion. Polygraph operators learn to be very good at what they do, and what they do is to intimidate and interrogate. The truth is, the polygraph examination should be referred to as an inquisition, rather than an examination.

The polygraph is an insidious Orwellian instrument of torture – one that I, as a polygraph examiner, wielded unmercifully. I, literally, scared the hell out of people with it. I learned the art of skillful application of terror and became a master inquisitor. I was very good at my job – very good, indeed. Efficiency is paramount in business, and I was more than efficient at breaking people. I was able to administer up to ten exams per day, and I obtained a confession or damaging admission with every exam. With my target in mind, my job wasn't really to run the polygraph machine. That was only part of the setup. My real job was to intimidate, dominate, and inter-rogate subjects and coerce them into telling me the truth. Let me clarify that statement. My job was to frighten and coerce human beings into telling me *what I had decided was the truth.*

My subjects were afraid of the little black box, and I went to great lengths to make sure those fears became reality. My victims quickly came to fear me, the machine, the room we occupied, and even, the very chair in which they sat. I knew that they were almost paralyzed by fear because I could smell it. Fear has a distinct smell. I have heard it described as a mixture of shit and spinach. But, one thing is certain. It is an unmistakable odor, the aroma of humanity in the throes of terror. Why is this emanation so unique, so recog-nizable? Because fear stimulates the apocrine glands that secrete fluids in the armpits and groin. These secretions come out through the hair follicles as a sour, pungent, musky odor that is easily and quickly recognized as stench that can only be produced by dread, panic, and foreboding.

I terrorized people every single day, and soon my office was permeated with this awful smell. Every morning when I entered my office, which was nothing more than a model of a modern-day torture chamber, I could smell it. And, every night when I left, the old odor that had accumulated mingled with the new batch left by that day's victims. This noxious smell was a constant reminder of the psychological trauma I inflicted upon people on a continuous basis. I worked hard to create an atmosphere that would produce fear and unrelenting terror in my subjects. This emotional turmoil was caused by a combination of two things: the polygraph and the operator – in this case, me. I repeat, I was good at my job. I was a great interrogator in relentless pursuit of the confession - the all-important confession. It was the prize, the goal, the ultimate ex-pression of the polygraphist's power. Nothing, and I mean nothing, would keep me from getting the confession.

After all, seven years of daily polygraph brain bashings will make one polish his craft to a blinding sheen. I had become so intent upon getting a confession from every one of my victims that I persisted until I succeeded. I would stay at it for as long as it took. As far as I was concerned, there was no clock, no time, just me and my subject...and, if they wanted this horrible experience to end, well then, just confess. In my interrogation chamber, it was a contest of wills, and I would always triumph because I would do whatever it took to win.

I cannot overstate the amount of power the polygraph operators wield over their subjects, and if one can exist without a conscience or a moral compass, one can probably continue the emotional butchery until retirement. Many did; I could not. The stress of being a professional torturer was too much for me to bear. Studies have noted that the nature of this particular work subjects operators to a disproportionately high amount of stress. As a matter of fact, one such study was done on me in 1973. It was a simple study conducted by psychology students from one of the local colleges. My blood pressure would be checked in the morning, and again at the close of the working day. My blood pressure was consistently 30% to 40% higher at the end of the day than it had been at the beginning of the day. On a few occasions, after particularly intense interrogation sessions, my systolic blood pressure shot up past 200. The students who were doing the study urged me to seek medical attention. They were probably afraid that my head might explode, or at the very least, I might be about to stroke out, ball up in the corner and start a drooling session. That my work as an interrogator was taking a toll on my health was no surprise to me because I knew that the polygraph interrogation system was just another form of torture, and I was also very well aware that the torturer, too, is punished in the process.

I am reminded of a story told by Frantz Fanon, a psychiatrist who served the French during the Algerian War of Independence. He wrote about the colonizer and the colonized, the oppressor and the oppressed, the torturer and the tortured. In it, he tells of a

French policeman involved with torturing Algerians. The policeman developed recurring nightmares and would often beat his wife and children for simply contradicting him. That was something he had never done prior to his role as an interrogator/torturer. The policeman is quoted as saying this about his role as a torturer:

We almost wanted to tell our victims that if they had a bit of consideration for us, they would speak out without forcing us to spend hours tearing information out of them. To all the questions they would say, 'I don't know.' So, of course, we have to go through with it. Today, as soon as I hear someone shouting, I can tell you exactly at what stage of questioning we've got to go. The thing that kills me most is the torture. You don't know what it is. It is very tiring. But, you can't let the bird go after he's softened up. It's a question of personal success. You have to be intelligent to make a success of that sort of work. You have to know when to lay it on and when to lead off. You have to have a flair for it.

I knew from personal experience exactly what this French policeman was talking about. And, like him, I, too, "had a flair for it." I seldom, if ever, failed to get a confession once I had set out to do so. I was not alone in this miserable condition. Many, if not all of the polygraph examiners I knew were developing the same mental disorders shared by all torturers, both past and present. The number of alcoholic, paranoid, drug-abusing polygraphists was alarming. They were all reacting to the haunting realization that their careers were based upon a pyramid of falsehoods. None of them would admit it or believed for a moment that they could trust the results of the polygraph. In fact, it was common knowledge that we could have gotten the same results from the toss of a coin, but we couldn't do that because it would ruin a very lucrative scam. Then, when you consider the damage done to people by falsely accusing them of deception – damage such as lost career opportunities, ruined relationships, and even, incarceration – well, at least in my case, the guilt became unbearable.

This false reality was highlighted by a retired CIA polygraphist named Sullivan who said in his book, *The Gatekeeper*, that the opinion of a polygraph operator regarding a subject's truthfulness was nothing more than SWAG, a scientific wild-assed guess. I agreed with Sullivan, except that I would leave off the word "scientific." To compensate for this awareness, polygraph operators work very diligently to become good interrogators in order to show that, even if the polygraph isn't a lie detector, it certainly is a valuable interrogation tool. I often felt that it would have been better and more compassionate to use a cattle prod to encourage people to confess, rather than to destroy them psychologically. At least, the physical burn would eventually heal. I knew that it was only going to get worse if I continued in what I had come to see as an evil occupation. So, I quit. Once I had decided, I didn't make a big deal out of it. It was plainly time to go.

CHAPTER SEVEN

Going Public

It was a Monday morning, as good a day as any to pull the plug on my draining job and start something a bit more brain-saving. I walked into my office for what would be the last time, placed my handgun and badge on the desk, and looked at them for a moment just a short moment, maybe just to make sure that what I was doing was what I really wanted to do. I guess you would think that someone who'd once felt so much pride putting on that badge would feel even a tiny bit of remorse at taking it off. But now, it was just a metal piece lying next to a revolver. Nothing more. It was like they were foreign objects - objects to be disposed of. I reached into my desk and pulled out a couple of pieces of typing paper, put one into the typewriter and crafted a letter of resignation. I specifically use the word "crafted" here instead of "wrote" because I used my military crypto training to embed a hidden message into an otherwise formal letter. It was simple and to the point. The message was "I am sick of this bullshit."

I picked up the letter and badge in one hand, and my service revolver in the other as I walked out of the room and headed down the hall to the Chief's office. I was actually feeling pretty good at that moment. It was that sense of relief that comes over you after you've finally made a decision that's been weighing you down. You almost feel like your posture is a bit straighter. I was clipping right along, headed for my destination down a fairly busy hallway, when I noticed that a lot of the clerical staff and officers were staring at me. I figured it was due to the fact that my weapon wasn't holstered, but in my hand...which was attached to my arm...which was swinging back and forth in cadence with my stride. I have to admit that it was an unusual thing to do, but this was an unusual day. So, what the hell. Let them stare. I walked into the Chief's front office and past his lady sentry, who was dumb-stuck that someone would have the audacity to pass her guard post and enter the emperor's domain without a proper blessing.

"Stop! Stop right now! The Chief is not available!" she demanded.

"Sure, he is," I responded, opening his door and stepping inside.

He was sitting at the same desk, same desk phone held up to the same ear, probably talking the same bullshit to the same person as he always did. His head rose up to see me and his face immediately went to pissed off, then to concern when he saw the revolver at my side. I tossed the badge onto his desk and it landed with a metallic 'clink.' Next, I tossed the revolver down beside the badge. It landed, displacing a few desktop items as it clunked and skidded a few inches.

"What the hell?" he questioned.

"Exactly," I answered, placing the letter in front of him and turning to walk out.

Behind me, he yelled as I exited, "What the hell is going on? Get back in here!"

I ignored him and walked through the outer office and was immediately confronted by his female portal protector in full confrontational bloom.

"You can't just walk into the Chief's office like that!"

"I already did," I answered, slipping past her to the next door to leave.

"There are rules, you know - rules for civilized human beings to follow," she said with a glare, pointing her finger at me.

I smiled back at her. "I used to think that, too," I said.

I walked into the general clerical area and over to a desk where a red-headed typist was busy clacking away at her machine. She was very involved with her work, so I didn't bother to ask permission as I picked up her telephone receiver, punched a line to the outside world, and dialed a number.

"City News Department, how may I direct your call?" a friendly, but hurried voice asked.

"Is Grif in?" I asked.

"Hey, Doug," the woman said, having recognized my voice. "Yeah, he's here - a little on the bitchy side today, but he's here."

"Thanks, Carla. Bitchy or not, I still need his ear. You still wearing those short little skirts to work?"

"No, had to lower the damn hemline. One of the editor's wives thought he was spending too much time evaluating the journalistic value of my lower appendages. You know how it is."

"I'd sure like to," I said.

"You've had your chances, Dougie," she laughed. "So, you want to talk to Grif, the grouch?"

"Want and need are two different things, my dear. This is a need kind of thing."

"Okay, well, if I ever hit your need-or-want category, call me, Baby." I heard another ringing, then a click.

"Yeah, Grif here. What is it?" a man's voice said.

"Boy, that's a sunshiny response to a phone call from a dear friend."

"Oh, great, it's you. Well, if you're calling for the five bucks on the Cubs game bet, forget it. Santo was safe. It was a shit call and you know it. Goddamn league is hiring blind umpires."

"That's not..."

"And, what do you mean sunshiny? I'll give you sunshiny. Brakes went out on my car this morning on the way to the publishing palace and I bumped into a car at the intersection. Do you want to know what kind of car it was?"

"Not really."

"I'll tell ya. It was a goddamn OKC cop car! No shit. Then, this new kid I don't recognize gets out and gives me a ticket."

"For what?"

"Bumping his ass! Hell, I don't know, and this all comes on the tail-end of a weekend spent with my mother-in-law on one of her booze-sucking visits where she spends the entire day telling me the evils of my breathing in air that would be better used to support the life of some more worthwhile creature, like maybe a vole. Then, I get here to the gutless newspaper I work at and there's a note for me from our illustrious Editor-in-Chief that says he thinks I'm being too snarly with people."

"Are you?"

"Am I what? Being too snarly?"

"Yeah."

"It's not even a goddamn word. He's supposed to be a professional journalist and he says shit like snarly?"

"So, what did you tell him?"

"I told him to put something in his ball sack besides air."

"How'd that go?"

"Probably won't be getting a raise this year. So, what pain in the ass stuff have you got for me, Williams?"

"I quit."

"Quit? Quit what? Smoking, drinking, screwin' around on your old lady? What?"

"I don't have an old lady."

"Oh, yeah. You're not as stupid as you act. So, what did you quit?"

"The department."

There was a moment of quiet. I could hear a lighter click and a long exhale on the other end before he finally continued.

"Trouble, Doug?" He asked with new concern.

"Not really. It was just time."

"It's that lie detector shit you told me about, isn't it?"

"That's it, Grif."

Another inhale, then exhale.

"So, what do you want from me? I mean, you've always been a top cop in the department, but just quitting ain't much of a story. No offense."

"It's not just quitting, and "ain't" isn't a proper term for a professional journalist."

"So, noted. Then, if it's not just quitting, what is it?"

"I'm gonna blow up the polygraph world. It doesn't work. People are getting shit on, and permanently shit on, at that. It's time to put a stop to it."

"Uh-huh. Very admirable. Also, quite moronic. What's wrong with just riding off into the sunset?"

"Don't have a horse."

"There is that. Okay, so what do you want to do? Some kind of news article?"

"That's up to you. What I want to do is call a press conference."

"Who do you think you are, the goddamn President?"

"No...met a couple, though."

"True," he said.

"I'm going to launch a campaign against lie detection in general and the polygraph, specifically. I need a press conference, and I know you can do it."

More silence.

"Shit like this makes it hard for me to cut down on smoking," he said.

"I didn't know you were trying to cut down."

"I'm not. Okay, I'll line it up. I need to interview you first, get a place for your gathering, put in some calls. You need to get my ticket taken care of."

"I told you I quit."

"Uh-huh. I gotta go. I'll line shit up and call your place with details."

"Thanks, Grif."

"Fix the ticket."

"But..." The line shut off with a click.

I rented a large meeting room at a hotel just down the street from the State Capitol Building where all the Senators and Representatives held their news conferences. My reporter friend had done his job well because all the local media, newspapers, radio, and television showed up. It was also quite obvious that word of my topic had spread beyond the media because I had some surprise guests.

Polygraph examiners from Oklahoma City and surrounding areas had showed up in force. I guess I shouldn't have been surprised because, after all, they were part of my topic. My concern now was to make sure that the meeting remained informational and flowed professionally. In order to keep things moving along once we started, I knew I would need a strong, but diplomatic person to manage the press conference. So, I had a friend of mine who was a police chief at a local department act as moderator. This was how I was going to launch what was to become a very lengthy and, ultimately, very dangerous Crusade.

I began by getting a volunteer to come forward to help me demonstrate the Sting Technique, as I called it. This marked the first time in the long history of the polygraph that anyone had demonstrated how simple it was to control tracings on the polygraph chart. The demonstration pointed out very graphically that the polygraph was just a crude instrument that could be easily manipulated. The audience was provided unmistakable evidence that the polygraph, when used as a "lie detector," was absurd, a joke at best. I stood in front of the packed room and let everyone – media, polygraph operators, and just interested bystanders – know that I was going to blow the whistle on the abusive nature of the polygraph test. I explained that well over 50% of honest, truthful people were falsely branded as liars by the people running these so-called lie detector tests. I told them that the evil Orwellian polygraph industry was guilty of perpetrating a massive fraud and that I believed this abusive, deceptive activity had to be stopped and banned forever. There was no sugarcoating my words.

I was well aware of the glares from the many polygraph operators in the audience. I knew all of them personally, and anger started to boil within me at the fact that they all just sat there silently. Were they all just willing to let this go on? Although they knew that what they were doing was nothing more than an outright lie, it was becoming quite apparent that they were willing to live with that lie. "Okay, fine, let's kick up a little dust," I thought to myself. I decided to challenge any or all of them to join me onstage and debate the subject of the validity of the polygraph as a "lie detector." When the cameras turned to pan the audience, every one of the polygraph examiners covered their faces and hid from the scrutiny of the lens. Some buried their heads in their hands; some ducked down behind the people in front of them; and, some even got up and hurriedly left the room. Not one polygraph operator accepted my challenge. Eventually, after I'd given them time to scurry from the room, I looked right into the cameras.

"That just about says it all, doesn't it, folks? Polygraph operators are like cockroaches - shine a light on them, and they run for cover. They know they are frauds, and they know that the polygraph is not valid as a lie detector. And, that's why they run from the challenge of a debate. If they could have defended their positions that the polygraph is valid as a lie detector, why didn't they take the opportunity to do so?"

I could see that the crowd of reporters were hanging on every word, so I shifted into high gear and continued with all the intensity of an evangelist at a tent revival.

"I'll tell you exactly why these charlatans won't debate me. It's because they know good and well that what I said is true. The basic premise upon which the polygraph is based is faulty. The reactions that they say indicate deception are often just caused by nervousness; and, nervousness does not always indicate deception. As a matter of fact, I've found that only about 50% of the time do these reactions indicate that a person has lied. The rest of the time, they are caused by a person's fear and nervousness. And, being afraid or nervous does not make you a liar! In order for the polygraph to be an actual lie detector, these reactions must always indicate deception – not half the time, not even 90% of the time – ALWAYS! And, truthfully, they don't. Most of the time, these 'lying reactions' are cause by any number of innocent stimuli that have nothing whatsoever to do with lying."

I continued my discourse by relating some of the horror stories of victims who had been abused by the unscrupulous people running the lie detector "scam," as I believed it to be. I began by telling the audience about polygraph operators working in the private sector, interviewing individuals applying for employment with a specific local company. I told how one particular polygraphist would brag about testing fifty people to fill just three openings. Others would tell similar stories, and they all would have a big laugh. "How about another beer, boys, ha-ha!" That's how it was, I told the audience - I know, because I was sitting at the table with them. I was one of them. And, what was our group saying? Well, we were openly admitting that truthful answers had been twisted so that the prospective employee's chance for an employment opportunity would melt down right before their eyes. Again, why? So that the polygraph operator would be paid for more and more tests! More tests, more results, more money. It's very simple - hideous, but simple. The machine and the operator joined together in one accord as judge and jury, rendering the opinion that a person was untruthful...for money.

I wanted the audience to understand the impact that this barbaric procedure had on people's lives.

"Imagine if you, your son or daughter were sitting in a chair being interviewed for a much-needed job. Then, imagine that behind the machine is a man who is deciding whether or not you are going to get that job. Imagine that he is making that decision not based upon whether you are worthy, but rather based upon whether or not he likes you. He may even disqualify you simply because he wants to make himself look good by showing how many terrible things he has discovered about you – even if those disqualifying admissions are completely fabricated. Or, he may call you a liar and disqualify you based upon some 'reaction' you had to one of his questions. Maybe, he doesn't like the tattoo on your arm, or the way your hair is cut, or, maybe, he's had a bad time with his wife lately, or, he's hungover. I could go on," I told them, "but just grab this thought: Imagine that you are a truthful person being called a liar and have no chance to appeal the decision. The sad fact is that millions of people in this country don't have to *imagine*. They've been through this nightmare, and many millions more will be facing it unless something is done to stop the madness."

I felt that it was important to give the crowd some foundation to my claims, so I explained my background and told them how I had come to learn about this abusive behavior. I explained that, aside from my job with the police department, I had also worked part-time for a private polygraph company, so I had firsthand knowledge of the abuses within the industry. I explained that the company I had worked for had actually encouraged us to fail as many people as possible in order to charge the employer more money for administering more polygraph exams. It was common practice among private polygraph examiners.

I could feel that I had their attention. However, to be as credible as possible, I made a point of emphasizing that I was not wrapping robes of righteousness about me and pointing a finger of blame at everyone else. Not at all. In fact, I wanted to close my news conference with my own confession. I freely confessed that I, Doug Williams, had transgressed just as the other polygraph operators, but that I was now doing my best to make restitution for all that I had done by bringing these atrocities to light.

My demonstration, my statements, and my admission were my earthquake. It shook up the room, but that wasn't going to be the big reaction. That would be the tsunami that would follow. Like every giant wave that follows a quake, it would come later, unpre-dictably later. But, there was no doubt it was coming, and it was going to crash the shoreline all around me.

The uproar caused by the news conference was immediate and intense. This was the first time any licensed polygraph operator had dared to expose the actions of these terribly abusive groups and call into account this corrupt and very powerful industry. The risk I was taking by doing this in 1979 was very great. The polygraph was nearing the height of its popularity. Millions of people hoping to work in private industry had to pass a test to get a job, and often, they had to periodically pass another test just to keep their job. The ordeal of the polygraph testing experience was dreaded by the people who had to submit to it. And, polygraph operators were a necessary evil for the owners and managers of the businesses that required their employees to submit to this grueling ordeal. Many of the business owners resented having to give the test; howev-er, they were required to do so by the insurance companies that covered their businesses against losses from theft by employees. Polygraph operators were raking in millions of dollars a year and, quite naturally, wanted to keep the truth from coming out. So, I pressed on with my damaging monologue, blissfully unaware of the dangers I would later face.

CHAPTER EIGHT

The CRUSADE

Because of my press conference, my mission had suddenly become a hot topic and I was invited to appear as a guest on a popular radio talk show on KTOK, the largest AM station in Oklahoma. The audience apparently wanted more information, so I laid out my reasons for leaving the police department and detailed my objections to the use of the polygraph instrument as a lie detector. I also explained that the goal of my crusade against the polygraph industry was to provide ample information to the public and legislative bodies that could pass laws banning this terribly abusive practice.

Now, I was out the gate and running hard – to where, I wasn't sure, because people's reactions to my freshly launched campaign were dubious, at best. Everyone, including my friends and family, thought that I was - well, let me give you a few quotes: "Stark, raving mad!" "Bat shit crazy!" "Fuckin' nuts!" My Dad even asked me, "Son, have you taken leave of your senses?" Well, I guess you get the idea. Many harbored serious doubts about my sanity and told me so in no uncertain terms.

To tell the truth, I had to agree with them. It was crazy to leave a career that I had spent years preparing for and striving towards. It was crazy to think that I could destroy an industry that was licensed by the State, one so heavily sponsored by employers and insurance companies in the private sector and relied upon by so many people in positions of power within the government. It was crazy to think that all I had to do was to tell the truth and everyone would believe me. After all, this was 1979, over fifty years since the polygraph had come into being. It had decades of promotion and endless propaganda supporting it, making it fully accepted as part of the American psyche. It was considered infallible by a vast majority of the population, as well as the media. All that culminated in making the polygraph the final, indisputable word on whether an individual was truthful or deceptive.

But, what the public did not know was that it was all just flat out smoke and mirrors. The few detractors it had were considered to be unpatriotic troublemakers, or just disgruntled people who were angry because their lies had been exposed by the polygraph. It was unheard of for anyone in a position of authority to question the polygraph, especially a police polygraph examiner. To do so would be an immediate career-ender.

As the reactions to my announcement at the press conference started to fly through the media, something became clear to me. Something was missing. I was sitting on my old rust-colored couch reading responses from the polygraph community in the local paper when one word kept jumping out at me. "Plan." People were being asked, "Do you plan on continuing to use the polygraph?" and, "Do you plan on responding to Doug William's allegation?" Plan! That was it. I could not proceed in any disorganized or chaotic manner. I needed a solid plan. If the reaction to what I was doing was as scorching across the country as it was right here in Oklahoma, I was definitely going to need to map out a strategy. I did have a sort of plan, but it lacked focus and direction, and it was obvious that I was going to have to hit this with everything I had. So, coffee and cigarette in hand, doing an all-night session, I devised a three-prong strategy. It became a strategy that would remain the same throughout my battle with the lie detection industry. *Education; Legislation; Litigation.* Although each phase of my three-point attack was detailed in description, the foundation of each was profoundly basic in nature.

The first prong, the Education Phase, was exactly what it sounded like. People needed to learn - and to learn from a reliable source. I had the knowledge and experience of thousands of polygraph testing sessions behind me, along with lengthy research into the history, uses and abuses of the polygraph. I would be that reliable source. Believe me, I'm not trying to sound arrogant here. I'm just stating fact. Besides, there was no other anti-polygraph hero on a white horse coming over the hill, so it was going to be up to me. Letting everything just continue unchecked was not an option. Okay, so I didn't have a white horse, but sometimes you just have to make do.

The second prong, the Legislation Phase, would be a different type of attack. Just educating politicians wouldn't be strong enough. I knew that I would have to get them to realize that it would not be politically injurious to them to sit, listen, and take a stand. Their education would have to include the fact that those being harmed were not limited to CEOs and high-ranking officials, but to the vast general population, as well - the vast *voting* general populace. Pairing that with proof that the polygraph didn't even work should garner enough attention for the Legislation Phase.

The third prong of my attack model was the Litigation Phase. This was, and still is the most complicated. I was hoping that once we were able to prove that people had been damaged by the falsehood of lie detection, legal recourse would fall into place.

When I had completed my written plan, I crushed out my last smoke into a nearly filled Hamm's Beer ashtray and gave a heavy sigh. Instead of going to bed, I leaned back on the couch and put up my feet. It was very quiet as I lay there thinking of the task ahead of me, wondering where this would all take me. I wondered where it would take the polygraph industry and the legions of polygraph operators who were going to fight me. It seemed a bit overwhelming for a moment, but then I began to visualize the faces of the people I had seen sit in the polygraph room with their pain almost palpable, and the concern of my own pending battle started to fade. I heard the woman's voice coming from the back of my mind like a cool, calm reminder of truth. "My God, what is wrong with you?" And, suddenly, any trepidation I had completely disappeared because now I finally had an answer. "There's nothing wrong with me – not anymore." As I lay there on my back, I saw the first glimpse of the morning sunrise through my East window. I rolled to my side and looked at the reddish-orange dance of a new day on the opposite wall and listened to the absolute silence and peace all around me. A gentle calm came over me. I closed my eyes with the thought that this might be the last peace for a long time.

To launch the Education Phase of my attack, I needed a text-book. So, I compiled information into a manual I called, *How to Sting the Polygraph*. It was a detailed, start-to-finish handbook on how to defend yourself from the polygraph and its operator. The tech-niques were simple, and a person could perform them with relative ease. But, I had one more thing to do in order to craft the manual into the ultimate textbook I wanted it to be. In order to round out my research so that the manual was completely authenticated, I decided to utilize all the techniques "undercover," as you might say. I would take polygraph exams from different polygraphists, pass them, document them, and notify the operators that had given me the test of the said results.

In order to do this, I would have to relocate. Oklahoma City wouldn't work. All the polygraph operators knew me, and they weren't going to let me anywhere near their little rooms of deceit. So, after I left the P.D., I moved south to Houston, Texas to launch my campaign. It was kind of like a beachhead onto foreign soil. During my first six months there, while testing my Sting Technique, I took over twenty polygraph examinations, each given by a differ-ent polygraph operator. I lied on every single question. Never once did I even get close to telling the truth. The results? I passed every test with flying colors and without the least bit of trouble. I was patted on the back and told that I was a perfect candidate, and an extraordinarily truthful person. The polygraph operators would even call me by name when they finished testing me, except they couldn't call me by my real name – *because I'd lied about that, too.* And, early on in this process, in addition to proving that the Sting Technique did work, I had an opportunity to prove that I could teach another person to pass the test very easily.

The opportunity presented itself one morning as I approached the building where I had an appointment with a polygraph operator at his office. As I started to enter the building, I noticed a young black man pacing back and forth just outside the entrance. He was obviously very nervous, so I asked him if he was there to take a polygraph test.

"Yeah," he said. "Second time in a few weeks. Had to take one before for a different job."

"How'd that go?" I asked.

"It didn't. Son of a bitch kept telling me I was a liar. I swear to God I didn't lie. There was nothing for me to lie about, nothing to hide. It's a damn low-dollar job, so why would I lie? After that, I figure the same thing will happen here."

He was quiet for a moment and I figured, let's see how fast I can teach someone to pass this thing. I introduced myself and told him what I was doing and that I thought I could help him.

"Huh?" he said.

"I'll show you how to pass the test."

"Hell, Mister, I haven't got time for that. I've got to be in there in 10 minutes." He said, pointing to the polygraph office door. "Besides, I can't pay you. If I had money, I wouldn't need this job so damn bad."

"C'mon," I said. "Let's head over to my car. I don't want any money from you and this won't take but a few minutes."

"Whatever," he mumbled, and followed me to my vehicle.

We sat in my car for about ten minutes while I explained the Sting Technique. He sat there staring at me with this look on his face like I was nuts – or, maybe this was some crazy *Candid Camera* episode he was in.

"Really?" he asked when I'd completed my training session.

"Really," I answered with a grin.

"That's it?"

"That's it."

We both went into the polygraphist's office. There were two polygraph operators in the office. I went with one and my new friend went with the other. I passed my test very quickly, then I took my time and gave the polygraphist my little speech explaining who I really was, and finally returned to the parking lot. When I got to my car, I saw a piece of paper lodged under the windshield wiper on the driver's side. I looked at the paper. In large capital letters, my first student had written the words, "I PASSED! THANK YOU!" A short meeting in the front seat of my car and the dreaded polygraph test had been exposed as a joke.

Every time I passed a polygraph exam, I would tell the operator who I really was and what I was trying to prove. My post-test speech would go something like this:

My real name is Doug Williams and I am an ex-police detective sergeant from the Oklahoma City Police Department. I am also a licensed polygraph examiner and have administered over six thousand tests. I have lied to you on every question you have asked, but you have determined that I was completely truthful. You, Sir, have been beaten, and beaten very badly. Remember my name. You will be hearing a lot more from me in the future because I am going to put you and your fellow conmen out of business.

Might as well get right to the point, I figured.

The reactions ran the gambit from fear to rage. One guy even threatened to call the police. I laughed at him and asked what he was going to say. That I beat his test? "Then, call," I told him. I had a lot of fun and a few scary moments, but I'd proven conclusively to other operators and to myself that the Sting Technique worked without fail every single time, and that there was never any doubt about the outcome.

It was now time to expand the Education Phase of my crusade and help those who felt threatened. I could – and, would - teach them how to protect themselves from being falsely accused of deception.

CHAPTER NINE

Crusading on a
Shoestring Budget

Without a regular paying job, I'd depleted my savings very quickly, and by the time I had proven the validity of the Sting Technique, I was flat broke. So, I had to find a way to make a living. I had no intention of embarking upon a new career path because I never once considered diverting my attention away from my primary goal. I started looking for a job that would pay me enough to get by, one that wouldn't take too much of my time and energy away from my crusade. I finally found a job as an apprentice machinist at Cameron Iron Works in Houston, and I have to admit, that was a humbling experience for a man of my age with my background and education. This place was a far cry from the White House Situation Room and the Oklahoma City Police Department. The factory was noisy, filthy, and filled with smoke. The people there were working at the only job they could find. It was nothing but a sweat shop. But, it paid well enough, and more importantly, it had a liberal leave policy, so I decided to hang with it for a while. I worked the second shift from 3:00 PM to 11:00 PM, which gave me plenty of time during the day to begin a phone calling and letter writing campaign.

I began a ritual. I would brew a pot of hot coffee, fire up a

Marlboro red, write letters and make phone calls to the offices of members of Congress and the Senate, both State and Federal, numerous unions, and the ACLU. I would include information about my background, my credentials as a polygraph expert, and a copy of my manual, *How to Sting the Polygraph*. I also contacted talk show hosts, television programs such as CBS News *Nightwatch, 60 Minutes*, and many others. In the letters and phone calls, I would spell out my objections to the use of the polygraph as a lie detector and explain exactly how I had arrived at my conclusions. I contacted anyone and everyone I could think of who could assist me in my campaign. I even gave the unions and the ACLU permission to copy my manual and distribute it for free to anyone who was subjected to a polygraph examination. It really wasn't very long before I started to receive responses. One of the first ones was from the American Civil Liberties Union. The ACLU told me that they had received more complaints about the polygraph than anything else they currently dealt with, and that they appreciated the attention I was giving it.

Not wanting to limit my attack with letters and calls, I decided to reach out to the public with impromptu and scheduled speaking demonstrations, as I guess you could call them. One of my favorite activities was to put on what I described as seminars. I would contact clerks at convenience stores and tell them who I was and what I was trying to do. Clerks were often targets of polygraph testing, so I figured this would be a good place to start. I would tell them to get a few people together and that I would bring my polygraph instrument, a few copies of my manual, and teach them how to pass the polygraph test. I started off holding the seminars in people's houses, but soon moved to union halls, church basements, and even conference rooms in hotels. I had a lot of fun demonstrating the Sting Technique, and I received an immense amount of gratification from people's reactions to the seminars. The reactions went from fear of the test - bordering on abject terror - to actually being able to laugh at it. And, after I had hooked them up to the machine and shown them how easily they could control every tracing on the chart, their fear of "the Box" changed to disdain and disgust at seeing what a sham it really was. I met one lady in her 50's who had already been subjected to a test before. She was thoroughly frightened and convinced that the machine had actually read her inner thoughts! After her friend got her to agree to sit with me and take the test again, she passed.

She looked at me and said, "That's it? That's all there is to it?"

"Yes, Ma'am, that's it," I answered.

Her wide-eyed fear turned to a delightful smile and a headshaking laugh.

I did everything I could think of in an attempt to generate interest in my cause, and over time, I began to gather support for my work. Although I was launching an assault on many fronts, I knew that to be the most productive, I would have to select one sector where the polygraph was doing a great deal of damage and focus on that. So, my first salvo was fired at the polygraph industry's use of pre-employment testing in the private sector. The emotional and economic damage done to innocent people because of testing in this arena was incalculable.

I was now receiving an increasing number of letters and phone calls. There were a few newspaper articles written about my crusade, and I was even being invited to appear on a few talk shows to debate other polygraph examiners – debates which, I might add, I always won. Many of the shows' producers told me that when the subject of the polygraph was announced, the call lines would light up with callers who were anxious to tell their own polygraph stories of torture. I would always encourage the talk show host to let the victims speak because their stories were so compelling, and these people needed to be heard. It was painful, however, to listen to these accounts of truthful people having been called liars, having lost job opportunities, having their life-long goals destroyed right in front of their eyes. Literally, millions of people every year who had simply applied for a job were being subjected to intrusive,

intimidating examinations administered by rude, overbearing, ob-
noxious, and sadistic polygraph operators.

During all the hundreds of radio and television talk shows I've
done, not one person who has ever called in has had anything positive to say about their polygraph experience. The reason for this is
obvious. The operators are able to ask any question they desire,
either relative to the job the person is applying for, or not. They're
even allowed to raise any other bizarre topic they wish to touch
upon. Increasingly, many of these professionals seem to derive a
sick satisfaction from delving into the sex lives of young people –
in particular, women applying for jobs. This is not an uncommon
practice. You've got to ask yourself what a clerk's job has to do with
one's sexual preference. These women - or anyone else, for that
matter - should never have to be subjected to this type of intrusive
and embarrassing interrogation just to get a job.

Yes, this was happening all the time and continues to happen
this very day. When the phone lines were opened, the victims of
the polygraph industry would vent their wrath upon the polygraph
operators. And, on those occasions when I was in the studio with
an operator and a caller brought up the bizarre questioning techniques, I really enjoyed watching the operator squirm and stutter
under those blistering and well-deserved attacks.

The Education Phase

Okay, class is in session and it's time for us to take a scientifically candid look at our subject: the polygraph. The word "polygraph" is a combination of two words: 'poly,' meaning 'many' and
'graphos,' meaning 'tracings'. The use of the polygraph as a lie detector is based upon the premise that when a person lies, certain
physiological reactions occur as a result of this lie and that this reaction always indicates deception. This "lying reaction" is shown on
the polygraph chart as an erratic breathing pattern, an increase in
blood pressure and pulse rate, and an increase in the GSR (Galvanic

Skin Response), which is nothing more than a measurement of the increase in sweat activity on the hand. Whenever I debated polygraph operators, I would simply point out that these very same reactions can be caused by any number of innocent stimuli. While it may be true that 50% of the time when you tell a lie, your breathing becomes erratic, your blood pressure and pulse rate increase, and your hands become sweaty, I would submit that it is also true that 50% of the time, that very same physiological reaction can be caused by something as innocent as simple nervousness.

It is important to understand that nervousness can occur in any number of circumstances: sporting events, weddings, doctor's appointments, etc. So, statistically, there is no more advantage to the polygraph than there is to the toss of a coin. I would ask employers to imagine how much money they could save by just tossing a coin into the air instead of using very expensive polygraph companies to test their applicants and employees. I would urge employers to consider just taking a quarter with them to the pre-employment interview. Ridiculous? No more so than paying huge sums of money to some charlatan with a totally fictitious claim about the validity of the scientifically faulty polygraph instrument being a valid and reliable lie detector, and who scams you into believing that half the people in the world are liars and he is the only protection you have. And, yes, I said "scam." I can't find a better word to accurately describe the polygraph industry – scam, fraud, con – take your pick. When you pay a polygraph operator, you are being duped, and you are the victim of the longest running con game in the history of our country. So, save your money and flip a coin.

CHAPTER TEN

Going into Battle

Armed with only the truth and my Sting Technique, I was pulled into the radio talk show circuit nearly full-time. It seemed that the more radio talk shows I did, the more I was invited to do. Occasionally, I was on some national shows, but at that time, most of them were local broadcasts. Each major city had its own group of radio talk show hosts, and I was rapidly becoming their go-to guy on the subject of polygraph testing whenever the subject was in the news. One producer told me that it was becoming more and more difficult to book a polygraph examiner who was willing to debate me. I explained to the producer that the operators preferred to keep the workings of their profession a mystery, largely because they knew that they could not explain to anyone's satisfaction how they could determine whether or not a person was lying by simply seeing his heart beating or her hands sweating.

Of course, whenever you start digging into the underpinnings of a billion-dollar industry, you're going to make some very powerful enemies. My enemies had deep pockets and a lot to lose if I were to become successful. Part of their anger and frustration came from the fact that, in the world of scientific fact, they had no defense against a truthful onslaught. And, that's what they were facing. They may have had numbers in their favor, but they were shut out when it came to scientific fact. Basically, I was throwing strikes and they were still trying to find a batter. But, I had declared war on a powerful and vicious enemy, and this was far from over.

I continued my letter writing and phone calling campaign while working the night shift at Cameron Iron Works. I also continued putting on seminars to teach people the Sting Technique, trying my best to put on at least one seminar per week. At the same time, I began coordinating with various unions – the AFL-CIO, the Teamsters, the Retail Clerks Union, among many others. To my surprise and relief, the popularity of my seminars soared. My crusade was progressing nicely, but I found that, as often happens in life, as soon as you get things on an even keel, they change. Cameron Iron Works manufactured oil field equipment, and in 1981, the oil boom went bust. I was laid off, and suddenly found myself without a steady income. So, one more time, I found myself faced with the challenge of trying to make a living while at the same time continuing my cause. I could not find another job that would give me the freedom of time off from work when I needed it. And, I was becoming fairly well-known in the Houston area, especially by polygraph examiners who hated me with a passion and were making their feelings known. Sounded like a good time to make another move on the battlefield.

It was 1981. I moved back to Oklahoma City where I renewed my friendship with an old pal, Chris Eulberg, a fellow police officer in the OKC police department. In fact, we had been in the same recruiting class back in 1969. Chris, now a practicing attorney, kindly offered me a job. He also said that he would even pay my way through law school if I would come to work with him. Since there was nothing else on the horizon and I didn't want to spend a lot of time looking around for a job, I took him up on his generous offer. Suddenly, there I was, Doug Williams, law school student at Oklahoma City University. I alternated this endeavor between working for Chris as a paralegal and continuing my fight against the polygraph industry.

Despite the fact that I was immersed in law school studies,

the move allowed me to embark upon the Litigation Phase of my three-pronged attack plan of *Education, Legislation, and Litigation*. Through some of my research, I discovered that there had recently been employee firings at a major business that relied heavily upon polygraph test results. It occurred to me that my new position would offer a great opportunity to pursue a wrongful discharge suit against that company and their polygraph employment practices. After speaking with one of the fired employees, I talked Chris into filing a wrongful discharge suit against Haliburton. Yeah, THAT Haliburton. I figured I'd just walk up to the porch, find the biggest, meanest dog of the bunch, and kick him before he could bite me. The lawsuit involved one of Haliburton's employees who had been fired from the purchasing department for the sole reason that he had failed a polygraph exam. This was the first lawsuit of its kind, which basically means that we were way ahead of our time. But, that was a problem in itself because, as any attorney will tell you, it is very difficult to build a case without the support of a former case law.

Even though we had no case law to back us up, we hit the legal ground hard and gave it our best shot. We filed the lawsuit, served subpoenas, and deposed the top executives of Haliburton at their headquarters in Duncan, Oklahoma. From the outset, our lawsuit was an uphill battle. It was like pushing a sled into the wind sideways up Mr. Kilimanjaro. Haliburton is a giant, and they had literally hundreds of lawyers in their corner and more money than the U.S. Mint. We never had a chance, even though I did get a lot of publicity for my crusade. More importantly, it gave me the opportunity to shine the spotlight on how one man's life had been ruined because a company had relied upon the results of a polygraph test and fired him. He had become another casualty in the lie detection war games. Well, at least he'd had a fight, which was more than anyone else had accomplished up to that point, so his case was a very big step along the way. The publicity of the case brought a great deal of national exposure, too, and, almost immediately, I was back on the radio talk show circuit, preaching against the horrors of an industry I so deeply despised.

As our media attention was growing elsewhere, television audiences were glued to their sets watching an attorney named F. Lee Bailey. Mr. Bailey had a syndicated series entitled *Lie Detector* that was produced by Ralph Andrews of Columbia Pictures. The premise of the program was to mesmerize viewers with the science of the lie detector as an impeccable piece of equipment that no one could manipulate, mislead, or escape. People were tested on air and, at the conclusion of the program, the audience was told if that person was deemed a truthful, honest, God-fearing American, or, if they were deemed a liar, tramp, or thief. This was dramatic stuff.

My attention was drawn to the show for obvious reasons, but one interview especially held my interest. One of the guests had been Jerry Ray. Mr. Ray was the brother of James Earl Ray, the man who had killed Dr. Martin Luther King, Jr. A short time after Mr. Ray had taken the polygraph on Mr. Bailey's *Lie Detector* show, Mr. Ray had this to say:

"I've taken five lie detector tests in my lifetime. I lied on all five, and I passed all five. One of those five tests happened back in the eighties, on a popular television show called, *Lie Detector*, hosted by famous criminal attorney, F. Lee Bailey. The person who actually administered the test to me on national television was a man named Ed Gelb, who was widely regarded as the best polygrapher in the business at the time. On that show, I was asked if I'd ever been involved in a bank robbery. I answered 'no,' which was a lie. I'm not saying that I'm proud of having been involved in a bank job. I'm just saying that I had been involved, and that I lied about it when asked that question on the show. At the end of the show, Bailey announced that I had passed the polygraph test."

However, F. Lee Bailey was a staunch defender of the lie detector, and he made it clear that his word was final in this matter. To back that claim of ultimate stature, he even went so far as to announce on his show that he would offer a $50,000.00 reward to anyone who could beat the polygraph. Really? It'd be pretty hard to turn that down. So, I didn't. My attorney friend, Chris, helped me draft a letter on Eulberg's law firm stationery to the producers and the network that broadcast Bailey's show. We challenged Bailey with the statement that I could beat the lie detector very easily and demanded the opportunity to prove it and collect the $50,000.00 reward he was offering. I signed the letter, and we sent it out UPS Next Day delivery. The very next week, the show was cancelled. Now, that's a real head-scratcher...or, maybe it isn't.

I continued with law school for a couple of semesters, but soon the money for tuition ran out. This didn't bother me much because my priority was my work against the polygraph, not becoming an attorney. So, Chris and I parted with a handshake and, once again, I moved on. Driving down the road, I realized that a lot of drastic changes had taken place in my life since my declaration of war on the polygraph industry. But, so far, I had just been kicking some dust into their eyes and forcing a game or two of legal hopscotch. I knew that it was time to either commit full force to this crusade, or to abandon it completely. Was I going to have a normal life, or was I going to continue the fight? It was obvious that I couldn't do both. I didn't ponder it very long before I decided that I had to make this crusade my top priority. I vowed to continue, and to do whatever it took to expose the abuse, no matter the cost. And, cost, it would.

I had no idea the mental and physical tolls I would face for all my endeavors, but sometimes, you have to make a run at the wall and keep at it until you start knocking some bricks out of it. This is true especially if you have a righteous cause, and I was convinced that I was on the side of the angels. I believe that if you see a situation where people are being oppressed and it is within your power to stop that oppression, you don't have the right to decide whether or not you are going to try and stop it. I am a Christian, so I am bound to that duty. There was really no questioning my future. It was time to crank up the pressure.

CHAPTER ELEVEN

Lobby with Moby

Some states had already outlawed or restricted the use of the polygraph as a condition of employment in the private sector. However, I was convinced that what was needed was a Federal law that would protect everyone from the insidious treatment of this industry. I believed that there was absolutely no justification for the continued use of the polygraph in hiring situations, and it was quite apparent that others knew this, as well. More people were realizing it all the time. The obvious conclusion was to enforce a Federal law banning polygraph use as qualification for employment.

After some research, I discovered that Congress had tried to pass such a law every year since 1972, but every time, the legislation had failed. The fact that some states had passed such a law didn't answer the definitive problem. Geographically separate and disparate legislation, although well-intentioned, wasn't a problem-solver as much as it was a philosophical first aid treatment. I was determined to get this Federal law passed, and soon. By now, thousands of victims had told me their heart-rending and, sometimes, horrifying stories of polygraph experiences, and I needed to follow through with my promise to stop this madness. Staying in one place would not get it done, so I had to become mobile – mobile on a big scale. An old buddy of mine from Iowa had told me that legendary

Hawkeye Coach, Hayden Fry, used to say, "You gotta scratch where it itches." Very simply, take the action to them. It was time to hit the road.

I outfitted myself with what equipment I could afford from a list of things I knew that I would need to carry on the battle, as well as to just generally live. Once I had done that, I suddenly realized that I would need a bigger vehicle than the one I currently owned. It wouldn't just be for storing all my new possessions, but a car big enough for me to live in, because in all likelihood, that was going to be the case for a while. So, I sold my old car and bought a 1967 Chevy panel truck. It was faded white with one side caved in from a dent that ran from the rear of the driver's side door all the way down to the back end. It had two front seats, no side windows, and two doors in the back. I put carpet down on the metal floor in the rear, rigged a cot that would fold down from the side, installed a small camping porta-potty, added a hotplate, an ice chest, and containers for drinking water. I also bought a large foot locker in which to store my papers and copies of my manual that could also double as a desk for my portable typewriter. It was, actually, quite efficient. I could sit on the edge of my fold-down bunk, and type. That way, I could continue my letter writing campaign, no matter where I was. I loaded up a file full of names and contact numbers for the media and anything else I could think of that I would need for this cross-country crusade. The last thing I needed to do was to name my war wagon. So, I called it Moby Dick because it was white and odd-shaped, just like the great white whale. It was, indeed, quite a sight.

I was now mobile in an, albeit, very Spartan command center. Instead of heading right out at first, I stayed in Oklahoma City. I had some contacts there, and I could start networking and build a support group composed of union officials, ACLU members, and others who would hopefully be willing to help me with my quest and give guided tours of my new "rolling central command and operations center." Okay, so I made that last part up, but I really was networking, and networking diligently. I knew that I was also going to have to support myself, and luckily, good fortune kissed me on the forehead once again when I met up with my old friend Tom Brown. Tom was one of those creative inventor types, and he was building a prototype energy efficient home. Although he was getting up in years, he already had two of the three things he needed to complete his project. He had a great plan, and he had the money to finance that plan. The only thing he was lacking was an able-bodied man to help him finish the job. I made a deal with him. If he would allow me to park Moby Dick on his property as my temporary campsite, I would help him build his house. He agreed, and even offered to pay me a small salary.

Having secured gainful employment and a place to camp, I got my campaign back on track and resumed working my contacts. I started with an organization with which I had not always been on friendly terms, the ACLU. I went to the headquarters of the American Civil Liberties Union in Oklahoma City where I met the State Director, a wonderful woman by the name of Shirley Berry. I began to tell her about myself and my crusade and described what I had been doing. Suddenly, about halfway through my story, she started clapping her hands and gave me a big hug. I thought this was a rather remarkable reaction, but then she told me that she had heard about my press conference and had listened to me on KTOK. Shirley said that if there was anything she could do to help me, she was up to the task. Before I could respond, she offered the use of her office and facilities whenever I needed. She also promised to introduce me to people in the ACLU community, both locally and nationally, as well as to local and national union leaders. Talk about jumping in with both feet – this lady was ready to help immediately, which was awesome news because I knew that all of her contacts would be incredibly important.

A game plan was starting to form. There would be meetings, phone calls and interviews in my future. Fortunately, this balanced out well with my personal life, which consisted of living in Moby Dick and working on Tom's house. And, yes, that's a bit of sarcasm.

The truth is, working on my friend's house was actually enjoyable most of the time, but living in the white whale was semi-miserable. Only semi-miserable, I told myself, because there were lots and lots of people who had it far worse - I just hadn't met any of them, yet.

Happily, my situation didn't remain that way for long. God, karma, or the patron saint of homeless, crusading home builders provided a solution. It came in the form of a beautiful nurse whom I met through my brother and sister-in-law. The young lady understood that I had a cause in my life; she had a real-life, human home; and, she liked me. I considered these things all signs of good character and, like I said, she was beautiful. This woman actually took pity on this burned out ex-cop - at least, that's the impression I got. We would walk and talk, and as I endeavored to explain my goals, she would politely nod and say, "Huh-hum," and, occasionally, shake her head ever so slightly. But, not once did she try to dissuade me from my self-appointed mission. Oh, yes, she thought I was crazy – but, good crazy. The only time she said anything critical was the first time we stopped in front of my mobile residence.

"What is that?" she asked.

"Moby Dick," I answered.

"You live in that?"

"Yes."

"And, you named it..."

"Moby Dick."

"Really?"

"Wouldn't make up something like that."

"Hmm. Doug, don't you think it'd be better to live in a real house or an apartment, or something?"

"I suppose, but..."

"Think about it. You're taking on this gigantic industry with thousands and thousands of followers, most of whom probably wish you harm, and these people have powerful connections in offices all around the country with every conceivable tool of new technology at their fingertips to use however they see fit on a moment's notice. And, along comes Doug Williams, crusader of the oppressed and beaten, waging a one-man war against these titans of tyranny from his headquarters inside…Moby Dick?"

"Yep," I said, smiling.

"Get your stuff, we're going to my place."

"Okay. You're sure on that, huh?"

"Yes, Doug, I'm sure on that. I think what you're doing is cool, and besides, on a more personal note, if this relationship is headed where I think it's headed, I don't want to tell my closest friend that we consummated it inside of Moby Dick. It just sounds so… Just get your stuff."

As a result of this sweet gesture, my living conditions improved immediately and gave me a stationary base from which to work. I had a phone, a place to keep all my records, and a table on which to put my typewriter – yes, a real table. It was like mentally shifting gears. Not only had she given me a place to live, but my nurse would become a great help to me in what had become my life's work.

I continued to be a very popular talk show guest as the skepticism about me gradually began to dissipate. I guess that it became clear to the producers that the polygraph industry was universally hated, and that I was able to present my case convincingly enough to a sympathetic audience. I was also no longer completely alone in my struggle. In addition to the assistance from my new friend, the nurse, I was also helped a great deal by some of the same people who had helped me in Houston: the ACLU, the Retail Clerks Union, AFL-CIO, Teamsters, the FOP, and other police unions. Then, I decided to utilize my background in religion to enlist the help of some of the United Methodist churches in the area.

I started giving seminars again and they became popular quite quickly. The number of people subjected to polygraph abuse was growing daily, and as a result, my training was in demand. As I mentioned earlier, in the 80's, millions of people had been forced to submit to polygraph examinations in order to get jobs in the private sector. In addition, in order to keep those jobs, periodic testing was required. Randomly chosen from the employee pool, he or she was tested to make sure of the worthiness of their minimum wage job, and, of course, to ensure that the polygraph examiner was amply paid. If one worked as a clerk in a convenience store, as a teller in a bank, a route salesman for a beer or soft drink company, or as a clerk in a retail store, these tests were a fact of life.

CHAPTER TWELVE

Spread the Word

The list of polygraph victims now numbered in the millions of employees throughout national, state, and local governments. Through the offices of the ACLU, the churches, and the unions, I was able to get access to union halls, church basements, and conference rooms in various hotels for my seminars. Anyone concerned that they might be subjected to a polygraph test at some point in their life was encouraged to attend. The seminars were free, and became one long march of spread the word, spread the word, spread the word.

At the beginning of each seminar, I would make sure that everyone in attendance had a copy of my manual, *How to Sting the Polygraph.* I would explain my title to the audience this way: a 'sting' is when you con a con man, and he never even knows he's been conned. The sting was the absolute goal: to beat them at their own set of game rules, and to do it without being noticed. It wasn't lying, I told them. The test was not reliable, so I was only teaching people how to protect themselves. I explained that the polygraph operators were the con men running the scam, and that when anyone in the audience had to take a test, they should just do what I would train them to do, and to never let on that they knew anything about the Sting Technique. I would then place my polygraph machine on a table in the front of the room and make the statement that, in five minutes or less, I was going to teach them how to control every tracing on the polygraph chart, and that when the seminar was over, they would know as much, or more, than any polygraph examiner. They would also have the added advantage that the examiner would not know *what they knew.* I'd look around the room and try to find the most skeptical person there. Then, I would look directly at that person and say, "You don't believe a word I'm saying, do you?"

Often, the simple answer was, "No."

Then, I'd say, "Well, let me prove it to you. Come up to the front and help me demonstrate my Sting Technique."

First, I would hook the volunteer up to the machine and, as I put the attachments on them, I would explain what the polygraph actually recorded. I would put the blood pressure cuff on the left arm and explain that the polygraph could record their blood pressure and heart rate. I would put the pneumograph tubes around the chest and stomach, attach the GSR electrodes to their fingers and explain what these attachments recorded. The audience would be directed to look at the exhibits in the manual, specifically Exhibit A, to see what these tracings looked like on an actual chart. Then, I'd begin my demonstration, which would go something like this:

The polygraph is not some kind of mind reading machine. It is not a magical lasso of truth like the one Wonder Woman used. Speaking of Wonder Woman, you may be interested to know that one of the self-proclaimed inventors of the polygraph – a man named Marston – actually wrote the comic book Wonder Woman. That fact, alone, should show you what a joke the polygraph is. Lasso of Truth, my ass!

That would always get a nervous laugh as the audience began to relax.

Marston, like all polygraph operators, was nothing but a fraud. In fact, he was worse than a fraud, he was a thief. He did not invent the polygraph, as he claimed. All he did was steal an idea from Dr.

John Larson, the true inventor of the polygraph. The real irony is that Dr. Larson called his invention a 'Frankenstein's Monster,' and he tried for forty years to stop it from being used as a lie detector. Why? Because he knew that it did not work.

Think about that. Let it sink in. The real inventor knew that the polygraph didn't work and tried to stop its use. The polygraph was invented in 1921 and has not changed since it was invented. It is, very simply, a crude reaction recorder and the reactions that brand you as a liar are often caused by nothing more than simple nervousness. What's more, I know how to control every tracing on the chart and I can produce a truthful chart, regardless of whether I'm telling the truth or lying. Now, I'm going to teach you all exactly how to do the same.

Let me tell you how I came to learn how to beat the polygraph. When I was on the police force, my only job was to run polygraph examinations. I learned early on in my career that the polygraph often branded innocent, truthful people as liars, simply because they had a nervous reaction on a relevant question. The so-called lying reaction is shown in Exhibit B in the manual. As you can see, this reaction is nothing more than an erratic breathing pattern, an increase in the GSR or sweat activity on your hand and an increase in blood pressure and pulse rate. Polygraph examiners will tell you that this reaction always indicates deception; but, I know for a fact that this very same lying reaction can be caused by any number of innocent stimuli: fear, embarrassment, rage at having been asked the question, simple nervousness, or even stress from taking the test, itself.

So, let's cut to the chase and get the answer to the question that you all came here to get. How do I pass a polygraph test? The answer is very simple. You learn how to manipulate a reaction to the control questions and how to avoid showing a reaction to the relevant questions. I once was asked if I could beat the polygraph. I began to seriously ponder that question. Remember, I was a polygraph examiner for the Oklahoma City Police Department for over seven years. I knew how the polygraph chart scored. If the subject showed a reaction to the relevant questions that was greater than the reaction to the control questions, they were presumed to be lying. If the reverse was true and they reacted more to the control questions than to the relevant questions, they were presumed to be telling the truth. I knew the difference between the relevant and control questions; that was easy. The relevant questions were obviously those that pertained to the reason the test was being given. On a criminal test, they were relevant to the crime under investigation. On a pre-employment test, they were those questions that would disqualify a person if he were deemed to have lied. I also knew what the breathing patterns looked like on the polygraph chart. I reasoned that it would be a simple matter to breathe calmly and evenly when answering the relevant questions, and to show an erratic breathing pattern when answering the control questions.

But, a fundamental question remained. How could I control the cardio and GSR tracings? How could I show an increase in blood pressure and pulse rate with an accompanying increase in the GSR tracing and produce this reaction on demand at the appropriate time? The answer came a few weeks later when a friend of mine was telling me about a pursuit that he and his partner had been involved with the night before. He told me that they had been chasing this bad guy at speeds of over 100 mph when his partner lost control of the scout car and they careened off the road into a ditch. He said, 'The pucker factor was so high, my asshole was pinching doughnuts out of the seat.' The pucker factor is a phrase used by cops and soldiers to indicate a very frightening situation. After my friend told me this, I realized that I might have just discovered a way to produce a blood pressure and pulse rate spike. I immediately hooked myself up to the polygraph machine and tightened my anal sphincter muscle like I was trying to stop a bowel movement. Not the most glamorous experiment, I'll admit, but very effective because, just as I had hoped, the tracings on the polygraph chart showed a dramatic increase in my blood pressure and pulse rate. And, much to my surprise, the GSR tracing mirrored the same response. In other words, by simply duplicating my body's physiological response to fear by implementing the pucker, I was now able at will to easily control every tracing on the chart. It was then that I knew the answer to the question was, 'Yes! I can beat the polygraph!'

As my attention turned back to my volunteer, I would ask him to demonstrate the Sting Technique by taking five to seven very shallow breaths and tightening up his anal sphincter muscle. When he did as he was instructed, right there on the chart for everyone to see was the evidence that he could do exactly what I had told him at the beginning of my talk - and, in five minutes, or less. I would tear off the chart, hold it up for the audience to see, and watch the surprised looks on their faces. I had proven to them that not only could they all do it, but they could do it easily. It was personally gratifying to see their relief when they finally realized that there was absolutely nothing to be nervous about. The polygraph operator was no longer in control. They were.

CHAPTER THIRTEEN

National T.V.

I continued to fine-tune my presentations, but now I realized that it was time to begin a new phase: Legislation, the second prong of my plan. I began to emphasize the need for new Federal laws banning the use of the polygraph in the private sector. I reasoned that it would be easier to get legislation passed to cover the private sector first, and subsequently try to get it expanded to include the government. The government wouldn't relinquish power easily, and those in positions of authority were adamant that they wanted to keep using the polygraph. However, many other people had started to adopt my conclusions, and I was encouraged by the unions and ACLU to become active in that pursuit. They believed that we finally had a good chance of success in enacting legislation.

There were high hopes that a bill could be passed into law because we now had the one element that had been missing in the past. For the first time in history, an expert polygraphist could be presented to testify in support of legislation forbidding the use of the polygraph. Everyone within the organizations involved agreed that I could really make a difference because I would be the first licensed polygraph operator to ever blow the whistle as an insider's insider. As such, I would testify as to the atrocities that I, myself, had committed, and to my own first-hand knowledge about the polygraph industry.

To further assist in our efforts to get legislation passed, I stepped up my personal correspondence to Senators and Representatives, offering my services as an expert witness to testify in support of legislation intended to stop polygraph use. In the meantime, as I continued broadcasting information, I was getting threats. Usually, they came from unidentified callers over the phone. I began to grow weary of the gutless no-names when they called, so instead of just hanging up on them, I found myself beginning to challenge them. "Listen, you gutless bootlicker, you know where I am...bring your ass on over here and let's see what you've got. Or, do you want to wait until I'm not looking?" I had a strong suspicion that the latter was exactly what they were doing.

For several years, I had been concentrating my efforts towards advancing the public profile of my campaign by contacting the major television networks: ABC, CBS, and NBC. Since there were no cable stations at that time, these networks dominated the airways. Of the three, CBS was by far the most popular and influential. I frequently wrote to *60 Minutes* and *Nightwatch*, since they both used the news magazine type of format. Besides, at that time, I was a big fan of Charlie Rose, the host of *Nightwatch*. So, very early on, I decided to find a way to enlist his help in my fight and pleaded with him to allow his program to spotlight the abuses of the polygraph industry. To me, he seemed to be one of the more open-minded late-night hosts, and I felt that he had a legitimacy about him. I also thought that his audience would primarily be composed of people who might very well be subjected to polygraph exams, so it was a hand-in-glove fit.

I pointed that out in my correspondence to him and repeated some of the stories I had heard from polygraph victims. Basically, I was putting forth to Mr. Rose the argument that I was also using with Congress. My request to him was very simple: let the facts play out on your show and let the evidence stand on its own, nothing more. That's all I was asking. Finally, my writer's cramp paid off and I got a response from CBS. I was invited to appear as a guest on *Nightwatch*. My first opportunity to appear in front of a national television audience. I was beyond elated, I was jubilant and a bit nervous, all at the same time. And, why wouldn't I be? This was a big deal. The show was produced in Washington, D.C. It was right near the top of the Neilsen ratings, and its audience was not only very large, it was very loyal. I could relate to how people felt about the show because I, myself, watched it at every opportunity. At that point in his career, Charlie Rose was a great interviewer and the program dealt with a variety of current events in the news. They also had celebrity guests and an occasional activist appear, providing that they were controversial and well-spoken. I felt like I fit that model, too. I couldn't help but realize that this would be a great opportunity for me and my cause.

CBS Nightwatch scheduled me for a fifteen-minute segment and sent me an airline ticket. I was ready. I had been waiting for this chance for over four years, and I was chomping at the bit and raring to go! I had fine-tuned my arguments on hundreds of radio and television programs, interviews for newspaper and magazine articles, and during my seminars. Even so, I decided to rehearse by looking into a mirror and going through my discussion points, one at a time. But, after about five minutes of this, I came to the realization that there is never a need to "practice" the truth.

I'll admit, though, that I was a little rough around the edges in appearance...did I not mention that before? Well, I had long hair and a mustache, and I looked every bit the wild-eyed, crazy crusader. I did, however, also have credentials, knowledge, and the truth. So, I figured it was time for me to put myself like a boat in the water and see if I would float.

When I arrived in Washington, D.C., CBS had a limo waiting for me at the airport. It took me directly to the *Nightwatch* studios where I was met by a group of people I presumed were with the program. What I had anticipated to happen next would be a professional, cordial meeting between the show's staff and my-self – but, immediately, I was struck by their skepticism. Actually, it was beyond skepticism. It was outright hostility. It was obvious that many of them were opposed to what I seemingly stood for and what I was doing in my quest to ban the use of the polygraph. They questioned my motives, made snide comments about my ap-pearance, and made it very clear that they doubted my sanity. They even went so far as to suggest that what I was doing was unethical, if not outright illegal. Some even asked me point blank why I was teaching liars how to beat the lie detector. To say the least, I was shocked, confused, and getting more than a little bit perturbed by their attitudes.

I began to wonder why I had even been invited to the show in the first place if everyone was so opposed to what I was about. It cer-tainly wasn't what I had pictured as the open-minded *Nightwatch* program I had viewed in the past. And, that's when I discovered the probable answer to that question. I was informed that Charlie Rose, host of the program and a man I admired greatly, was going to be off that night. His replacement was a CBS Supreme Court reporter by the name of Fred Graham. The word was that Graham had made it very clear from the outset that he was not a fan of mine and that he wanted nothing to do with my cause. It quickly became appar-ent that I didn't have a friend in the house – nor, an objective mod-erator for the show.

I can only presume that Charlie Rose would have been more sympathetic to my beliefs, or, at the very least, more open-minded. My correspondence with him had indicated that he was aware of what I was trying to do and why I was trying to do it, which was probably why I had gotten the invitation in the first place. But, re-gardless of the surprise change, and in spite of the hostility, I tried to be as diplomatic as possible under the circumstances. I did take comfort in the realization that I had finally made it to the big time. I was in the studio, and I was determined not to blow my chance at my first national television appearance, despite the fact that everyone was treating me like something foul they'd found on the bottom of their shoe. Things could be worse – and, maybe they would be. I'm a pretty tough guy, but the truth is, I was nervous. After all, there was a lot riding on this, not just for me, but for all the victims, and it seemed like the deck was stacked against me. Their plan seemed to be to put this whistle-blowing loud-mouth from Oklahoma in his place. Nope. They obviously didn't know with whom they were dealing. They weren't getting a virgin, here. After what I'd already been through, I was a veteran at dealing with this kind of behavior. I was prepared. Of course, I couldn't compete with Fred's manicured nails and somewhat inflated ego, but I was in the game. That was the main thing.

I realize how corny this must sound, but I really did feel a responsibility to the victims of the polygraph industry. I'd heard so many of their stories, and yes, I could feel their pain. I had promised them that I would do my best to stop the abuse, so I would try. I figured that this was going to be a balancing act, a give-and-take situation. So, for now, I would take their attitude. But, that would only be temporary...because once the cameras were on, it would be show time.

I attempted to get control of my anger, put on my happy face, and smile at everyone with my most sincere smile. I told them that I would be happy to prove to them that the polygraph was not as valid as a lie detector as they seemed to believe. Just as I had claimed in my letters to Charlie Rose, I said that in only five minutes or less, I could train anyone to control the tracings and provide proof that the polygraph was not a dependable method of lie detection. Then, I stopped, pointed at them and reminded them that they didn't have a damn thing to lose – that the risk would be all mine, every bit of it. If I failed, they would be congratulated for exposing me as a fraud. And, if I proved my point, well, they would have a scoop on all the other networks with a controversial and interesting program. Then, with my good nature melting down a little, I said, "So, if you're not afraid, pick someone to be my subject. Then, stand back and watch."

They looked at each other as though they were trying to figure out what to do with me. It was a bit bizarre. I was standing all by myself while they huddled up in a little cluster on the other side of the room. Lots of whispering and nodding, rolling of eyes, bodily twitches, flinches and gyrations were going on. So, while they were involved in their summit meeting of the stressed and sensitive, I took the opportunity to look around the studio. It was a very large room, surrounded by glass-enclosed offices along the sides. The set was a small platform in the center of the room, with three chairs lined up behind a small table. It was surrounded by metal poles with lights attached to them, and there were yards and yards of cable all around. There were four T.V. cameras on rollers, and several monitors were scattered about the room. It was the largest studio I had ever been in, and, believe me, it was intimidating.

However, what drew my attention even more than the show's set were two men in suits who were standing off to the side in the shadows. My cop's eyes were immediately drawn to the bulges beneath their jackets. It was obvious that they were armed. Probably my ever-present FBI surveillance team. It was becoming a real drag having a couple of Feds around glaring at me all the time, but, by now, I was becoming accustomed to it. Apparently, the crime rate must have been at an all-time low for them to spend so many tax dollars following me around. And, they made no secret of the fact that I was under surveillance. The presence of the FBI agents in the studio was possibly one of the reasons that most of the staff were so hostile and unsure about how to deal with me. They had to wonder just what the hell they were getting into. The government was clearly in support of the polygraph, and President Reagan had just signed a presidential directive expanding its use in an attempt to stop leaks to the press and to strengthen national security. So, I'm sure they were not wild about the idea of me actually teaching people how to beat their test on national T.V.

After a while, the group of staff people came out of their huddle and approached me with my first test subject in tow. He was a young man in his early twenties, and it was apparent that he was quite nervous. I tried to put him at ease by smiling, shaking his hand, patting him on the back, and telling him that I was going to make him a star. One of the producers led us to a small room off to the side of the studio. Once we were both seated and away from everyone else, I explained to my young volunteer what I was going to do. Then, I gave him all my normal instructions. I asked if he could follow the instructions and execute them on the count of three. He gave me a rather surprised look and said that he thought he could handle that. I hooked him up to the polygraph and all its equipment. After a couple of tries, he got the correct tension level with his sphincter muscle and produced a perfect cardio rise. We looked at each other, and I saw the same reaction on this young man's face as I had seen countless times before.

It had only been about five minutes when I opened the door and motioned the group to come and look at the results. I pointed to my watch and said confidently that this new volunteer was already an expert on how to beat a polygraph test. I showed them the chart and explained that this was exactly what I intended to do on their program. They appeared to be somewhat impressed by my demonstration, and one of them even admitted that it would make a very compelling visual effect on T.V. However, I could see that, impressed or not, many of them were even more hostile than they had been previously. I was now convinced that many of these people were not network personnel, at all, but were really government plants. To make matters worse, the FBI agents were still lurking in the shadows and glaring at me with those same malevolent looks on their faces.

The production staff told me that was all they needed for the moment, and that the limo would take me to the hotel. So, I started packing up my equipment, which was no small task. It was not the sleek computerized model of today; it was the analog model, the same kind that had been used for over fifty years. The pens were hollow metal tubes that drew ink from their own plastic containers.

In order to pack them up, I had to drain the ink from the pens and clean them thoroughly. It was a messy, time-consuming job, and no sooner had I finished than a woman I hadn't met came up to me and said they thought there was a problem with the volunteer that I had just trained. She said that the union refused to allow him to appear on camera, so there would have to be a new subject. I figured this was probably bullshit, but what was I going to do? It was their show and I was only a guest. Clearly, this was becoming a contest of wills. I thought to myself, what choice did I have. It's their kite; they can fly it any way they want to. Besides, I had been in situations much more pressure-packed than this, and I was determined to hang on until the wind quit blowing.

The producer made it clear that there was no way around the problem and that I would have to train someone else. So, I clenched my teeth, nodded, opened up my polygraph case and began getting it set up to train another volunteer. Apparently, this was their way of performing due diligence, or, more likely, attempting to beat me down before the program even began because over the next three hours, I trained at least six more people. And, much to the chagrin of most of the staff, it took less than five minutes per person to train them. By now, this had become a test of my endurance, and they were obviously enjoying themselves immensely. I noticed that many members of the original group had left and that there were new people showing up all the time. Many were asking if they could take a turn at trying to "beat the box." I was exhausted. I had been at it non-stop for several straight hours. But, wanting to be a good sport and keep everyone happy, I kept at it until they all got tired of playing polygraph games.

Finally, the woman in charge told me that they were all completely satisfied that I could do what I had claimed and that we could call it a day. She did seem a bit more enthusiastic now, and some of the hostility had disappeared. Curiosity had replaced much of the animosity that had filled the room earlier – and, oh, by the way - remember the FBI agents? Well, it seems that they had left the building, which gave the group cause to relax a bit more, too. I was told that the limo would pick me up at 9:00 A.M. for the taping of my segment the next day. Man, what a relief that was. It had been a long, tiring, and very weird day, and I needed some rest.

I arrived at the hotel around 9:00 P.M., got a bite to eat at the restaurant in the lobby, went to my room and unpacked my suit. People probably thought that I was partial to that suit because I wore it so much. But, there was a legitimate reason for wearing that suit. It was my only suit. Yes, I had been running around the country doing seminars and radio and T.V. shows with only one suit. If you were to look closely at the television programs I did in the early to mid-eighties, you would see that my ensemble never changed. I might have long hair and a mustache on some shows or my hair would be cut short with no mustache on others, but the one constant was that I would always be wearing that same brown suit. I had been desperately poor most of the time, and what money I could earn by working odd jobs was used to support my crusade. There certainly was no money in my meager budget for a collection of good suits. Hell, there was no money in my budget for a collection of good socks! Yet, one has to be adaptable in the world of poverty-stricken crusaders, so I had purchased a nice brown suit from a Goodwill thrift store for my appearances. Actually, it was a very nice suit, and I think I only paid about $3.00 for it. For an additional $2.00, I had picked up a nice pair of lightly used wing-tip cordovans. The Goodwill had kept me looking sharp, and all on a $5.00 clothing allowance. I have to admit, no one ever asked me who my tailor was, and packing sure was easy.

After I had performed my pre-event ritual of unpacking my wardrobe and ironing out the wrinkles, I went into full relax mode and the weariness of the day hit me full on. I was mentally and physically whipped, and nothing but sleep had any appeal, whatsoever. I sat down on the edge of the bed, too tired to move, and replayed the events of the last many hours in my mind. Almost immediately, my reverie was rudely interrupted by the ringing of the phone next to the bed. The last thing I wanted at that moment was to talk to anyone, but I answered it. Instantly, I regretted having done so as I recognized the voice on the other end. It was she, the woman from the studio. It was becoming a never-ending saga, and my irritation rose from "What the hell is it, now?" to a red hot "Are you shitting me?"

I realized that she was boozed up, and in the background, I could hear the chirps and burps of a noisy downtown bar as she slurred and giggled through her new request. It seemed that, once again, there was a problem with the volunteer I had tested and trained. But, she laughed, not to worry. She, being the always alert and all-attentive executive that she was, had located another volunteer that would be perfect. The bartender. Yes, the bartender from her current watering hole would be just perfect. She wanted to send a limo to get me and have me train this one last volunteer.

For a moment, I just sat there not saying anything as I analyzed my response possibilities. I could say 'no,' in which case I could very well lose my nationally televised T.V. time. Or, I could say "Yes, Ma'am, you bet, whatever your heart desires. I am your servant, day and night." Or, I could describe an anatomically impossible position I would like her to attempt and then, upon its completion, I would agree to return to the studio. Of course, the particular move I was contemplating might hurt her neck, or her head might get stuck and the show would never get off the ground, so I said, "Fine," and hung up. Okay, so I'm a softy. But, really, the crusade needed this T.V. spot, so if I had to bend over a few times – within reason – I'd do it. Like I said, within reason.

When I got back to the studio it was about 10:00 P.M. and the group that I had presumed were sent to intimidate and frustrate me had grown considerably. Reinforcements had been sent in. There were at least two dozen people in the room, and it was obvious that many had been hitting the sauce pretty hard. Looking back on it now, I'm sure my suspicions at the time were correct. Most of them were probably just bar patrons, or winos, or government agents, and I was beginning to wonder if there was any difference. But, assuredly, most of them were not associated with the network. If two agents can't intimidate the Williams guy, let's fill the room with flakes, no-neck thugs, and bully boys and see how he likes that. The flakes irritated the hell out of me. They were just a bunch of clueless clowns skipping through life in a pink-hued fog on someone else's bar tab. The bullies didn't bother me a bit – they could flex and puff all they wanted. The truth was that when I was on the police force, I'd probably spent more time in bar fights than any of these guys had ever spent away from home.

The woman in charge stepped up with a slight stagger and proudly produced her latest volunteer. I noticed that he was not nearly as drunk as the rest of them, so I hoped that I could get this over with quickly and drag my ass back to the hotel for some heavy sleep and light dreams. I took my new subject into the office and set up my machine for the third time that day and went through the little training exercise with him. He told me that he was very interested in learning about the polygraph test since he'd had to take one to get his job and had to take it again every six months to keep the job. He really wanted to know how it worked, or if it worked. I was pleasantly surprised by his polite and respectful manner. Thankfully, his comments reminded me of what I was there to do and gave me a little boost to get through the late night.

Five minutes later, I reported to the group that I had, once again, trained a person to control every tracing on the chart. I tore off the chart and showed it to them. I asked them if I had finally convinced even the most skeptical among them that the polygraph was not a lie detector. They all looked at each other as if to see whether they were all in agreement and reluctantly conceded that I had, and that the next day's program would truly be a history-making event. I, myself, found it a major endorsement from the American Society of the Drunken Stupor.

CHAPTER FOURTEEN

Reality T.V. – Really?

When I arrived at the studio the next morning, the alcohol in-duced gaiety of the previous evening had subsided. It had been re-placed by an atmosphere that one could best describe as dark and unpleasant, almost ominous, similar to an afternoon sky before a severe round of thunder. The clouds in this particular "sky" came in the form of two more armed men standing in a poorly lit area just off the set. These were different men from the previous day's events, and they were presenting me with their best sinister stares as I walked around the area, prepping for the show. These guys worked harder at looking tough than the first two guys. They didn't look tougher; they just worked harder at it. Obviously, the A-team had arrived. Or, maybe the other guys were just hung over.

But, on the brighter side, today there was a new producer. I had not met her before and I was delighted to see that, unlike the woman from the day before, she had a much more professional at-titude. Everything about her – her demeanor, her clothes, and even the way she walked – was professional. And, she was sober, which I took as a bonus.

One thing, however, hadn't changed from the day before. She, too, had another subject for me to train. This new subject, however, was very different from the others. Not only was this "volunteer" dressed in a very nice business suit, but there was something else about this man that made him unlike any of the other people I had tested earlier at the studio. Where the previous day's participants had been curious and a tiny bit willing, this person was openly hostile from the very beginning. The producer finally told me that this man was an Assistant U.S. Attorney. Coincidence? I think not.

This just confirmed my suspicions, and I was now certain that this was another attempt by the government to sabotage what I was trying to accomplish. A good scout is always prepared, so I really had no issue with this; it was just a reminder of whose tail feathers I was yanking on. There wasn't much time to think about it, though, because today, things were moving much faster than they had during my prior visits to the set. The large studio was much hotter than it had been the day before, too.

There were people running around, shouting orders at one another, camera positions were being adjusted and lights being tested. It was controlled chaos, bordering on mayhem. I was immediately directed to the set and told to use it for my training. I did as I was told and began getting my polygraph instrument ready.

My subject, the U.S. Attorney, came up onto the small stage and took a seat next to me. He sat there while I worked and studied me with an air of prosecutorial superiority, complete with a snide little smile and upraised nose. I continued working with the polygraph and figured, what the heck, I'll try a little small talk with the guy. It actually worked, for a little bit at least. He told me his name was Jonathan, and over the course of our short conversation, I discovered that Jonathan was an aspiring thespian and was involved with a local amateur theatre group. The rest of the conversation, however, was markedly different and dealt with his being very critical of me and my efforts.

"Mr. Williams, I'm not completely certain what it is that you are trying to accomplish, but have you ever considered the damage that you could very well cause?" he asked.

"Damage?" I answered, as I readied the polygraph for show.

"Yes, damage. And, serious damage, at that."

"And, what would that damage be, Jonathan?"

"National Security, obviously."

"National Security?"

"Yes."

"I'm showing people that the polygraph doesn't work and teaching them how to protect themselves if they are ever forced to take one. Most of these people are employees in private industries like store clerks and delivery truck drivers, and you feel that they could be damaging to National Security?"

"Absolutely."

I stared at his pompous expression for a moment as I turned and leaned back against the table holding the polygraph machine.

"Jonathan, do you hear crickets in the background sometimes after you speak?"

"What?"

"'What' is correct...as in, 'what' the hell are you talking about?"

"Listen to me, Mr. Williams. If you attack the polygraph, which is a very valuable tool, then foreign spies and their ilk will be allowed to roam the streets of this country at will because they have not been detected."

"Ilk?"

"Yes, ilk."

"Okay, Jonathan, name one spy or any of their ilk that has been detected by the polygraph. I'll wait. Go ahead and give me one name. Do you need more time? How about I whistle the theme song from *Jeopardy* while we wait."

"Now, you're being ridiculous. I can be ridiculous, too."

"You've already proven that."

Jonathan sighed. "Mr. Williams, you are missing the point."

"Agreed."

"The point is that the government must maintain some control, even in a basically free society. That's what tools like the polygraph do – maintain an element of control over the population."

"And catch spies and their ilk."

"Yes, of course. That, too."

"And the store clerks and truck drivers? They would just be inadvertent casualties?"

"Well, yes, some people will be damaged, but you can rest assured, that is kept to a minimum."

"Kinda hard for me to rest anything on a guarantee like that."

"You're making a bigger issue out of this than it need be."

"Well, Jonathan, if you happen to be one of the minimum that gets damaged, it's probably a big deal."

"Again, you are missing the point."

"Again, I agree."

Jonathan sighed again slightly, then leaned a few inches toward me.

"Mr. Williams, you worked for the government. I've seen your resume; we all have. Very impressive I might add. So, surely you understand that the government needs to protect the people, and the people rely upon the government to do that. It's about control and protection."

"From the government and the polygraph."

"Now, you're getting it."

"Oh, I think I got it a long time ago."

"But..."

"It doesn't work, you know," I interrupted.

"The government?"

"Well, that, too, but I'm talking about the polygraph."

"So, you say, Mr. Williams, so you say."

"And, so you also will say, Jonathan."

He raised his eyebrows. "And, Mr. Williams, how do you propose to convince me of that?"

"You will convince yourself, Jonathan. I can teach you in less than five minutes how to pass the test. Just five minutes. How about it?"

"Well, I guess it would be interesting," he said, though, I could tell that his government-controlled heart wasn't in it.

Before he could change his mind, I went right to work, hooking him up to the machine and giving him the same instructions that I had given all my previous subjects. I carefully explained to him that when the program started, I would count to three and he was to tighten his anal sphincter muscle and, at the same time, take five rapid shallow breaths. I told him I wanted to run through it once to practice.

"You want me to do what?" he asked. "Tighten my anal sphincter muscle? You are certainly joking. I am not going to do that, especially in front of millions of television viewers."

"You're going to do it. You're the volunteer. Besides, Jonathan, no one is actually going to see you do it. I mean, we're not going to point your naked ass at the camera."

He did as he was told and produced a perfect reaction on the cardio, pneumograph, and GSR tracings. When I showed him what had happened, he looked for a moment at the chart and then up at me.

"But…"

"Exactly," I said.

My U.S. Attorney, Jonathan, was obviously shocked and chagrinned at how easy it was. I told him that when I gave him the cue by counting to three, all he had to do was to duplicate that maneuver to demonstrate the Sting Technique for the cameras. I heard him mumble, "Whatever," as he sullenly nodded agreement.

We all sat around the set awaiting the arrival of our fill-in host and were finally blessed as Fred Graham made his appearance. The producer introduced us, and while he had very little to say, it was clear by his attitude and curt demeanor that he wanted absolutely nothing to do with me or my crusade and that if it were up to him, my appearance and demonstration would be cancelled. He looked at the polygraph and muttered something like, "I wonder what the Justice Department thinks about this." Then he turned and walked quickly away, yelling at the makeup girl. They say you can't tell a book by its cover. Yet, when you first lay eyes on Fred's perfectly attired, manicured appearance as he walks nose in the air past you, acknowledging only himself in a window reflection as he glides by, you might think he was a pompous wimp. You would be correct. So much for reading beyond the book cover theory.

When Graham had finished verbally drubbing the makeup girl and tossing casually rude comments to everyone he could reach, he returned and took his place in the chair next to me on the stage. We were just a few minutes from the start of taping when Fred apparently felt he had warmed up his internal engine of conceit sufficiently on the staff and it was now time to commence with the guests. Creating the perfect impression of an arrogant Oxford-educated lawyer, he made it very clear that he was not the least bit happy to help a long-haired, wild-eyed crusader attack and question the validity of such a valuable tool as the polygraph. He immediately tried to put me in my place. He looked at me bending over my machine, and with an imperious tone, angrily asked the producer, "Is he going to have his ass in my face the whole time?" He, then, looked past me and began a conversation with Jonathan as though he were the guest instead of me. He asked Jonathan what the Justice Department thought about the polygraph and what he, as a U.S. Attorney, thought about what I was doing. Jonathan looked at me with a smug look on his face and told Graham that he did not agree with me, and that he thought what I was doing was dangerous to National Security and a hindrance to criminal investigations. Despite the fact that Jonathan now knew that the lie detector could be manipulated, he made the same ridiculous comments he had made earlier, neglecting, however, to mention the dangerous store clerks and delivery drivers whom he must have forgotten.

Graham mumbled something and asked the audio technician to put a microphone on Jonathan. He told the producer, "I think the audience would be interested in hearing the Justice Department's view on this." The producer glanced over at Graham with an exasperated expression on her face and told the audio man to hold up as we were less than a minute away from taping. By now, I was completely frustrated, my rage bubbling up to the surface, and I knew I had to become more aggressive. If there's one thing I'm good at it's getting aggressive. I took advantage of the moment of indecision, jumped to my feet, glared at Graham.

"No! Do not put a microphone on Jonathan. He is not being interviewed, I AM!"

I leaned down with my face about four inches from Graham's, locked my eyes on his with a predatory glare, my voice seething with anger.

"Fred, I can prove everything I'm going to say here today. You can feel free to ask me any question you like...you can challenge me on any statements I make, point out anything I say that you feel is wrong or out of line in any way, but *I am the guest here and you will interview me – and, only me.*"

By the time I had finished, Fred didn't look quite so pompous. His face was pale, his eyes wide, and he looked like he was in dire need of a pair of clean underwear. It was as though his mind could not comprehend how I could have changed in an instant from being Mr. Nice Guy to this crazed wild-eyed ex-cop. He'd gotten a glimpse into the eyes of what was perhaps the meanest SOB he had encountered in his genteel profession, and it had scared the hell out of him. Taken aback, he turned to the producer with a subdued, almost pleading voice.

"Is he going to be an unguided missile up here? Are there going to be any controls on what he can say?"

All of his arrogance had evaporated into thin air and he seemed to wilt down into his chair. The producer just shrugged her shoulders, turned to the cameramen and the crew in the booth behind her and said, "Thirty seconds." She, then, grinned at me with an expression that seemed to say, "Damn, I wish I'd had the cameras rolling during that little exchange!"

The clock on the wall showed only fifteen seconds left. At this crucial point, Jonathan must have felt like he had to defend Fred's honor or some idiotic thing like that because he leaned over to me and whispered into my ear.

"What if I just sit here and do nothing when you tell me to show a reaction?"

Now, little Jonathan wants to be a bully. How cute. Little Jonathan should have thought through this little maneuver. So, now the U.S. Attorney, in all his hypocrisy, was determined to sabotage my demonstration by being dishonest. I was suddenly more furious with him than I had been with Graham. I got up out of my chair and, loud enough for everyone to hear, and said,

"Looks like I need to adjust that cardio cuff - won't take a second."

Then, I leaned over in front of Jonathan, got in his face with my nose almost touching his, and in my most menacing stage whisper I hissed,

"Jonathan, if you don't do what I trained you to do when I tell you to do it, I'll beat your fucking face into a bloody pulp right here on national television. I'm tired of your silly-ass attitude, and, Mister, if you don't think I'm serious, just screw around with the test, Pencil Dick."

I was thoroughly pissed off and as serious as cancer. Jonathan's face turned ashen. He, too, had now seen the true attitude behind the mask, up close and real personal. It terrified him because he knew without a doubt that I would do exactly what I said I would do. I figured that for someone like him, who probably had never been in a fight in his life, the threat would hit twice as hard as it would a normal person – especially, since he was a thespian who took great pride in his looks. I watched him withdraw like he was about to ball up into a fetal position and crawl under the furniture. I gave my best Dirty Harry half-grimace, half-grin and sat back down. I took a deep breath, composed myself, gave the producer my most reassuring smile to let her know that everything was fine and that I was fully prepared for my demonstration.

So, now the three of us had taken the time to establish the fact that I was the alpha male on the set, and that both Johnny and Freddy were no more than distant "also rans." There were no guarantees, but when I saw the look frozen on Jonathan's face – a cross between *Holy Shit!* and *Get me the hell out of here!* – I was certain that I was in control. I thought it ridiculous that I'd had to go to that much trouble just to get an opportunity for a fair interview, but this fight had been a knock-down, drag-out brawl from the beginning, so why should I have expected anything different?

Suddenly, the producer shouted, "Quiet on the set!" and all became very still. Graham and Jonathan sat there stone-faced and I put on my best Sunday School smile as the countdown began: Ten, nine, eight, seven, six... And, so it was that I began my first national television broadcast. When you watch the video of that segment, you never would guess that there had been so much drama behind the scenes. But, that, they say, is show business.

During the broadcast, Fred Graham's demeanor altered entirely. He was very professional and courteous when he interviewed me. And, Jonathan? Well, he produced a perfect reaction right on cue. Even Fred Graham was impressed when Jonathan showed how easy it was to manipulate the polygraph chart tracings. My little demonstration had graphically proven my point, and even my host and volunteer had to admit it. To say that I was immensely relieved and very proud of the results would be an understatement. At that moment, I felt like I could walk on air.

After the producer called it a wrap, she congratulated us all on a wonderful performance. Fred and Jonathan both bolted from the set without saying so much as a word to me. In fact, they didn't even hazard a glance in my direction. I smiled to myself and started to pack up my equipment. I was elated that I had made my point and didn't give a tinker's damn whose feelings I had hurt in the process. I did laugh a little at their intimidation efforts, though. I'd already had five years of hard fought battles tied up in this war, and I was not going to let a couple of arrogant assholes ruin my first appearance on national television by making me look like a fool.

As I was about to leave the studio, the producer came up to me with a warm smile on her face. She shook my hand and said, "I'll give you this much, you certainly know how to handle yourself... and, you look great on T.V." Hey, it doesn't hurt to have your ego stroked a little now and then. So, I left that day feeling pretty damn good.

CHAPTER FIFTEEN

Texas Busters

I returned home to Oklahoma City and my life returned to normal - normal, as in back to the seminars, letter writing, and phone call sessions. But, now I had an addition to my presentation package that added to my ever-growing credibility. Anyone who has ever been involved in a war of propaganda knows how important media validation can be. My girlfriend, the nurse, had recorded the *CBS Nightwatch* segment and I decided to include it with some of my correspondence, so, I made some copies and mailed them out. It's amazing how much credibility a successful national television appearance can afford a person. If you can make your case with that kind of exposure, you suddenly become sanctioned as a media expert. I was even asked to speak as a guest lecturer in some criminology and psychology classes at a few colleges. Whenever I made the appearances, I would emphasize that the person I had taught to beat the polygraph on *Nightwatch* was, in fact, an Assistant U.S. Attorney.

However, I knew that eventually my notoriety would come at a price because I had begun to notice quite a few more polygraph examiners attending my seminars, and they didn't seem to be there to shake my hand and wish me well. They were easy to spot. They always came late, stood in the back of the room, and were conspicuous not only because they looked different from the clerks and route salesmen who normally attended, but because they always seemed to have a tense look on their faces, a combination of contempt and concern. Inevitably, they would leave early – but, never without making sure to take at least one copy of my manual before they left. They were either curious about it or threatened by it because sometimes they would take three or four copies. I made a point never to recognize them publicly, nor did I call them out to debate me. However, I always made it clear that I intended to put each and every one of them out of business.

My friends with the ACLU and other various unions began cautioning me to be careful. They explained that things were starting to heat up, and that there were some rumors floating about that "something" might be planned for me. It was more than slightly obvious that, between these comments and some of the threatening phone calls and letters I had received, what I was doing was becoming very dangerous. Some of my friends even suggested that my life might be in danger. I appreciated everyone's concern, but all I could do was to assure them that I was, indeed, fully aware of the circumstances. And, anyway, who was I going to call? The FBI? There was no way that I was going to run and hide. So, it was business as usual for me – but, my police training told me that a periodic look back over my shoulder for security purposes couldn't hurt.

During this time, I became acquainted with a private investigator by the name of Jim Humphreys. Quite a character, Jim was! He always claimed that the T.V. series *Magnum, P.I.* had been based upon his life, which seemed to be a bit of a stretch to me, but after a while, I became inclined to believe that he might have something there. I had to admit that he bore a striking resemblance to Tom Selleck – his walk, talk and clothing, right down to his mustache. I finally decided that either Selleck was portraying him or he was impersonating Selleck. When I met Jim, he was already working a case down in Dallas involving the polygraph, the Lenell Geter case. The Geter story had captured the public's attention and was the subject of a *60 Minutes* report at the time. Jim had done all the behind-the-scenes investigation for the program, and his work ultimately resulted in Geter being found innocent and freed from jail. I am not easily impressed, but I have to admit that I was very intrigued with Humphreys and his zeal for justice. He told me that despite passing two polygraph tests, Lenell Geter had been tried and convicted for an armed robbery that he had not committed. After his involvement in that case, Jim said that he had become certain the polygraph was an abusive tool and offered to help me in any way he could. Since professional allies were scarce, I was delighted to have a chance to work with him. I also wanted to pick his brain about his own experiences with *60 Minutes.* To appear on that program was one of my goals, and any information would be useful to me. Although Jim had not actually appeared on camera, they had relied heavily upon his investigation, claiming credit as though it had been their own. Another lesson learned: you can accomplish a lot if you don't care who gets the credit.

My little construction job with my friend Tom Brown was about finished and my girlfriend and I were having a parting of the ways. Not that there was anything seriously wrong – actually, we were getting along great. The issue was that we each had a different idea about the future. She was going off to graduate school in another state, and I was bellybutton deep in my work, which would take me who knows where, so we decided that this part of our relationship had ended. Like Waylon Jennings said in a song once, "The time had come to bum, again," and off I went. It was a lifestyle transition time, once more.

The first thing I needed to do was to come up with a new way of making a living. The second was moving back into Moby Dick. Although I had become used to sudden changes, this time it seemed more of an unfortunate setback because I had enjoyed living with my lady friend nurse. I'd also particularly enjoyed having her apartment for my headquarters. But, truth be told, the timing was probably right because things were getting a little hot for me in

Oklahoma City. I'd heard that the FBI and local polygraph examiners were determining the best way to halt my crusade. So, I loaded my portable typewriter, my brown Goodwill suit and my polygraph into my faithful steed, Moby Dick, and hit the road. Destination: Dallas, Texas.

For the next couple of years, I divided my time between Dallas and Houston. Some of the time, I would live in Moby Dick; once in a while, I could afford a cheap apartment; and, now and then, I would be taken in by one or another kindhearted lady who had sympathy for me. I worked various jobs from construction to truck driving and just about everything in between, but I also continued my writing campaign. Often, I would spend hours crouched over my little typewriter in the back of Moby Dick, typing letters to Congressmen, Senators, and media. I concentrated my efforts on *CBS 60 Minutes*, which to me was the brass ring, the pinnacle of success for anyone trying to bring an injustice to light.

I teamed up with Jim Humphreys for a while. Sometimes I wasn't sure if that was a good idea or not, but I certainly had some very memorable adventures with him. Jim was, indeed, a charismatic figure. Just like in Tom Selleck's show, he, too, drove a fancy car, only Jim's was a blue 1966 Jaguar XKE convertible. I had a blast riding around in that classic car! In those days, it was called a chick magnet, and since we were both eligible bachelors, we played the role for all it was worth. What helped, too, was that Jim always seemed to have plenty of money. He dressed well and had the fancy ride, so I presumed he was a very successful private investigator. What I also discovered was that Jim was a very creative man, especially when it came to promotion. He came up with the idea of our forming a partnership, a joint venture we called GRAPH BUSTERS. He even went so far as to have T-shirts made up with a picture of a black polygraph with a red circle around it and "NO" drawn through it to indicate no polygraphs were allowed. I figured it was worth a go.

Jim had quite a few contacts in the media due to his work on the Geter case and his involvement with *60 Minutes,* and he used these contacts to get us some appearances on local television shows to promote GRAPH BUSTERS. We'd go to the studios wearing our T-shirts and I would demonstrate the Sting Technique using Jim as my subject. Yes, Jim was a hell of a promoter; however, we did some things on various occasions when we got together that sometimes bordered on insanity. His theory was that there was no such thing as bad publicity, and he hatched some hilarious activities for us. Sometimes, they were a bit too far out for my taste, but Jim believed - as a much later President would also believe – whether good or bad, always keep your name in the press. That's quite a theory, but sometimes the bad can be a little *too* bad.

One such embarrassing escapade happened in 1984. President Reagan had just signed a presidential directive requiring polygraph examinations of thousands of government employees. It was an election year and since Reagan was running for re-election, there were a number of fundraising events in the Dallas area. So, Jim and I saw this as an opportunity to have a little fun. We learned that a large fundraising event was to be held at one of the more prestigious hotels in Dallas and thought this would offer a good opportunity for us to get some publicity for GRAPH BUSTERS. We immediately formed a plan and were off and running. We went to a costume store and purchased two Reagan masks – not the cheap plastic ones, but expensive rubber masks that covered our entire heads and looked very realistic. We got to the hotel early and set up the polygraph on a table near the podium in the front of the room where the event was going to be held, and Jim used his connections to tip off some reporters who were already there with their cameras ready to roll. Dressed in suits and ties and our Ronald Reagan masks, we entered the gala. We must have been quite a sight, apparently, because one of the cameramen described it as 'visually-great T.V.' Jim pulled up an armchair next to the table and I hooked him up to the polygraph. As the people began to arrive for the fundraiser, they were amazed to see their candidate, himself, undergoing a polygraph test! Some were amused, some were surprised, but most people did not appreciate the humor, while still others became angry and indignant. We were soon escorted from the room by a chuckling security staff. I don't think we made much of an impact with that little stunt, but we did get publicity and have a little fun. Sometimes, you've just got to have some fun in life, no matter how serious the fight you're engaged in happens to be. Besides, how often do you get a chance to play a President in front of a paying audience?

From the outset, my relationship with Jim was destined to be short-lived, despite our fun times together. Aside from a couple of T.V. appearances and our little Reagan skit, on the professional/crusader basis, we hadn't done much else. There were several reasons for our parting, but it was primarily due to our disagreement on what we hoped to accomplish. Jim thought we should make a business out of my crusade. He wanted to charge admission to the seminars, sell the manual, and add a full marketing blitz to increase sales. My plan was to continue giving free seminars and to distribute the manuals free of charge to attendees. As with many partnerships, financial disagreements and dissimilar ideals often become unbreakable barriers, and our situation was no different. The partnership pretty much folded and GRAPH BUSTERS faded away.

I was thinking about heading out-of-town for a while when I was asked to perform a favor. One of the local unions had arranged for me to have access to a large conference room in a Dallas hotel to conduct one more seminar before I left the Dallas area. The union official told me that he had used his contacts in media to get me a five-minute spot on an AM radio talk show to promote the event. So, I hit the airwaves, explained what I would be doing at the seminar, gave the address of the hotel, and invited anyone who was interested to attend. As a result, we had very good attendance, and I noticed that the polygraph community was well represented in the audience – once again, glaring at me from the back of the room. As usual, they left early with their arms full of free copies of my manual. Damn, these guys were getting expensive.

After the seminar, I packed up my equipment and briefcase and went out the back door of the hotel. I had parked close to the door in the back so that it would be easier for me to haul my equipment out of Moby Dick. I walked across the near-empty parking lot to my faithful steed and just as I reached my destination, a man stepped out from behind my living quarters/office where he had apparently been lurking.

"You've put on your last show, asshole," the man said as he jammed the barrel of a gun into my gut. I guess when someone sticks a gun into your gut, they feel like they can talk to you like that. And, me? I'm weaponless, surprised, and alone...so, who am I to argue?

I have to admit that there have been times through the years when I have pondered the manner of demise I would experience when the time came for me to hitch a ride on the Pearly Gate Express. It's safe to say that being gut-shot in a dimly lit parking lot was not my preferred way to receive a welcoming hug from old St. Peter, the Greeter. But here I was, and there was no doubt that I had a situation on my hands, a precarious one, at that.

"So, big shot, do you know what this is about?" Mr. Lurker asks.

"You want my car?"

"No. I don't want your car."

"You want my wallet?"

"No! I don't want your damn wallet."

"Is that your wife back in my room?"

"No! I don't have a wife, asshole!"

"Then, I guess I don't know what this is about."

He was huffing like he'd just run the final leg of a mile relay, and his breath was a pungent mixture of dime whiskey shots and perpetually non-brushed teeth. I squinted through the odor to get the first good look at my assailant in his wrinkled white sports coat, lime green shirt, white pants, and blue bowling shoes. His face was contorted and pinched in, and his eyes looked too big for his head.

He reminded me of a damn weasel, or, maybe a ferret. Either way, he was a mean-looking bastard. Well, mean-looking because he was holding a gun - actually, he looked ridiculous. I concluded that his parents must obviously have been intoxicated on the night of his conception. The only thing worse than my being killed by this guy would be to have the cops catch him afterwards. If they were to put his picture in the news, the whole world would think I had been murdered by a cartoon character!

In order to avoid dying in such an embarrassing way, I needed to assess my predicament and examine my options. There are always options. My foe had only one hand free because his other hand was holding the revolver against my belly. I was much bigger than he, and with his stick-man build, obviously stronger and, actually, sober. There was a bonus on my side, as well. In my not-too-distant past, I had been skilled in numerous self-defense tactics, one of which was disarming weapon-wielding weasels at close range. He, on the other hand, appeared to have no discernable skills other than consuming bargain basement booze, engaging in erratic behavior, and boycotting proper dental hygiene.

"Do you want me to raise my hands, or something?" I asked.

"You being cute?" he growled.

"Sometimes, it just comes out."

"I'm gonna put an end to your bullshit right now," he said with a drunken slur. He was repeating his earlier threat, but now it became more ominous because he was trying to talk himself into it by saying 'right now.' This concerned me because it meant something was going to happen, so I knew I needed to take the initiative.

I took a quick scan of the area in search of some kind of assistance. A cop would have been great, but that would have been too much to ask. Hell, I would have settled for a nosy neighbor, or even a wino with a bottle of MD 20/20 and a good throwing arm at this point. But, there was not a soul to be seen. The whole damn world had gone to bed except for Lurker and me. Speaking of which, he was starting to act a bit more skittish as we stared at each other, and that couldn't be good, I thought. I was getting a bit tense, my-self, standing there with an inebriant holding a projectile launcher pointed at my pancreas. If he were to start flinching or twitching, things could go south in a hurry.

"So, what is it that I've done that has you so pissed off?" I asked, searching for an opening.

"Ain't me. It's my boss. You're trying to shut him down with all your high and mighty horseshit talking and these seminars," he said as he pushed the revolver into my belly harder to emphasize his point.

My assailant staggered into me, causing him momentary loss of balance, which in turn, gave me the opportunity I needed to ad-just the scales of power. I dropped my briefcase and machine, both landing with a resounding crash. Quickly, I reached down, grabbed the gun's cylinder and squeezed so that it wouldn't spin and pop off a round into my still-breathing carcass. He grunted and strained as he tried to pull the trigger, but he couldn't move it. This is where the advantage of bigger and stronger comes in handy. I twisted the weapon sideways, wrenching it up and away, pulling it out of my adversary's small, sweaty hand while trapping his finger in the trigger guard and bending it backward. Mr. Lurker let out an an-guished howl of pain that sounded like someone had just shoved a hot poker up his ass, and then as fast as our dance of disarming had started, it was over.

My rat-faced foe stood there holding his former gun hand with his uninjured one while he stared at me with a surprised, fright-ened, but still booze-glazed look in his eyes. What he had discov-ered was that life can change in a hurry. One minute you're the Ferrari, the next you're the speed bump. You might say that his po-sition of authority had diminished greatly.

"You aren't much of a hit man," I said as I examined the small handgun I now held.

"You broke my fuckin' finger!" he replied with a whimper.

"Goes with the lurking business. Who sent you, anyway?"

"Nobody."

"Uh-huh. Well, you best tell 'nobody' you quit. Be better for you."

"What about my finger?" he whined.

"Don't believe you're in much of a bargaining position for health care right at the moment."

Apparently, he had arrived with a bucketful of stupidity because with the last couple of drops floating through his booze-drenched brain, he decided to take back control of the situation by grabbing for the gun! In reaction to his slow-motion reach for the weapon and my ever-eroding patience, I struck the gun onto the left side of his skinny head.

"Oww! Goddamn!" he shrieked as he ran.

"It's not my fault about all this," his voice yelled from the darkened dumpster area.

"Well, you were going to shoot me!"

"Yeah, I was. But, I ain't got nothing against ya. They were paying me to do it."

"That's where we're different."

"How's that?"

"I'm doing this for nothing!"

"Man, you're a mean bastard," he whined again.

"Listen. You go on back and tell your employer to step up his game. Keep sending them, cause I'm waiting. Now, go."

"Maybe I won't," the voice said.

"Maybe I'll tie your nuts to my bumper and drag your ass around the lot for a while," I said, taking two steps towards the voice. There was a sudden scurrying sound followed by a crash and the bark of a distant dog.

CHAPTER SIXTEEN

An Invitation from Congress

The Legislation Phase

After Jim and I went our separate ways, I went back to Houston and got a job working as a cornice carpenter subcontracting jobs on a large apartment complex. I liked the flexible schedule because I could set my own hours and have plenty of time off. In return for my being a sort of night watchman, the construction superintendent allowed me to camp out in Moby Dick and hook up to one of the electrical power poles on site. I had free electricity, running water, and my choice of numerous porta-potties scattered throughout the construction site. Not exactly all the comforts of home, unless this was your home – which, in this case, was pretty close. Despite the living conditions, I developed another tactic to help people with the polygraph and, in general, to get the word out with a whole new line of communication.

There were a few convenience stores located within walking distance and I made it a point to get acquainted with many of their employees. I told them about my little project and that I was trying to get a Federal law enacted that would protect people like them from the polygraph and outlaw its use as a condition of employment. In other words, they would not have to take a polygraph exam in order to get a job, nor to keep the job they already had.

They were pretty enthusiastic about my crusade, so I gave them copies of my manual and asked them to find a suitable meeting place large enough to accommodate a hundred people, or so. Once they had acquired a location, they could invite anyone they knew who had to take a polygraph test. I would meet with them, demonstrate the Sting Technique, and teach them how to pass the test. It was a very simple, very basic approach.

With all my increased activities, I felt that I needed an office and an answering service of some type, so I came up with a plan. It was the early part of 1985, and back then, every convenience store had anywhere from three to six public telephone booths lined up in front of it. As was usually the case, one of the public phones also rang in the store and the clerks could use it for store business or personal use. I made friends with the clerks at the store closest to my campsite, and it became a sort of center of operations. At my request, they decided to help me out and let me have the number of the phone that was accessible from the store. I asked the friendlier clerks if they would even be willing to take messages from anyone who might call that number asking for me. Although it was a strange request, the word spread amongst the other convenience stores, whose employees also agreed to help me out. Suddenly, the Doug Williams Anti-Polygraph Crusade had a chain of satellite offices.

I was back in business! During the day I would contact some of the producers of the radio talk shows I'd been on in the past and let them know how they could contact me. Since most of the interviews were done over the telephone, I was able to respond to questions from my phone booth studio at the convenience stores. Admittedly, there were some minor problems in handling interviews this way – people walking by chatting, drunks yelling at each other, children crying, and constant traffic noise while I was on the air. But, without question, the worst part were the numerous clouds of Kamikaze mosquitoes that seemed to be alerted by the ringing of the phone. Success comes with the ability to overcome many obstacles. So, in spite of numerous obstacles and a great deal of scratching during those few months, I was a guest on over twenty shows, and all except one were syndicated nationally.

As I received more attention, I decided to use my parents' address and phone number in my correspondence, as well. Even though I had a new contact system, I was fully aware that I still needed a home base from which to handle the most important issues. I figured, what better home base than home. My parents lived in Oklahoma City and my father, a Methodist minister, was now the director of the United Methodist Foundation for the Oklahoma Conference. I would check with them regularly to see if anyone had responded to my letters. Usually the responses were the same, with occasional letters from the ACLU or other unions encouraging me to continue my work.

It was in June or July of 1985 when I got some very exciting news. My parents had received a letter from a U.S. Congressman by the name of Martinez. He was the Chairman of the Subcommittee on Employment Opportunities for the Committee on Education and Labor in the House of Representatives for the 99th Congress. He had sent an invitation for me to testify in hearings on HR 1524, and HR 1924. These were House Bills designed to ban the use of the polygraph in the workplace for the purposes of hiring and firing. My mother gave me the contact information and phone number for Representative Martinez, and I excitedly called the Congressman's office to accept the invitation.

Finally, there was once again some interest in Congress to pass a law that would outlaw the use of the polygraph, or at least restrict its use. Things were changing; minds were changing; and, it seemed that something was really going to happen this time. When I contacted Congressman Martinez' office, I was forwarded to a staff member who filled me in on the details of HR 1524. She told me that it was a Bill, the purpose of which was to "prevent denial of employment opportunities by prohibiting the use of the lie detector by employers in business that were involved in or affected by interstate commerce," and that HR 1924 was a Bill designed "to protect the rights of individuals guaranteed by the Constitution of the United States and to prevent unwarranted invasion of their privacy by prohibiting the use of the polygraph equipment for certain purposes." She promised to send me copies of both Bills as soon as possible.

I can still remember how I felt, sitting in the back of Moby Dick after a hard day's work, sweating my ass off in the heat and humidity of a summer day in Houston, drinking a cold Budweiser and smoking a Marlboro while I carefully read the Bills. I was so delighted that I literally laughed out loud at some of the language and almost clapped my hands with glee! Surprisingly, these Bills had some teeth to them! They were quite lengthy, but I didn't care. I sat, read, reread, and smiled. Something was starting to happen. As sure as I was sitting there, I knew that something was starting to happen.

CHAPTER SEVENTEEN

Testimony Before Congress

What follows is my testimony taken directly from the transcript of the hearings before the Subcommittee on Employment Opportunities of the Committee on Education and Labor in the U.S. House of Representatives 99th Congress first session on the HR team 24 HR 1924. Hearings held in Washington, D.C. on July 30, 1985:

Mr. Douglas Gene Williams:

My name is Douglas Gene Williams, and I plead guilty to crimes against humanity. I was a right-wing terrorist. I tortured thousands of people, documented more forced confessions than most Gestapo agents, violated countless constitutional rights, and had absolutely no regard for human dignity. I was often rewarded for my skillful use of terrorism. There are some truly grim stories behind those official letters of commendation I earned as a police detective sergeant. I was a highly trained, well-equipped terrorist agent. My specialty was psychological trauma and my weapon was the lie detector. I am here today to try and undo some of the damage I have done by telling the truth about the lie detector.

The polygraph has been cloaked in shady scientific jargon for over 50 years. Lie detector operators claim an accuracy rate of 96-98 percent. It has been endorsed by such bastions of journalism and law as F. Lee Bailey and Jack Anderson. The polygraph has received media validation on a national level. The polygraph has developed into a multi-billion-dollar business since its invention in the late 1920's, and it is now the longest running con game in the history of this country.

The polygraph is not a lie detector and it is not a truth verifier. The polygraph is simply a crude reaction recorder, and the reactions it records can be indicative of just about anything – anything except deception. Let me share with you how the polygraph works, and, incidentally, I have a machine here with me if anyone wants a demonstration.

Please look at Exhibit B. That is what the polygraph actually records. I think you have been supplied with these. What we have here is a machine that can watch you breathe, watch two fingers on your right hand sweat, and watch your heartbeat. That is all the machine is capable of recording. During the test, the examiner will ask a series of questions and watch for any changes in your breathing, perspiration, and blood pressure. These changes are called reactions. A casual look at this diagram shows a person's breathing has become erratic, blood pressure is elevated, and the hands are sweating. Does this mean the person is lying? Although it is absurd to come to this conclusion based upon such flimsy evidence, that reaction is what polygraph operators refer to as indicative of deception, and that reaction has been the start of many tear-jerking sob stories because that reaction does, in fact, mean you have lied. I would submit that this exact same lying reaction can be caused by many things other than a lie. As a matter of fact, any number of innocent stimuli can and do cause this exact reaction – fear, rage, embarrassment, a phone ringing, pain from the cardio cuff, and even the tone of the examiner's voice.

The validity of the lie detector is based upon a phony set of 50-year-old pseudo-scientific principles. And even the polygraph experts do not have the temerity to refer to the polygraph as a lie detector preferring words like "investigatory tool," instead. It is certainly a tool, or more correctly, a psychological billy club that allows even the most pusillanimous polygraph operator to become a terrorist. These con men know their profession is a fraud; that it is impossible for them to explain to anyone's satisfaction how they purport to be able to detect deception by simply recording a person's fight-or-flight response.

The piles of propaganda produced by the polygraph profession rival Hitler's propaganda machine. But the largest and most odoriferous pile is their theory of the control question. Simply stated, the control question technique is a method of comparing reactions. For example, if you happen to breathe in short, shallow breaths, your fingers start sweating and your blood pressure increases when the polygraph operator asks you what you have stolen from work and you breathe calmly and evenly when he asks you if you ate breakfast this morning, you will fail your polygraph test. The unadulterated stupidity of the control question technique presumes two things that are impossible for the polygraph experts to prove. One, they must prove that only the questions cause a reaction. That it is impossible for any other stimuli to give you that little shot of adrenaline necessary to trigger a reaction. Two, and this is even more ridiculous, the polygraph experts must prove that a truthful person will only react to a control question and never react to a relevant question. It seems to me that the accusatory nature of the relevant question is a great deal more likely to elicit a response than some imaginary control question. Perhaps I am being too harsh. Here are some examples of control and relevant questions. You decide which are the more threatening of the two, which is more likely to cause you to have a fatal reaction. Can you name anyone in the company who is stealing? Can you drive a car? Have you ever used or sold marijuana? Have you had anything to eat today? Have you violated any of the company's rules and regulations? Do you drink coffee?

Remember, the polygraph operator will compare your reactions to these two questions, and if you react more to relevant than to control, he will call you a liar. Despite what polygraph proponents may say, the whole concept of lie detection via polygraph is nothing but a crock of propaganda.

The pre-employment polygraph examination is a setting for some of the worst cases of polygraph abuse because, unlike the criminal suspect, the job applicant cannot refuse the test without suffering as a result of their refusal. These polygraph examinations are simply an interrogation. The only part the polygraph plays is to sufficiently scare you enough to disclose the sordid details of your past indiscretions. I could make a good case for the proposition that we have an inalienable right to lie when confronted with a lie detector. Employers routinely circumvent federal law by simply asking employees to take a lie detector test. Even the government says it is illegal to ask about arrests and sexual habits in pre-employment tests. In fact, many areas are off-limits to employers. But the employers can disregard the law by paying a "hired gun" to ask questions that, legally, he is prohibited from asking.

Unfortunately, many people feel they can afford to tell the complete truth to every question put to them on the polygraph test. Their blind faith in the machine is sadly misplaced. The joke is on those who think the system is fair because the lie detector has a built-in bias against the truthful person. As a result, the more honest you are, the better your chances of failing the test. And the real irony is that the reverse is also true.

Anyway, I can tell the complete truth or complete lie or anything in between and still pass any polygraph test given at any time, by anyone, anywhere. Mark Twain said, "If you've done it, it ain't bragging." I have done it hundreds of times and I have instructed thousands of people to do the exact same thing by simply teaching them to distinguish between the control and relevant questions and to duplicate the physical response to fear on demand at the appropriate time. By following the instructions in the little manual that I have published, thousands of people have learned to consistently *produce a truthful polygraph chart.*

The polygraph profession has accused me of having a myriad of sordid motives for writing this manual. Perhaps their anger stems from the fact that the only power they have is derived from the fear and ignorance of their victims. I only hope I have been successful in tipping the balance of power from the terrorists to the victims by telling some of the tricks of this terrible trade.

As to my ex-colleagues' criticism, I would offer this thought for consideration: It would, after all, be the ultimate irony for a lie detector operator to object to the truth.

Mr. Martinez:

Thank you, Mr. Williams. I have one question and it stems from what you said near the end of your testimony. I assume that what you said was that you can fool the polygraph examiner and you can teach other people to do it, too.

Mr. Douglas Gene Williams:

Yes, Sir, I can and have consistently. The polygraph records breathing, blood pressure, and your pulse rate, sweat activity on your hand. This is what you should look like when you are answering a relevant question – calm, even breathing patterns. When you answer a control, you should indicate that this upsets you.

All I do is teach people: one, how to distinguish between the questions; two, I hook them up on a polygraph and teach them to physically manipulate their responses to fear. Now, what happens when you are afraid? The autonomic nervous system kicks in a little bit of adrenalin and what happens? You start to breathe erratically, panting and gasping for breath, your hands become sweaty and your blood pressure increases. Any erratic change is what the polygraph profession labels as a staircase breathing pattern. There are about five breathing patterns. I just teach a person to duplicate that breathing pattern when they are confronted with a control question, and to duplicate the response to fear.

Now, it took a while. I was asked by a friend of mine on the police force when I was running these, "Bearing in mind that you are an expert, if you were confronted with a polygraph test, could you pass it?" I said, "Well, I can certainly control my breathing. I can appear to be calm and reasonable when I am answering a relevant question; and I can appear, through my breathing tracing, to be upset when I answer a control question. But, how do I handle the sweat activity and the blood pressure?" I couldn't figure that one.

About three or four weeks after I had confronted myself with this problem, one of my friends came in and said, "Hey, we got in a chase last night. Man, that guy was going well over a hundred miles an hour. And, my partner was driving the car and he lost control. We went out across a bar ditch, tore out a barbed wire fence and went out into a pasture at 100 mph." And, he said, "Man, I was just pinching the donuts out of that seat." I said, "What?" He said, "Yes." He said, "You know how when you get upset you just kind of pucker up like that?"

I sat down immediately after he left, hooked myself up to a polygraph machine and duplicated what your body normally does when it is confronted with stress. It looks exactly the same on the polygraph, and there are at least 2,000 documented cases that prove that a polygraph examiner cannot tell the difference.

Mr. Martinez:

Thank you. The reason I asked that question is because, if you remember, earlier I stated that we had a particular individual in a department that could teach people to do it. And, he did it in precisely the way you have described. So, I know for a fact that you teach people to fool the lie detector.

The prepared statements of Douglas Gene Williams, Ex Police Sergeant/Polygrapher, Oklahoma City, OK, and a copy of my manual were entered into the official transcript as part of the official Congressional Record of the Hearings.

No sooner had my testimony begun when I'd begun to hear mumblings, and even a few audible gasps, from those in the gallery who were there to witness or to report on the proceedings. And, I could see by the startled looks on the faces of the Congressmen that my testimony was certainly getting attention. That's when I'd had my first *uh-oh* moment. Maybe I was being a little too intense. Maybe what I was saying was too much for the crowd to handle all at once. Up to this point in the hearings, the use of the polygraph had been discussed in an orderly, business-like manner, as if there were no pressing problem. But, I also knew that discussing it calmly and reasonably wouldn't be sufficient. I had to impress upon the Congressmen that the victims of this terrible industry needed protection and they needed it now. To treat it as though there were no emergency would be like going to the hospital because your leg was cut off and having the doctor tell you, "We'll start with a band-aid and work up from there." So, I'd decided, enough of the cozy bullshit, it's time to shake things up. I'd pressed down on the gas pedal and held it there.

After I finished my testimony, the Chairman of the Subcommittee, Representative Martinez, called for a recess. As I was gathering up my things and preparing to leave, he came down from his position with the Committee and approached me.

"Congratulations, that was an excellent job, and you made a big impression on me and the rest of the Committee."

"Thank you, Congressman. I'm grateful for the opportunity to testify in support of what I consider to be much-needed legislation."

"I wanted to ask you, what organization are you with? I haven't been told who you represent," he said.

"Well," I answered with a little smile, "I don't have an organization. But, like you, I have a constituency, and a very big one, at that. I represent all the millions of people who have been beat up and victimized by the polygraph thugs. And I must tell you, Sir, this abuse has been going on for far too long. I will tell you that thousands of people are enduring the trauma of polygraph testing. Those are the people I'm here to represent. And I'll tell you something else, you are going to be hearing a lot more from those very people in the near future."

He stood and looked at me for a moment as if he were trying to comprehend a story about a terrible tragedy that had just occurred. I don't think he had ever had it put to him that way before.

"Do you mean to tell me that you have no organization backing you and that you are not employed by anyone to be a spokesman?" he asked.

I looked him straight in the eyes.

"That's exactly what I'm saying, Congressman." I took a quick look around the room and added, "Truth be told, I'm probably the only person in this room who is not being paid to be here."

He glanced at everyone moving around the room, and then intently back at me for a moment. He nodded his silent agreement, took my hand in both of his.

"Mr. Williams, I promise you we will do our best to get this Bill passed into law. And, I want to thank you, personally, once again, for your excellent testimony. It will go a long way towards making that happen."

I didn't say anything else - I didn't think there was anything else I could say – so, I nodded at Congressman Martinez and turned to leave. My progress to the door only lasted a couple of steps because, as I turned, I noticed for the first time how much the crowd in the gallery had grown. Dozens of people armed with notepads, still cameras, news cameras and microphones were now gathering around me. I was literally blinded by the camera lights and flashes as I waded through the group, polygraph case in hand. About half way to the door, I heard Congressman Martinez' voice call out to me.

"Hey, Doug. How about giving me a demonstration of your Sting Technique? Show us how easy it is to beat the test before you leave."

I was part-way through the throng of reporters. I turned to look at the smiling legislator, realizing immediately that the cameras were rolling. I smiled back.

"I'll be happy to Congressman, but on one condition."

I looked over to an area with several pro-polygraph experts mumbling to each other. And, there was Mr. Barefoot, the president of their Association. He had earlier testified as to the incredible and wonderful proficiency of the polygraph and how useful it was for a myriad of business and law enforcement purposes. He was now conferring with the Association's attorneys. I figured, what the hell, why not. So, I looked back at Congressman Martinez and yelled loud enough for Barefoot and everyone in the room to hear me.

"Get Mr. Barefoot there to agree to be my subject. I'll hook him up and ask him if he lied during his testimony here today. This shouldn't be a problem for Mr. Barefoot. After all, he did testify in great detail about the validity of the polygraph as a lie detector. And, he is President of the American Polygraph Association, a duly elected, fearless leader in the industry. He should certainly jump at the chance to take a polygraph with America watching..."

I was still in the middle of my challenge when Mr. Barefoot made a run for it. I don't mean he said, 'excuse me' to a couple of people and slid by nonchalantly. No. He picked up his briefcase and walked quickly to the door. I mean, this guy was *moving*. His rapid escape to the outside world was followed by jeers and laughter from the reporters and even some of the Congressmen. As the snickers and *Can you believe that?* comments started to fade, I took my polygraph and papers and walked toward the door. Again, my steps were interrupted by the shouts and hand-waiving of the reporters who were determined to ask me more questions. So, I held an impromptu news conference in the hall, which lasted well over an hour. I reiterated many of the points I had made in my testimony and told some of the stories I had heard over the years. I pointed out that my opponents were more than a bit conspicuous by their absence at our sudden gathering. I wondered aloud why they would make such bold assertions about the validity of the polygraph and, yet, be unwilling to take questions from the press. My closing statement was very simple:

"Listen, folks, I've got nothing to hide. In fact, I don't want anything hidden because I can positively prove the truth in everything I testified to here today."

CHAPTER EIGHTEEN

Threat and Confrontation

As I was leaving the news conference, I was approached by two professional-looking women in their thirties. The first one identified herself as a producer from the Carol Randolph Show and her companion introduced herself as a staff member from Congressman Pat Williams' office. As we did some quick handshaking, the first woman made it plain that she wasn't there for idle chit-chat. She offered me an opportunity to appear on their television show. Before I was even able to give her a response, she dove right in to the reasons I should accept the invitation.

"Mr. Williams, Carol Randolph is a no-nonsense type of person with a strong media and international news presence in this city. Her show is broadcast on Channel 9, which is a local CBS affiliate. Keep in mind when I say 'local,' I mean Washington, D.C. Our program is the top-rated daytime show in the Capitol, which my friend here can attest to."

"That's absolutely correct, Mr. Williams," the second woman said. "The Carol Randolph show is a vital link between the media and government officials at all levels. I can tell you with complete confidence that Carol Randolph's viewers include nearly all the Congressmen, Senators and their staff members on a daily basis."

"I came here today to hear all the speakers in preparation for tomorrow's show. The topic will be polygraphs and the political and social impact these instruments have on our culture," the first lady said.

The second woman added, "My boss, Pat Williams, will be on that program. We would like you to join him."

"Okay," I answered. "Sounds like a good idea."

"Larry Talley will be a guest, as well," the first lady added with a smile on her face. "Larry Talley? As in Larry Talley, Vice President of the American Polygraph Association?" I questioned.

"Yes," she said. "I thought you were familiar with him."

"You just reeled me in," I said.

She then filled me in on the details of time and transportation, and the deal was done. As they walked away, I began to realize that this was a much larger occasion than just another television interview. I'd heard of Representative Williams before, and what I had heard and seen was pretty good. Sharing a stage with him would be worthwhile and interesting. But, it was the idea of sitting next to Larry Talley that intrigued me most. Although I had spent years debating polygraph operators, this would be different.

Talley was at the top of his organization – well, almost. Barefoot was the President of the Association, and even though Talley was Number 2, he wasn't at all like Barefoot. Talley was an "in your face," hard-core defender of his money-making machine. Barefoot had run away today at the end of the hearing when I'd challenged him. Talley had not run. He had stared at me from a distant corner of the room while his associates ran past him. Talley's dark, motionless stare was one of hate. Not just hate for what I was doing, but for me personally. No, Larry Talley would not run. Neither would I.

The limo picked me up from the hotel the next morning and took me to the television station. I walked into the studio and was immediately confronted by Carol Randolph, a professional-looking African American lady who made it clear right from the start that she was the person in charge. She directed me to a set in the studio where all the lights were on, the cameras and crew in place.

"You say you can teach a person how to beat a polygraph test in five minutes or less. Let's see you do it."

Without a word, I began to prepare for the demonstration. When everything was set up, I asked her to take a seat. I hooked her up to the machine and gave her the same instructions I had given so many times before. She just shrugged, did what I asked her to do, and produced a magnificent reaction. I tore off the chart, held it up to the camera and pointed out her reaction on all three tracings. I pointed to my watch and said that I had used only about three of my five minutes to train her to beat the test. When I finished removing all the attachments from her, she picked up the chart and shook her head slowly.

"I am very impressed!" She motioned to the crew to bring another chair to the set. "Mr. Williams just earned himself a place on the panel." And, turning to me with a slight smile, she said, "I have to confess something, Mr. Williams."

"Call me Doug. I'm not old enough to be Mr. Williams, yet."

She smiled, "Okay, Doug."

"Confess away," I smiled back. "No sin is too great."

"Well, I had you invited here today in order to prove you are a fraud." "Uh-huh."

"That's why I met you at the door. That's why I was a bit abrupt with you."

"A bit?"

"Okay, very abrupt. I figured I would catch you in an unprepared state, force your hand and expose you to my viewers."

"So, how'd that work for you?"

She laughed. "Well, I don't think it would be possible to catch you unprepared. There's no hand to force because you're so open about everything, and the only thing to expose is the fact that I was wrong."

"I wouldn't be so hard on yourself. You probably got some less than accurate information."

"Yes, I would say my information was less than accurate."

"You know, where I come from, we call less than accurate

information 'bullshit'." She laughed again. "Well, Doug, you're the real deal. And, I do like the way you handle yourself. So, I definitely want you on my show."

We both looked over at several people walking into the studio, one of whom was Larry Talley. She watched him stride over to the makeup girl. "Yes, I definitely want you on my show."

Carol Randolph opened the show by saying, *At 8:25 this morning, I walked into the studio and met Doug Williams, a former police polygraphist who became disenchanted with the polygraph. And, since 1978, has taught thousands of people to beat this machine. Watch what happens.*

The show began with the entire video of my meeting her, training her, and showing the results of the training, with the camera zooming in on her reaction that she had manipulated on the chart. It was a step-by-step tutorial featuring the Sting Technique. I watched Talley's face as the video ran and grinned at his deflated expression. He knew he could never explain that away. And, when the video showed me tearing off the chart and holding it up for the camera, he actually put his face into his hands, rubbed his eyes, and began rocking back and forth.

"If I can teach a person to control every tracing on the chart, that is *prima facie* evidence that the polygraph is not a lie detector."

Facing the camera, Ms. Randolph told the audience that she was an attorney and that the fact I could do that would, indeed, constitute such evidence. When we went to a commercial break, I looked at Talley as he sat stone-faced, grinding his teeth. Much to his dismay, my demonstration had taken up well over half the time allotted for the segment and had set the tone for the entire program. To make matters worse for Talley, Ms. Randolph was obviously no longer on his side.

After the break, Ms. Randolph began by asking Representative Williams why he had introduced legislation intended to ban the use of the polygraph. What follows is dialog taken verbatim from the video tape recording of that program:

Ms. Randolph:

Why are you opposed to the use of the polygraph machine? What's wrong with it?

Rep. Pat Williams:

You know, Carol, you are a wonderful talk show host, but when I look at you, I don't think you would make a very good liar. And yet, Doug Williams took you aside for ten minutes and taught you how to beat this gadget. In other words, they don't work; we have millions of Americans subjected to them, losing jobs and being denied employment because of a gadget that doesn't even work.

At this point, Larry Talley interrupted the conversation and began the first of his attacks against me, personally.

Larry Talley:

Doug Williams did not teach you how to beat the test. All he did was teach you how to add distortions to the chart. I think the most appropriate question to ask the viewing audience is what they think about how a person who, by his own admission, goes around the country and has written a book about how to beat the test, and how to lie and cheat during the course of a polygraph test. And I don't even want to make any more comments about that because I don't want to give any credit to someone who doesn't deserve any credit.

Ms. Randolph:

Well, Doug, you were a police officer and now you are going around the country doing this. How do you respond to Mr. Talley's charges?

Doug Williams:

Well, the part about me going around the country is quite correct. I do go around the country and teach people how to pass their polygraph tests when I'm able; but that is not my profession, since I do not get paid for it. I would describe it more as an avocation, rather than a vocation.

Ms. Randolph:

Why are you doing this? Why are you so opposed to the use of the polygraph? What is wrong with it?

Doug Williams:

There are three things wrong with it. Number one, it is an invasion of your privacy. Number two, it does not work. And, Number three, I can teach anyone to control every tracing on the polygraph chart. Contrary to the statement that was just made, I did not simply teach you how to distort the chart. I taught you how to produce what any polygraph examiner would say is a truthful polygraph chart...

Talley interrupted again.

Larry Talley:

What you did was teach her to add distortions to the chart, every polygraph examiner knows how to detect those countermeasures.

Doug Williams:

There's only one thing wrong with that, and that is it is just not true. I have taught thousands of people how to pass these tests. I have personally used what I call my Sting Technique to beat every polygraph examiner in Houston, Oklahoma City, and Dallas. There are thousands of people who use this Sting Technique daily to pass their polygraph tests...

Again, Talley interrupted.

Larry Talley:

Ask Mr. Williams how many polygraph licenses he has in the United States. To my understanding, he is not even licensed to do this.

Ms. Randolph:

If a person reads Doug's book and does what it tells him to do, it seems to me that they could beat it. I mean, how accurate could the polygraph be if they know how to control the tracings on the charts?

Doug Williams:

Let me respond to the question about licensing. I was the first person licensed to conduct polygraph examinations in the state of Oklahoma under the Oklahoma Polygraph Examiners Licensing Law passed in 1972. I was a licensed polygraph examiner for some seven years and conducted over six thousand polygraph examinations. Simultaneous to that, I took my degree in psychology from Oklahoma City University and later found that what I did for a living was a fraud. What the polygraph records is known as 'fight-or-flight' response. The polygraph industry says that when you show symptoms of this fight-or-flight response, which is simply nervousness, you have told a lie. They equate nervousness with deception. And that is wrong! The reactions that would brand you as a liar – this nervous fight-or-flight reaction to an accusatory question – can be caused by a number of innocent stimuli. Fear, embarrassment, or just plain nervousness can cause the exact same reaction that the polygraph industry says indicates you have lied.

Larry Talley:

But, Carol, the polygraph has been proven to be a very valuable tool to the American businessman. Forty-billion dollars a year in thefts are attributed to employees in this nation. And we need the right to protect our assets, as the Federal government needs the right to protect their national secrets.

Doug Williams:

I'll agree with that. It is a great tool, if by tool you mean a psychological billy club that will coerce a person into a confession. But, there is no evidence that the polygraph can detect deception. I cite the OTA (Office of Technology Assessment) report which proved this. I can also cite any number of congressional studies over the past twenty-five years which have proved that the polygraph is not a lie detector.

Carol Randolph:

Mr. Talley's argument about saving money – isn't that a valid consideration?

Rep. Pat Williams:

Yeah, you bet it is. The loss to American business from alleged employee theft is pretty large, and Larry may be right, it could be as much as forty-billion dollars. By the way, it's nothing compared to the crime of businessman against businessman. I mean stock thefts and rip-offs that are going on in the Board Room against their competitors, illegally, are a lot more than forty-billion dollars. But, nonetheless, Larry's right, there is a lot of employee theft. There's an old country singer by the name of Tom T. Hall, and there's a line from one of his songs which says, 'If they hang 'em all, they get the guilty.' And that's what the lie detector does. In order to catch a few employees that might be stealing, they hang 'em all. That isn't the way the American system is supposed to work.

That pretty much ended the program. Although Talley tried to interject more points in support of his position, he also took off on a tirade against me, personally, stating that the polygraph did work - all this without the tiniest bit of available proof to offer. Talley was floating in a sea of frustration and was in a panicked search for some type of support as he began a new rant. Representative Williams and I just looked at him and shook our heads. Even Ms. Randolph stared at him in disbelief. It was obvious she wanted him to end his rant so that she could wrap up the show.

Talley and I were driven to our hotels in the same limo. Apparently, the show's organizers weren't used to guests that were true antagonists. Talley was obviously very angry – or, maybe even mortified by the events of the day. As soon as we were seated in the limo, he decided it was time to heat it up a bit.

"You think you're pretty big shit right now, don't you, Williams?" he said.

"I'd say fairly big is all."

"Oh, really? So, you think you won? You didn't win anything."

"Does that include your undying friendship and devotion?"

He made a sound like a growl as his face turned red and beads of perspiration began to form on his forehead.

"You don't get it, do you?"

"Get what?" I asked calmly.

"You're by yourself. You get that? You are by yourself?"

"Okay, got it."

"And there are lots of us."

"Lots?" I smiled.

"Lots. Like a whole damn army."

"A whole damn army, huh?"

"Yeah, tough guy. A whole damn army and they are just like me."

"Wait – do you mean to tell me you've got a whole army of short, pot-bellied guys that spit when they talk and sweat a lot?"

"What?!"

"Do you guys do parades, because I'd like to see that."

"Listen, Smart Guy," he screeched, "this organization goes all the way to the top!"

"So?"

"So...?"

"I said that already."

"You have no idea who you're dealing with, Williams."

"Oh, I know exactly who I'm dealing with. Right at this moment, I'm dealing with a guy who is about to let his 10-dollar mouth overload his 10-cent ass."

Talley raised his eyebrows for a moment, then gathered all the courage he could muster, leaned toward me and pointed his finger toward my face.

"Williams, bad shit is gonna happen, and it's gonna happen real soon."

"No," I said, raising my voice from pleasant to hard. "Bad shit is going to happen, and it's going to happen *right now.*"

"What?" he asked, leaning back a few inches.

"If you don't sit back and put that finger down, I'm going to shove it up your ass so far you'll be able to scratch your tongue."

"But..."

"Then it'll get worse."

"But..."

"Great come back. Here's the deal – you want to do something, well, let's get with it. Otherwise, send the boys from the top. They never seem to show up on their own."

Talley's face turned as red as a beet and he looked at the chauffer, his terrified eyes appealing for help. Right then, the limo pulled into the driveway of my hotel. I looked at the driver in the rearview mirror and handed him a ten for a tip. He waved it off, smiled, and winked at me in the mirror.

I grabbed my polygraph, opened the door, and gave Talley one more shot. "Enjoy all that money you're making, asshole, because your parade is about to get pissed on."

Just as I was about to slam the door, I stopped and stuck my head back in the car and looked at him.

"Promise me one thing," I said.

"What?"

"If that army of guys like you ever goes out on maneuvers, promise you'll call me. I've just got to see that."

I slammed the door shut and walked into my hotel. I heard the muffled sounds of Talley cussing me and smiled as I turned to see the mottled face of a frightened little man glaring at me through the window of the limo.

CHAPTER NINETEEN

A Beer and A Bribe

As a result of my Congressional testimony, I had begun to gain some notoriety and my popularity with talk show producers was on the rise. One thing, however, had not changed. Despite the resulting demand for media appearances, all my radio interviews were still being done from public phone booths in front of convenience stores. A penniless crusader has to be flexible and adapt to the conditions at hand. But, thanks to the opportunity I'd had to testify before Congress, I now had another weapon in my arsenal. I had a way to capitalize on all the publicity and to involve the general public in my battle. In each of my interviews, I encouraged the audience to write to their Congressmen in support of the pending legislation and also made them an offer. If they wrote or called their Congressman, they could request a copy of my manual and it would be mailed to them free of charge. I'd already spoken to many Congressional members who'd agreed to handle the mailings. So, in actuality, I had enlisted Congress as a partner and marketer of my crusade!

The crusade was really getting up a full head of steam, things were moving quickly, and it looked like we would soon be successful in getting legislation passed. However, this prospect of success also brought with it a lot of negatives. The primary negative reactions came from my enemies who stood to lose a very lucrative business. The more I exposed these people, the more desperate they became, and the more vehement their attacks. Each debate was the same: my facts versus their fabrication and hostility. Their personal attacks against me grew with every encounter. And, although their attack philosophy never varied, the intensity increased. They were in full-blown panic mode, and I'd have been a complete fool to say that it wasn't starting to worry me. Panicked people do stupid things. Since they were so determined to shut me up, I fully expected one of their boys to come after me. I pondered Talley's threats, and although Talley, himself, didn't scare me, I figured that sooner or later, somebody was going to take a whack at me. You don't poke a finger into the eye of a giant ogre who's trying to protect his pot of ill-gotten gold without experiencing some kind of retaliation – and, I had been doing some serious eye-poking.

Much to my surprise, a new approach must have been decided upon. There was no attempt to shoot me, stab me, or run me off the road. Instead, they pressured me with something much more devious and, in many ways, more frightening. They changed their tactics from threats to something they must have perceived as more professional. They decided to use a method they hadn't yet tried. They had threatened me, yelled at me, and stuck a gun into my belly, with no affect. Now, their planning committee had, apparently, come up with a new strategy.

One day after I finished work on my construction job, I tossed my leather tool bag into Moby Dick, sat down on the back bumper, and twisted the cap off a cold bottle of Bud. I had just taken a swallow when I was approached by a well-dressed man who handed me a business card and introduced himself as an attorney associated with a law firm in Houston.

"Mr. Williams, I represent a consortium of polygraph companies that includes manufacturers of the instrument all the way to professionals that use them in the course of their daily business."

"Professionals." I stated.

"Yes, professionals. And, these companies have authorized me to offer you a position as a consultant with their firms."

I took another swallow of beer. "You sure you've got the right construction site?"

The whole scene was bizarre, to say the least. Here I was, sitting on the back of the bumper of a 1967 Chevy truck, drinking a bottle of beer, shirtless, wearing old cut-off jeans and ragged tennis shoes, dripping with sweat and covered with sawdust from head to foot, my vision partly blurred by my long hair, while in front of me stood an impeccably dressed lawyer wearing a suit that no doubt cost more money than I had seen in a year. Well, it was a scene right out of Ripley's Believe It, or Not. Hell, old Ripley, himself, might not have believed this one.

It was hot, so I took another swig of beer, pointed to a sawhorse and told him to take a seat. He flashed a quick smile at me – the kind a Great White shark would flash at a passing surfer. He pulled the wooden sawhorse up next to the back of Moby Dick, dusted it off, sat down, and began his presentation.

"Mr. Williams, my clients, the polygraph firms, prefer to remain anonymous." "I'll bet."

"However, I can give you my personal guarantee that the offer I am extending to you is entirely real and completely valid."

"Nothing like a personal guarantee," I said.

"Uh, yes, of course." He placed his briefcase on his lap. "I have all the necessary documents with me to finalize our agreement, once we have reached a satisfactory conclusion for all the parties. All I have to do at that point is to fill in the amounts agreed upon, have you sign the documents, and we have a done deal, as they say."

"Wow, great opening and a great close. So, what's in the middle?"

"Middle?" he asked.

"What is it we need to agree on?"

"Oh, yes, of course. Very astute of you, Mr. Williams. There are, of course, some details."

"I've always liked that word."

He raised his eyebrows, "Word? What word?"

"Astute."

"Astute?"

"Yeah, astute. Always liked that word."

"Uh, yes, a very fine word, I'm sure. Now, as to the details to which I referred. First of all, my clients realize that the polygraph has some problems – minor problems, of course – that need to be addressed."

"That's very astute of them."

"Yes," he cleared his throat. "Secondly, they are also aware of your efforts and are completely convinced that you, Mr. Williams, would be the best person to offer some solutions to these problems."

"Minor problems."

"Minor problems, of course. Your position, which I'm sure you will find quite rewarding, will be to head up research and propose ways to improve polygraph testing, both in terms of validity and fairness for the benefit of all involved, including those persons that would be required to submit to a test."

"Even them?" I said with raised eyebrows.

"Everyone. Now, for these services, the compensation package would be very generous. Furthermore, I am authorized to make a binding offer of employment immediately."

I was waiting for him to get to the point. I knew there was something that smelled of fecal matter in this box of chocolates, so I decided to remain quiet until he revealed it to me.

Of course, as in any negotiation, there is give and there is take.

"Of course," I said.

"This offer is contingent upon your agreement to cease any and all opposition to the use of the polygraph in any manner or form."

So, there it was. The polygraph industry was going to buy my silence. They had tried arguing; they had tried threatening; and, now, for strike three, bribery. A gag-order. For my opening move,

I said, "I'll need a five-year contract at two-hundred grand a year."

"Agreed," he responded.

"Okay. I'm also going to require a hundred-thousand dollar signing bonus."

"Agreed."

"Payable immediately."

"Agreed."

"And a company car - preferably, a Mercedes. Something in the SL Class would do nicely. And a new one every year for the duration of the contract. You can lease them if you prefer, but you will need to take care of the insurance and tags."

"Agreed."

"An expense-account. Two grand a month sounds like a nice round figure." Once more, "Agreed."

I added that I would expect them to provide me with a place to live and from which to work. Perhaps, a three-bedroom, two-bathroom house on the beach with a study and a nice ocean view — something on the beach in Malibu or Miami would do nicely. Again, he agreed without hesitation. I then asked him if there was anything I could demand that would not be granted. He gave me a cold smile, shook his head.

"Let me put it this way — they will do whatever is necessary to stop you from trying to destroy their industry."

I knew that the polygraph industry was probably bringing in well over a billion a year, and this lawyer was making it clear that they would pay me a small fortune to shut up and go away. So, for good measure, I tossed in a couple more perks to which he responded, "agreed," and jotted down notes on his pad.

Apparently, this attorney's main job was to say 'agreed' and to nod occasionally. He was really good at it, but I was getting tired of the little game and wanted to get back to work. Besides, I wouldn't seriously have considered taking the polygraph mafia up on its offer. (Yeah, yeah, I know...I'm batshit crazy.)

"You'll need to sign these forms here on the bottom where I've marked it," he said, holding some papers and a pen out to me.

"Nope," I said.

"Nope?"

"No," I said. "Nope is just a slang term. 'No' with a 'pe' at the end. Same meaning." "What?" His voice raised for the first time in our talk. "Aren't you supposed to say 'agreed'?" I asked.

"Are you crazy?"

"Funny, you're not the first person to say that."

He shook the papers he was holding to dramatize his point. "This will be your last chance."

"You're trying to flag down the wrong truck, man. You'd think your asshole clients and their friends would know me a little better by now."

"Whatever do you mean?"

"C'mon, man, they've been hanging so close to me we could bump ass cheeks."

"You've made a big mistake."

"You're right. Damn beer is warm. Should've iced it down longer." I swirled a drink of beer around in my mouth, then spit it on the ground.

"Can you be serious for at least a moment," he almost screeched.

"Mr. Lawyer, this is about as serious as I can get with the maggot-infested world you represent."

"You don't understand."

"No, you don't understand. I have a hate for what those jerkoffs do to people that just boils inside of me. I don't give a digger's damn what they think about me or what they want to do about me because they always hide behind somebody's skirt."

He stood up, dusted off the seat of his very expensive pants, looked at me with eyes as cold as a rattlesnake's.

"You will be lucky if you live long enough to regret this."

"Don't believe luck has anything to do with it," I said. "And tell your friends I'm not hard to find if they want to seek me out for confrontations, and such. But, they should think long and hard before they do anything stupid. I haven't got much left in this world but a will to fight, and I do have a truckload of that. Hate to see anyone get their feelings hurt," I said.

"Is that some type of threat?"

"Hell, Mr. Lawyer, I don't care if you call it a party invitation. Just relay it to whomever you need to relay it to."

"Well..."

"Best get moving, Mr. Lawyer. I believe I hear an ambulance siren in the distance...you might be able to chase it down, if you hurry. You might be riding in it, if you don't."

"There's nothing for me to do but take my leave, then," he said.

"You're very astute."

He shook his head, turned and walked away.

"Astute," I mumbled to myself. "Yes, sir, always liked that word."

CHAPTER TWENTY

Rest and Religion

In the 1980's, President Reagan greatly expanded the use of the polygraph within the Federal Government. Don't get me wrong, I liked Reagan. He came along at a time when the country needed him, but, in my opinion, he got this wrong. The Defense Department was vastly expanding its polygraph training school and graduating as many polygraph examiners as possible in order to meet the growing demand for tests. So, in turn, the polygraph industry within the government was becoming even more powerful and pervasive. As the Executive Branch gave more authority to the lie detection machine and Its supporters, I found myself under greater surveillance than ever before.

Beyond all these issues, something else was bothering me – something that seemed a bit more insidious than just the gaining of power. The offer from the lawyer was a shot across the bow. Even though I had brushed it away like a mosquito who had made it past the repellant, the message and its delivery had been clear: We have deep pockets. Ask for anything and we can provide it. Deny us, and you'll find out how deep we are in other ways. It had all been there in the offer. They were willing to pay anything...anything to stop my crusade. Although the offer was a sign of desperation, the way in which it was handled was quite different. That had been calculated desperation. They had sent an attorney. He'd brought an offer. Then, he'd brought a threat. "You will be lucky if you live long enough to regret this." Pretty clear. Pretty simple. A good old fashioned 'or else.' So, the warning wasn't buried very deep. If they were willing to pay anything, they were willing to *do* anything, as well.

The reality of my current situation was blatantly obvious. Despite all I had done and all the support I had garnered from rank-and-file employees to politicians across the country, the one fact that remained constant was that the polygraph people still owned the store. Was I becoming a little paranoid? Hell, yes, I was paranoid! I was fighting a growing giant of an industry that could afford anything, say anything, and do anything it wanted. And, it had the support of the President of the United States to back it. As for me? Hell, I lived in a truck. I wasn't freaking out, exactly. But, I definitely realized that I had to be more aware of my surroundings at all times. An old saying crept into my mind. *Just because you are paranoid doesn't mean they're not out to get you.* I decided that I would adhere to that mantra for some time to come.

Other things started to happen, as well - unusual things. Some people who had been close supporters of mine began to avoid me. Some went to great lengths to stay away and to act as if we didn't even know one another. My friend, Jim Humphreys, wasn't one of them, though. Even though we weren't working together, he was still the outspoken Jim that he'd always been. Then, he got arrested on a cocaine charge. Jim might very well have been guilty, but the odd thing was that the warrant was already four years old when it was finally used to arrest him. He'd been in the city all that time and suddenly this charge appears? Hmmm.

Then, too, things around my living quarters began to appear tampered with - nothing major, just little 'Hey, Doug, we were here' kind of tampering. These things combined to remind me that, perhaps, it was time for me to prepare some type of defensive barrier - a high-tech barrier for my self-protection. So, I bought a 12-gauge

Remington pump shotgun and a few boxes of .00 buckshot to load it with. That's about as high-tech as I get.

Still, even with the gun, I was feeling a lot of pressure. After a while, it started to build up, and although I needed to remain alert, I didn't want to get too leery about everything, which was where this was headed. So, I decided to take a break. Not a break from my crusade – at least, not totally – but, a break to regroup, re-evaluate my plan, and get a little rest. I needed to go somewhere I could focus without interruption, and this 'somewhere' would have to be a safe haven of sorts. Oklahoma City. I headed for home. All gamblers and athletes know that the home field has advantages and can tilt things in their favor. I needed some tilt, so I went home.

Part of going back was also to enable me to attempt a self-over-haul. I was getting a lot more national attention recently and was beginning to feel that my long-haired-rebel-crusader image may have run its course. No doubt, it had been effective in the early days of my endeavors, but now I was being heralded in the national arena as the spokesman for the polygraph oppressed, so maybe it was time to adjust my appearance.

Sometimes, a self-overhaul is more easily accomplished when you get an assessment from someone whose opinion you truly respect. That someone was my Dad. My father was a direct kind of guy. He was not cruel, but if you asked him a question, you would get an honest answer. Sometimes you might not like the answer, but you could be certain that it was straight-from-the-heart honest. When I told him that I was home to recuperate, rebuild, relaunch and get some type of job to hold me over until I'd completed all these tasks, his response was simple.

"You need a haircut."

"I know."

"Then, clean and iron that brown suit of yours."

"Okay."

"I'm going to take you to see the Bishop."

Dad was talking about the Bishop at the Methodist Church,

which for most people, would be a welcome surprise. Unless, of course, those people knew my father. Then, most people wouldn't be surprised at all. My father was the Director of Planned Giving for the United Methodist Foundation and his office was just down the hall from the Bishop's office. But, that wasn't the reason Dad wanted me to go. There was another reason, and I'd have to wait until the next day when I went with him to learn what that was.

So, with a clip here and a snip there, the makeover was completed prior to the morning of the meeting with the Bishop. I looked at myself in the mirror and realized that the person looking back at me actually looked like a real professional. Hell, I cleaned up pretty good.

The next morning, I arrived at the Oklahoma Conference Headquarters located on the campus of my alma mater, Oklahoma City University. I met Dad at his office and we went together to the Bishop's office. When your Dad has a little juice – and, my Dad did – it didn't hurt to take him along on a mission such as this, especially when you weren't sure what topics would be discussed, or exactly what the mission was.

Bishop John Wesley Hardt was a very impressive looking man. He was sturdy, and he had the appearance of someone in authority - not someone who had been given authority by mere virtue of his position, but someone who had earned that authority and a substantial amount of respect to go along with it. He had kind eyes, but he had an air about him that let you know he was not a man to be trifled with. He and my Dad had been friends for quite some time, and the Bishop greeted me kindly. He opened the conversation by getting right to the point.

"What can I do for you, young man?" he asked.

I was a little surprised by the question, mostly because I had presumed that I was in for a teacher/student type forum and that the Bishop was going to advise me. On the other hand, John Wesley Hardt did not fool with unneeded words. So, I responded by giving him a brief rundown about the past several years of my crusade.

I explained to him that I had a very strong sense that this was my mission, even my Christian duty to put a stop to the oppression I'd witnessed. The Bible said that Christ had come to remove oppression, heal the sick, preach the gospel, and I believed that I was behaving as Christ would if He were in my situation. I continued by telling him some of the highlights of my campaign and where they had led me thus far. I also filled him in on some of the problems I'd encountered with the industry, itself, and the surveillance I'd been under.

He sat back in his chair directly across a large brown desk from my father and me. His hands were steepled in front of his face and his eyes locked onto mine as he listened.

"So, Bishop Hardt, I guess I'm home to recuperate for a bit and to fine-tune what I have to do going forward."

"First of all, Douglas, you may call me 'John'," he said.

"Uh, no. No, Sir, I can't," I stuttered.

The corner of the Bishop's mouth showed a tiny, almost imperceptible smile. I couldn't call the man 'John.' Not just because he was our Bishop, but because he was *Bishop Hardt*. I've only met three men that drew everyone's attention the moment they walked into a roomful of self-absorbed, cackling people. One was President Lyndon Johnson. The second was John Wayne. The third was Bishop John Wesley Hardt. No, I couldn't call him 'John.'

"Well, Douglas, let's discuss your efforts. The United Methodist Church has a long and honored tradition of social and political activism. And, I must say, I am in full agreement with your position against the abuse of people by the polygraph industry. I also agree with you that something needs to be done to protect those who are victimized, and I applaud your work on their behalf." I noticed that he and my Dad were smiling a bit. "Your father has kept me informed of your activities over the years, and I have seen you on television from time to time. You've been very busy, Douglas."

"Only out of necessity for the cause, Bishop. I'm not trying to be a star."

"Never thought for a moment that you were, Douglas. There is no doubt that you realize, possibly more than most, that the viewable media is the new battleground for causes and debates, political or theoretical."

"Just reaching the masses, Bishop."

"And very effectively, I might add. You've become a skilled debater, Douglas." "The facts are on my side, Bishop."

"Yes, that would seem to be the case and I would expect no less from you. However, there is an issue, is there not?"

"Yes."

"Enemies at the door."

I nodded. No one spoke for a moment. "I'm not frightened," I said.

"I believe you," he answered. "But, you are tired."

"Yes, Bishop, I'm tired. I'm tired of looking over my shoulders and peeking around corners. I think it's starting to wear me down."

"Well, we can't have that." He got up and walked over to a window and momentarily peered out at the campus of the college and the city beyond. "Douglas, I have a position in the Church I would like you to take on."

"I don't want any charity, Bishop, with all due respect."

He turned from the window to face me. "Oh, it's not charity," he said with a growing smile. "I want to use your talents. You're a good speaker. You make your case very well. You feel deeply about people and you care about their struggles and their needs." He walked back and took his seat. "I need a pastor in a rural church here in Oklahoma," he continued, "and, you're it."

"A pastor?"

"You have the background. The Church needs you. I need you. And, the Lord needs you. How can you say 'no' to that?"

I looked at my father seated to my right and he was beaming. That's when I realized all this had been discussed well in advance of our meeting.

"Well, you do know, Bishop, I'm going to continue my work."

"We wouldn't have it any other way," he said. "And the community you're going to plans on being very supportive."

"Plans on? Like they already know?"

"One of God's messengers may have let it slip."

"Bishop, I hope I'm up to this task. I've been working in a little bit different forum lately, you know."

"Douglas, I have no doubt about your abilities. Besides, you were raised in the Methodist Church. You know we Methodists appreciate the simplicity and beauty of God's work. Our Church is here to spread the word and support people. That's pretty much what you've been doing. The only difference is that we provide refreshments after services."

"I'll do my best, Bishop."

"I'll pass along some advice an old pastor gave me many years ago. 'Bring the message on Sunday, marry and bury as needed, God will do the rest'."

"I think I can handle that."

We all shook hands. "One last thing, Douglas. You will be able to rest where I'm sending you. It's a very, let's say, protective community."

As my father and I walked to the door, the Bishop added, "Douglas..."

I turned to face him. "Yes, Sir?"

"Nice haircut."

I thanked the Bishop, but again, he waved off my thanks and grinned at me. "Let's see if the FBI can climb over the church steeple to get to you."

———————◆◆———————

Fargo. A slice of Americana, Oklahoma-style. A good place for me to settle in for the time being. Now I had a place to live, a regular income, and an office out of which to work. I had a respectable professional position and, most importantly, plenty of time to devote to my crusade. Also important was the fact that I was assigned to a church in a very small town where any strangers would be easily spotted. That, alone, gave me a strong sense of security. All in all, it was an absolutely perfect scenario. I believe God does things to nudge us along the way, and I believed His hand was involved in this – along with my Dad's. Dad had a way of setting things up for you, then when it all came together, making you think it was all a coincidence or of your own doing. This was a classic example. I had a need; Dad had an answer.

Despite the fact that my arrival to this new community was designed as a sabbatical of sorts, things really didn't slow down. My testimony in the U.S. House of Representatives, and the many articles that had been written about it, were still generating a great deal of national attention. Interestingly enough, it had become easier to respond to interview requests now that I had a permanent address and phone number, and even an office chair to sit in. Inadvertently, my new role as a crusading Methodist minister was a pretty big hit, bringing with it a lot of positive publicity. *Methodist Minister Crusades Against Polygraph Abuse.*

As long as I was making some changes, I decided to make one more. I finally put Moby Dick to rest and bought a good car and a nice, clean Classic C motor home. Old M.D. had served his purpose and I figured this was as good a time as any to retire him. Besides, as the years go by, a little more comfort in one's travel becomes significantly more important. After all, just because I was a pastor in a small community now, didn't mean that I wasn't going to be on the road. So, I used my new motor home to go back and forth to Oklahoma City for media appearances and to confer with my friends in the unions. I could easily live in the motor home during the week when need be. In fact, my new schedule and living arrangements were the most comfortable I had experienced in years. And, Fargo - well, Fargo was a cool little town.

CHAPTER TWENTY-ONE

60 MINUTES, At Last!

One crisp, clear morning in February of 1986, it finally happened. I was sitting in my church office going over some notes for Sunday service and the weekly event schedule when the phone rang. I answered with my standard church pastor response to a phone summons, and the reply came in a woman's voice.

"Good morning. I'm looking for Douglas Williams."

"Well, your search is complete, Ma'am, you're speaking to him."

"Great," she said. "Mr. Williams, my name is Gail Eisen. I'm a producer for *CBS 60 Minutes.*"

At this point, I realized I was supposed to respond, but quick-witted Doug just sat there. When she'd begun to speak, I had been raising my white United Methodist Church porcelain cup half full of Folgers to take a sip. Now, I just held it part-way up and stared at it. It was sort of a half-mast coffee cup salute.

"Mr. Williams, do you have a moment to speak?" she asked in an ultra-professionally polite voice.

Well, let's see...I was torn between typing the bake sale notice, the Sunday School announcements, the adult choir schedule, or talking to a *60 Minutes* producer.

"Absolutely," I said.

"Perfect. What I'm calling about, Mr. Williams, is this. *60*

Minutes is exploring the possibility of doing an investigative report on polygraph testing."

"Okay," I answered with an attempt at a calm voice. So, it was only one word, but it was calm.

"Part of this investigation would deal with accounts we have come across dealing with abuses in polygraph testing."

"I see," I responded. Two words, still calm.

"May I call you 'Doug'?"

"Sure," I blurted out. Losing calm now.

"Well, Doug, what we would like is for you to come to New York City to discuss the possibility of your involvement in this investigation."

"I'd jump over the moon to get there." Calm is completely gone.

"We'd fly you, instead," she said with a smile somehow coming through her voice. "I do want to be clear, Doug. This is preliminary and we, at this time, are only looking to see if this would be a worthwhile project."

"Understood."

We discussed a date and other arrangements for a few moments...and, then it came. "Doug, when you arrive at our studio, you will be meeting with Diane Sawyer. She will have some questions for you, and then you'll meet with our investigative and production people."

"Diane Sawyer." I could barely breathe. "Sounds great." I made a vague attempt to collect my wits about me.

"May I ask you a question?"

"Sure," she replied.

"Did you select me because of the letters I've been writing to your show?"

"Partly. But the main reason was your background, the attention your topic is drawing and how well you've done on some recent interviews."

"Oh, I see."

"But, the letters – well, yes, they had something to do with the decision, as well."

"I thought so."

"You were very diligent in your letter writing campaign."

"Yeah, there were a lot of 'em."

"An understatement."

"I bet you folks were surprised a person would write that many."

"The word would be innumerable," she said.

I laughed. "Probably could have rebuilt a tree out of all that paper I used."

"I'm thinking Redwood."

When I arrived in New York City, a CBS limo met me at the airport and took me to the suite of offices assigned to *60 Minutes*. Once inside, I was ushered into a plush, carpeted room where I met Diane Sawyer and a group of producers. It was obvious during our introduction and handshaking session that they were surprised by my newly professional appearance. I presumed that they had watched the *CBS Nightwatch* program and that the producers of that show may have told them to expect someone who looked quite different from the man they saw in front of them. I began to wonder what else the producer of *Nightwatch* might have told them, and suddenly began to regret some of what I had said and how I'd behaved before and during that program. Oh, well. What was done was done. However, I did feel that I had to somehow rehabilitate my image in these peoples' eyes if I were ever going to take my crusade to *60 Minutes*. After all, it wouldn't help my objective at all to have Harry Reasoner open the Sunday night show with "This week on *60 Minutes*, anti-polygraph activist and expert Doug Williams hisses, yells, and beats the living shit out of a pro-polygraph panel." Nope. Couldn't have that.

I immediately liked Diane Sawyer. It would be difficult not to. She was very kind and did her best to put me at ease when I was introduced to her. I was a bit nervous and unsure of how to proceed when she noticed the Presidential Service Pin in the lapel of my brown Goodwill suit. The pin is a replica of the Seal of the President of the United States. It is awarded to every member of the military who has served in direct support of the President for one year or more. When Diane saw the pin, she exclaimed, "You were with WHCA!" It was clear from the looks on the faces of the staff that she and I were the only ones who knew what she was talking about. She commented how impressive it was that I had worked in that department and asked me to explain to the staff what exactly WHCA was. I explained that the initials stood for White House Communications Agency, and that I had been assigned to the Situation Room from 1966 through 1969 as a communications advisor to Presidents Johnson and Nixon. Diane added that she had worked for President Nixon on the staff of Press Secretary Ron Ziegler from 1970 to 1974. Apparently, we had just missed crossing paths by a few months. I suggested that we probably had some mutual friends because I had worked in the Situation Room down the hall from the Oval Office in the West Wing, which was just a few feet away from the office of the Press Secretary. I mentioned working with Alexander Haig and Henry Kissinger when they were with the White House National Security Council. Our similar experiences helped form an immediate bond between Diane and me, and I could tell that the staff was beginning to relax. They might even have started to think that this segment might work, after all.

For the next two or three hours, I sat with Diane and several members of the staff while they conducted a wide-ranging, in-depth, and very exhaustive interview with me. It was obvious they were going to leave no stone unturned. These people were as good at conducting interviews as any cop I had ever met. They certainly gave the concept of due diligence a whole new meaning. But, after all, this was *60 Minutes* and the program had a well-earned reputation to protect. Furthermore, I was a controversial person and my crusade was a volatile subject, so they had to be very careful. I answered all their questions as candidly and completely as I could. I tried to be polite, but also as persuasive as I could be about the need to stop the abuse perpetrated by the polygraph industry. It may sound like grandstanding, but this was my chance to tell them stories about real-life experiences that victims had related to me over the past several years, and that's exactly what I did - and, in great detail. At one point in the conversation, I made a point of saying that not only were innocent, truthful people being called liars, but that the polygraph industry was so corrupt that employers could actually 'call in' their polygraph test results. That comment immediately caught everyone's attention. "What do you mean 'call in' their results?" one young man asked as we sat around the conference room table.

"Exactly that," I answered. "I guess to put it into the simplest of terms, the scenario would go like this: An employer of a delivery company or a retail company - it doesn't matter - would hire a polygraph company or operator. Let's say this employer had someone working for them that they didn't like, or that they were suspicious of, or just didn't want around for some reason – but, didn't really have a reason to fire that person. What Mr. Employer would do is mention to the polygraph operator that there was a problem with that particular employee."

"Like what?" a young lady producer asked.

"Normally, they tell the operator that there's been a theft, or something similar, and they think 'Jimmy John' had something to do with it."

"Jimmy John?" she asked, eyebrows raised.

"The employee. Anyway, once the polygraph operator has that little bit of information, his job becomes easy. He hooks up the various employees to his machine, and when the testing is done, guess who is called a liar?"

"Jimmy John," the same young lady producer said, "give the lady a box of chocolates. She is correct."

Diane asked, "It's that easy? Truthfully?"

"Actually, it's easier than that. The employer doesn't have to have a theft, or even a misconduct issue. They can just tell the polygraph people 'I think we have a problem with Manny, or Jimmy

John, or whomever' and, sure enough, the polygraph operator will verify that problem."

"Without proof of any wrong doing?" asked the young man.

"Proof has nothing to do with it." I responded.

"That sounds absolutely incredible," Diane said.

"What's even more incredible is the fact that some employees are subjected to this stuff every six months, just to keep their jobs."

"I can understand security measures, but this is pretty extreme," the young lady commented.

"Extreme? It's not even reality-based," I said.

"I just can't believe this can be happening. Not today," she added.

"Oh, it's happening. In fact, it's been happening while we've been sitting in this room. I can assure you of that."

After the interview, they thanked me for my time and told me that they would be in touch with me soon. As I was leaving, Diane Sawyer came up to me.

"Doug, before you leave, can I have a moment?"

"Sure thing," I answered.

"Doug, I don't see any way you can come out on this. I have been doing this for a long time now, and I think you probably are the only true crusader I have ever met. I can usually see how most people profit from their crusading, but I don't see how there is anything in this for you."

I looked at her for a moment, gave her my best 'devil-may-care' smile.

"Come out on this? At this point, I'm gonna be surprised if I even come out of it alive."

She looked at me for a moment, gave me a faint smile, then we shook hands and parted.

As I was walking away it occurred to me that I had just said something I never thought I would ever say, and I was surprised to realize that I truly, truly meant it. Not in a paranoid way or a T.V. tough guy kind of way, but in a very matter-of-fact kind of way, I knew deep down inside that there was a possibility that I might not come out of this alive. That reality was now a part of life for me.

A couple of weeks later on a Friday around the middle of March, I got another call from Gail Eisen, the producer from *60 Minutes*. She told me that she and a film crew were coming to Fargo to visit with me, and that they were going to film an entire Sunday morning church service, if that would be okay. I told her I would be delighted to have them visit. She said they would meet me sometime in the middle of the following week.

When I announced to my congregation that *CBS 60 Minutes* would be there the following Sunday to film the service, a rush of excitement filled the pews. Fargo had a population of approximately three hundred people, and this would no doubt be the biggest thing that had ever happened there. Most Sundays, the little Methodist church usually had about fifty people in attendance. They were kind, generous, loving, and supportive of my crusade, and I looked forward to showing them off to the *60 Minutes* people.

Gail Eisen and her crew arrived in Fargo on Thursday and spent the entire day filming outside the church and getting footage of me at work in the office. Over the course of the next couple of days, they also filmed and interviewed just about everyone in town. On Sunday morning, they hit the church – Hollywood-style. The little structure we used for worship was suddenly filled with cameras, lights, and microphones. It truly looked like a movie set. The reason for all the gear was that the show filmed everything with movie cameras, just like those used to film motion pictures. When they completed filming, they would then edit the film and make a VHS tape of the edited version so that they could have a near-perfect, first generation version. That gave them the highest quality tape available at that time for broadcasting. It also had a depth and color quality not found on a regular VHS tape. So, on that Sunday in March 1986, the United Methodist Church in Fargo, Oklahoma became a working movie set. They filmed the entire service from the opening prayer to the closing hymn. They filmed everyone coming into the service and me shaking hands with everyone on the way out.

After the service, Gail Eisen told me she would be in touch and they all packed up and left. It had been quite a production, and I'm sure it cost CBS tens of thousands of dollars. But, nothing about the polygraph or my crusade had even been mentioned.

Then, very abruptly, they were gone. What the hell was this all about? At first, I'd thought that they were going to do a human-interest type of story on me and my crusade. That really wasn't what I had been hoping for when I'd met with them in New York – I'd been hoping for a discussion about the issues facing the polygraph industry. But, given this turn of events, the human-interest angle was the only reason I could think of for them to go to that much trouble. Soon it dawned upon me exactly what was going on...the entire trip, all the hype, filming the service and interviewing seemingly everyone in town. The main goal had just been a very thorough background investigation on Mr. Doug Williams. They had been there to check me out and to make sure that everything was exactly as I had described it. They had researched the past, and now the current state of my life was getting the lens of scrutiny passed over it. Well, that was okay by me.

Ultimately, not one minute of the many hours of filming they did in Fargo was shown on the *60 Minutes* segment when it finally aired.

CHAPTER TWENTY-TWO

60 MINUTES – The Sting

The following Thursday afternoon, I got another call from Gail Eisen. She told me that the decision had been made and that *60 Minutes* was going to do a segment targeting polygraph abuse. She said that she would be the producer, with Diane Sawyer as the correspondent, and they wanted to confirm that I would be interested in working with her. I told her to count me in! Her main question was how much time I would be able to devote to the project. My duties as a pastor required me to be in Fargo on Sunday mornings, but I would be available to devote the rest of the time to the show for as long as she needed me. She agreed that would be workable and said she'd arrange transportation and lodging and asked me to catch a flight to New York the next Sunday afternoon. She said she would meet with me first thing Monday morning and we would begin planning our strategy. When I hung up the phone, I stood there for a moment, mentally trying to digest what was transpiring. FINALLY, *60 MINUTES* – a chance to share with millions the atrocities I'd been telling smaller groups about all these years! I was overjoyed – and to say the very least - even a bit on the giddy, goofy side because I couldn't stop myself from clapping, laughing, and thrusting my fist up towards the sky. I think I might have even jumped up in the air a couple of times. Awe, hell, who cares? IT WAS *60 MINUTES!*

The following Monday morning I met with Gail Eisen in her office to discuss how best to proceed with the segment. The more we talked, the more impressed I became with her. She was the ultimate professional – intelligent, creative, and most of all, gutsy. We sat across from each other in her office and she got right down to business.

"Doug, you told us in our first meeting that the polygraph industry was so corrupt that you could – and, these are your words – 'call in your test results'." She paused, looked me straight in the eye. "You are here to help me prove whether or not that is true."

I have to admit that I was a little surprised by her direct approach and, for the first time in this long journey, I wondered for a moment if my adrenal glands may have overworked my mouth on the previous trip and if I had possibly overstated my case with that bold assertion. No matter. I knew I was correct.

"Everything I said before was true, and it's true now," I said.

"You've seen this happen?" she asked.

"Numerous times. It's common practice – normal operating procedure in the industry."

"Prove it."

I sat there for a moment looking at the determined, no B.S. woman with her beautifully styled hair and direct eye contact, seated in this chamber of major network production, and I realized that I had better have a good response.

"Huh?" I said. Okay, so that's all I had. Give me a chance – it'll get better.

"You were a police investigator, Doug. So, investigate. If what you say about the polygraph industry is on the line, you should be able to prove it. Actually, Doug, you have to be able to prove it, because if you can't...well, I don't think I need to say anything more about this situation."

"No, you don't."

"So, for the purpose of this investigation, you are the detective in charge. This is your case. Where do we go with it?"

I had to smile for a moment. I was amazed at the fact that during this entire polygraph struggle, I had endured men threaten, curse and call me names – but, almost always from a distance. Here, the women - these women - were right in your face. If I ever needed back-up again, to hell with the guys. I'd call Gail.

"Okay, I get the message. That's what you want - an investigation."

"That's what I want."

"There's something I want, too."

"Such as?"

"I want some of the victims to have their stories told. Lives have been ruined. They need their say."

"Agreed. The victims' stories will be an integral part of the program. Okay, Mr. Williams, you're the one piloting this plane. You're the one who made the accusation that the polygraph operator was greatly influenced by the person paying for the test. So much so that you said they could 'call in the results.' So, having made this accusation, it is up to you to prove that it's true. I'm sure you know that, in the eyes of the law, the burden of proof is on the accuser. You are accusing the industry of evil and fraudulent activities, and now we're giving you an opportunity to make your case against them."

"All right, then, there is only one way to do it," I said.

"Which is?"

"We would need to set up a real-life situation in which the polygraph would be used to test people just like they get tested thousands of times every day."

"I follow you so far."

"To avoid criticism from the polygraph industry that we are not being fair, I think it's important that we make our investigation as objective and realistic as possible."

"We are of one mind on that topic," she said, leaning forward from her seat and resting her forearms on her desk.

"Let's break this down," I said.

"Commence breaking."

I, too, leaned forward and put my forearms on her desk, closing the distance between us.

"The polygraph industry contends that the test referred to as the 'specific issue test' is the most accurate of all the testing models."

"Go on."

"So, if that's their best, that's what we go after. Go right to their number one, beat them on their home court."

"I take it you have a plan."

"Oh, I have a plan if you have the ability to put it into place."

She raised an eyebrow. "Mr. Williams, we are *60 Minutes*. We have abilities you've never dreamed of."

I liked Gail Eisen more all the time. With that bit of prodding, I laid out the details of the plan I'd already formed in my mind. I told her we would need to find an actual business that would allow us to use their facilities and test actual employees about a certain theft from that particular business. I also suggested that we go right to the top of the polygraph pyramid and choose the largest and most prestigious polygraph firm in New York City to be the subject of the investigation - no one from below the top tier of companies and examiners, no second-teamers. Big dogs, only.

Gail and I spent the rest of the meeting brainstorming, pacing the room and bouncing ideas back and forth like tennis players. Gail was creative, she was innovative, and it was clear that she had a great deal of experience in setting up this type of sting operation. After about three hours of exchanging ideas, we had the basic outline of our plan in place. The next step would be to put the pieces together and put the plan into motion. Even though over a period of days we had worked out the details of the operation, I was still a little bit nervous and unsure about how this would all work out. One glitch could be disastrous. There would be no gray area here. This was a win/lose situation, and when it was over, there would be no friendly handshakes or better-luck-next-time speeches. There would be no next time for me. There would be no next time for the crusade. There would be no next time, period.

We moved with our staff into a staging area. For our sting, we used the offices of *Popular Photography*, a magazine owned by CBS, so the people there really had no choice but to cooperate with us. Actually, they seemed pretty curious about what we were doing, but since secrecy was important, we let them continue to be curious. We took over three of the rooms in the company's suite of offices. In one room we installed pipes in the ceiling to disguise our microphones, cut holes in the wall and covered them with pictures made from a special photographic gel, the kind that cameras could see through. This would be the room where the polygraph test would be administered. In the room next to it, we set up cameras to record the polygraph tests as they were being conducted. From yet another room, Gail and I, along with some of the staff, could monitor everything the cameras were recording in the polygraph testing room. I've got to admit, it was really fascinating to watch the technicians and set design people work. They were fast, efficient, and there seemed to be no obstacle they couldn't overcome. There was no doubt in my mind that this was the major league and I was on deck – and, soon would be up to bat.

Finally, the day arrived when we were scheduled to administer the first polygraph test. I knew everything was on the line – my crusade, my reputation, and more importantly, the fate of the potential victims of the polygraph industry. If I could prove that it was as fraudulent and corrupt as I claimed it was, it would go a long way towards putting an end to the abuse. To say that I was on edge would be the understatement of the century! I had barely slept at all the night before, and during the night, my blood pressure had gone crazy. In fact, it had been so high that it had blown blood right out of a small mole on the side of my face and had soaked my pillow. I'm surprised that I didn't stroke out right then and there! It looked like a homicide scene. After a personal triage session and a quick trauma recovery, I'd prepped myself by shaving, showering, spilling hot coffee on my stomach, re-showering, banging my knee on the car door, and driving to our location.

When I arrived, I sat in the car for a moment and took inventory of myself. Aside from the fact that I was limping, scalded, and needed a blood transfusion, I was also nervous as hell. Okay, maybe I'm a bit overboard on all that. Maybe, not.

I met Gail in our observation room in the offices of *Popular Photography*. We were both excited, and she seemed to be as full of nervous energy as I was. I paced the floor, prayed quietly and hoped that my antiperspirant didn't break down. In setting up our sting, we had asked an assistant producer by the name of Janet Tobias to assist us. Her job was to act as the personnel director for the magazine. Janet must have had an acting background or, perhaps in her younger days may possibly have made a lot of prank phone calls, because she was a convincing operative. She contacted a polygraph company called Spartan Security Services and explained that her company was currently having a problem with possible employee theft of company property. They agreed to send Kevin Cassidy, a polygraph examiner from their company, to administer the tests. We used four actual employees of the magazine as our subjects: Julia, Bob, Lorraine, and Paul. We told them that they were going to be given polygraph examinations to determine whether or not they had stolen a Nikon camera belonging to the magazine. Bear in mind, of course, that no camera had been stolen, no crime had been committed. All they had to do was to tell the truth when asked if they had stolen the camera. As a little incentive, we even promised them a reward of $50 if they could pass the test. We had instructed Janet, our 'personnel director,' to give Mr. Cassidy a little tip. She was to tell him that the thief might very well be Paul, although she had no proof. So, the stage was set, and we were off.

Mr. Cassidy was a very detailed operator and worked through each step of his testing carefully, making sure that he put on the lie detector "show" as I had done so many times before. He was doing his best to convince his subjects that the polygraph was the final word in lie detection. As he completed each subject's test, he would tell them how it had turned out. He thanked Julia, Bob, and Lorraine for their cooperation and truthfulness, and sent them on their way.

When it came to Paul, it was a different story. You remember Paul? He's the one that our fake personnel director told the polygraph operator might be the thief. And, sure enough, Mr. Cassidy, our professional polygraph operator, told Paul, "You come up very shy as far as truthfulness goes." Yes, Mr. Cassidy had his man. The case of the stolen camera was solved - except for the fact that Paul hadn't actually stolen the camera because *no camera had been stolen.* Mr. Cassidy had called an innocent person a liar. As soon as the polygraph operator had made his pronouncement, Gail and I looked at each other – I with a smile, and she with a look of astonishment. The crew got excited and momentary bedlam broke out. Success! Everyone was happy; I was vindicated; and, Paul was in shock at having failed the test and being called a thief and a liar.

After the examiner had left, we all looked at the tapes again and were satisfied that we had good video and audio on all four of the examinations. The staff was congratulating me on accurately having predicted what the examiner would do, and everyone was as excited about the outcome as was I - everyone, that is, except Gail. She was standing off to the side of the group with a pensive look on her face.

I walked up to her and said,

"Well, it certainly looks like I have proven my case."

I was hoping for a 'way-to-go, Doug' or 'great job' or something. Instead, she motioned for me to come with her to the other room. She closed the door, walked over to a small desk and sat on its edge.

"Doug, I think we need to have a different polygraph examiner administer the test to our volunteers."

Was she serious? She was.

"Why in God's name would we do that? What's wrong with this guy? He came from a top-flight firm and they vouch for his capabilities, so..."

Gail put her hand up to interrupt and gave me a sympathetic smile.

"Don't you get it? Believe me, I know how this works. If we don't do another test, they will say this was an isolated incident. They'll say that it was a mistake made by an incompetent examiner, or that it was an abnormality and that Mr. Cassidy does not accurately represent the polygraph industry. You can count on it. They will have an escape route if we only use one test session and one operator."

My heart sank to the bottom of my stomach, and all my pride at having been vindicated vanished. But, deep down inside of me, I knew she was right. I knew that her assessment of what my critics would allege was correct. I walked to the desk where she was sitting and perched next to her. We both stared straight ahead, deep in thought.

"Okay, I agree. I hate saying it, but I agree."

"Good. I hate saying it, too. And, maybe if circumstances were different, we wouldn't have to do anymore."

"Meaning what?" I asked.

She looked at me. "Meaning what? Are you kidding, Doug? You've been fighting this conflict all this time and you have to ask that question? This is a Goliath-type institution we're investigating. They have deep pockets, high level contacts, and resources most foreign countries would love to have access to. On our side, we've got a bull-headed, wild-eyed minister from Fargo, Oklahoma and some cameras."

"But, you forgot one thing."

"What would that be?"

"You are *60 Minutes*."

She gave me a big, confident smile. "Yes, we are. So, let's line up the next operator and do this right."

It took twenty-four hours for Janet Tobias to get another polygraph examiner scheduled in accord with my request that he be chosen from one of the largest and most prestigious firms in the city. I muttered to Gail that the phrase 'prestigious polygraph firm' was an oxymoron, but I wanted to deprive the polygraph industry of any excuse to complain.

Our second polygraph operator was Joe Diaz from Intelligence Services, Inc. This time, Janet, our 'personnel director,' was instructed to say that Bob might be the potential thief. We decided to make the change as a safety measure, and as a control factor in the testing. Again, none of our volunteers were aware that one of them had been pre-selected to be the guilty party, and, as before, they were instructed to be truthful in answering the test questions.

I was nervously confident, if that makes any sense, as we sat in the control room while Mr. Diaz conducted standard polygraph procedures on the four employees. Mr. Diaz was very thorough, and his results were conclusive. Paul – our previous 'liar' – had passed, and, guess what? This time, Bob was the deceptive party in our missing camera case.

"From what I see right here," Diaz said, indicating Bob's polygraph chart, "I know I'm right on the money."

Bob was incredulous. "I don't care if your lines are off the page, I didn't take the camera."

But, Diaz was adamant that the polygraph had proven Bob guilty of the theft and called in our Janet Tobias to discuss the results. Diaz warned that to fire Bob based only upon the results of the lie detector could result in a lawsuit, so they should fire him for other reasons. Diaz said, "I told him, hey, I'm 100% sure that you got the camera, and he wouldn't even look me straight in the eye."

That afternoon, we all met to discuss the day's events. Again, everyone was amazed that another different, innocent person had been labelled a liar when they had, in fact, been telling the truth. So, I was now two for two, and although I was feeling pretty good, I had this nagging feeling that we weren't done yet. I looked across the small conference room and saw the expression on Gail Eisen's face, so, this time, I beat her to the punch.

"You want to go for three out of three, don't you?" '
She gave me that sly, half-grin and nodded her head, 'yes.'

Our third polygraph operator was Ed Sullivan from Sterling Polygraph Systems. You guessed it, he also called a different, innocent, truthful person a liar. When the program aired, Diane Sawyer described it this way:

When he came in to test our four people, we told him something different. We told him we thought Lorraine might have taken the camera. Ed Sullivan passed Paul and Bob – the two who had failed before – and, indeed, his candidate for deception was Lorraine.

I grinned at Gail. "I think that's what they call a hat trick – three out of three. Have I proven my case to your satisfaction?"

"You most certainly have, and this program is going to be a classic." Then, she looked at me with that quizzical expression in her eyes and I held my breath, waiting for the other shoe to drop.

"What now?" I asked, trying to hide my irritation and wondering what else it would take to satisfy her.

"Something just hit me. Doug, do you think you could go in there right now and beat him?"

"Sure," I said with an ear-to-ear grin. "I told you, I can lie about everything and anything – including my name – and pass a polygraph test."

I turned to one of the guys on the crew, "Would you be kind enough to get the camera and lens we have been questioning everyone about having stolen?"

"Why do we want that?" a staff member asked.

"Well, if I'm going to be questioned over a stolen camera and pass the test, I should at least steal the camera and take it into the test with me. Should make it easier for him. It won't...but, you'd sure as hell think it would."

The crew member nodded and got the camera and lens out of the cabinet in the storage room. I asked Gail to put the items into the briefcase and give it to me. Then, they called Janet Tobias and told her to tell Ed Sullivan, the polygraph examiner, not to leave. I told her to tell him we had one of the possible prime suspects for him to test, a man who she believed had been involved with

Lorraine in the theft of the camera.

I took the briefcase containing the camera and went into the room with Sullivan, where I underwent a polygraph exam with questions about the theft of the camera. I lied in response to every question he asked me. I lied about the camera, where I worked, and my name. Hell, I could have lied about the time of day, if he'd asked. At the conclusion of my test, he got up from behind the desk, came around to me, and shook my hand.

"Mr. Jones, it is a pleasure to meet you. You are the most honest person I have ever tested."

It was all I could do to keep from laughing in Sullivan's face. Instead, I turned and walked toward the door. As I was leaving, I could not resist turning to our hidden camera, giving a thumb's up sign, a big grin, and a couple of exaggerated winks.

Later, the show's producers asked the three polygraph companies involved in our investigation to come in and be interviewed about the tests that had been conducted. Only one of them agreed. William Winblat of Sterling Polygraph Systems accepted - an error in judgement on his part. It is worth watching the entire *60 Minutes* segment just to see Winblat fidget and squirm and offer his lame explanation for the actions of his polygraph operator, Mr. Sullivan. At one point, Diane asked Winblat how he could explain the fact that his polygraph operator had called an innocent, truthful person a liar simply because we had indicated to him that she might be a thief. He hung his head, looked down at the floor and simply said, "It shouldn't be."

Diane also interviewed my arch enemy, Larry Talley, who attempted to explain away the fraud and corruption that we had exposed in the program.

"The polygraph may not be perfect, but it is the best thing we have now, and it is better than nothing."

To that, I would say that it is *not* better than nothing; in fact, it is *much worse* than nothing. Three out of three different polygraph operators called three different, innocent, truthful people liars about a crime that *had never even happened.* In this, the first ever independent, nationally televised test using a polygraph, it was 100% wrong, 100% of the time.

60 Minutes did a wonderful job on that program, and I was extremely grateful. But, in my opinion, one thing was lacking. For some reason, they cut out the part where I beat the polygraph test. I was very disappointed, and to this day, I still don't know why it was cut. Gail once indicated to me that they couldn't get it past the lawyers. In the final analysis, the way I saw it, they had put the nails into the coffin of the polygraph industry, but they had left out the stake through the heart. The vampire was injured, but he was still able to limp away.

Diane Sawyer concluded the *60 Minutes* program by reporting on the legislation that had been introduced in the House of Representatives intended to ban the use of the polygraph as a condition of employment in the private sector, an expose that caused an immediate uproar in the media. The episode was first broadcast on Mother's Day, Sunday, May 11th, 1986 and aired repeatedly over the next two years. The title they gave the episode was TRUTH and CONSEQUENCES. Very appropriate, I thought...very appropriate, indeed.

CHAPTER TWENTY-THREE

From Wild-Eyed Crusader to Well-Dressed Lobbyist

Over the next several months, I made a number of trips to Washington, D.C. to lobby members of the Senate in hopes of persuading them to join the House in support of the Bill to ban the use of the polygraph. Yes, I had become a lobbyist, but with some distinct differences. While other lobbyists had support teams, staff, money, paid transportation, and inside contacts...well, I had myself. Despite that slight difficulty, things were starting to happen. The House of Representatives had already voted to pass a Bill that would become the Employee Polygraph Protection Act. However, the Senate would have to approve the Bill before it would become law, and that would take time.

In June of 1986, I was invited to come to D.C., once again. This time I was going to be empaneled as a member of the Office of Technology Assessment. This panel was charged with the task of studying and reviewing the Department of Defense's polygraph program. It was a prestigious assignment because the OTA was a key resource for members of Congress who were dealing with technical issues. Its purpose was to provide information to guide them in crafting legislation and public policy. The research and writing of the report submitted by the OTA to Congress was accomplished by a staff of about two hundred, most of whom had a Ph. D. For the actual studies of specific areas under investigation, they relied upon specific individuals with experience in the area under investigation. When I received the letter inviting me to be a contracted member of this study group, I couldn't help but grin when I thought of how it must have galled them to recognize me as an 'expert.' After all, this was an elite group, or so they considered themselves. It's a safe bet that most of the steno pool had more education than I did, so I was certain that they really didn't want to hear my 'expert' opinion. But, I was going to give it to them, anyway.

When I arrived at the designated meeting place for the OTA panel, I was very impressed. Outside the main meeting room was a sort of reception area where members of the panel were chatting quietly and helping themselves to drinks and goodies from trays of fruit and pastry. I peeked into the meeting room and saw that it was filled with chairs for spectators on both sides, and in the center was a long, very beautiful horseshoe-shaped wooden table. At the head of the table was an engraved nameplate with the name of the person, and underneath was the word, CHAIRMAN. Others had names on them followed by "Ph. D." I couldn't help but to notice that no one in the group seemed interested in talking to me, and that even those who might have been, looked at me quickly, then looked away again. So, I grabbed a cup of coffee, went into the conference room, and began looking for my name on one of the engraved nameplates. Why not? It's not every day that they engrave your name on a shiny nameplate, especially just for some meeting. After searching to no avail for several minutes, I glanced toward the very end of the table on the right-hand side nearest the door. My eyes were drawn to a piece of folded white poster board that had my name scrawled on each side with a black magic marker. What? No nameplate? No distinguished seat at the table? Shocking. I wondered if this meant I was not an 'honored guest.' Maybe they were just being prudent and cautious with taxpayers' money. Didn't really think that was it, though.

I stood there and chuckled to myself because, by now, this was becoming an ongoing element of disrespect. I understood why they felt the way they did about me - I really didn't fit in with this group. I wasn't even sure if I fit in with any group. To those in the world of academia, I suspected that my little undergraduate B.S. degree was so insignificant that they were almost embarrassed to be seen with me. I presumed that, as far as they were concerned, I didn't deserve to be a member of such an august panel of highly educated people. And, further, it was no doubt that their unanimous belief was that, whatever I had to say, it would simply be the opinion of an uneducated man and, as such, would be of little or no interest to them. As far as those in the polygraph industry were concerned, I was nothing more than a traitor, a malcontent who was slandering their good reputation and making unsubstantiated accusations against an industry that was vital to the protection of our national security. I guess you might say I was the sand in their Vaseline jar. But, regardless of their opinions about me, I decided that Mrs. Williams' son needed a title under his name, too. So, I pulled out my pen and wrote CRUSADER in large capital letters under my name on my little cardboard nameplate. Ah, now I was officially 'somebody.'

Alas, I reminded myself that there was a bright side. I was getting paid. I'd been fighting this fight for almost eight years, but in all those years, I had never made one thin dime. Now, for the first time, I was being paid to give my opinion. The contract they had sent me from the OTA was for $200, plus expenses. If they'd bothered to consider how much damage I'd done for free, it should have scared the Ph. D. out of them to imagine what I could do with $200!

The meeting finally commenced. As the Chairman began outlining the purpose for the gathering, it became clear to me that it was to divide up hundreds of thousands of dollars in contracts available from the Department of Defense to study their own polygraph program. I was absolutely baffled! That was it? All these intelligent people were here to plead for government grants...taxpayer's money.

As the Chairman went around the table calling upon each member to make his presentation, I became aware that a group of men had gathered behind me. They were sitting on metal folding chairs that they had moved from the spectator's area to form a semi-circle very close to the back of my chair. I had been so intent upon listening to the sickening display of avarice that I had not noticed that I was being surrounded by 8 to 10 large tough guys. They began making snide remarks, whispering to each other and giggling like a bunch of third graders. It was obvious they were trying to intimidate me or to distract me in some way. They were so close to me that I could feel their breath on the back of my neck. One of them leaned even closer and whispered into my ear, "You know, Doug, you could afford a decent suit if you'd come to work for us; we could start you as a GS 14." I knew that was about a $50,000-a-year salary. I didn't bother telling him that I had already turned down much more than that from a hotshot lawyer wearing a much better suit than his. But, just as I tried to refocus my attention on the panel, the Chairman called my name and asked if I would care to present my proposal.

"Yes, thank you, Mr. Chairman."

As I attempted to stand, I realized that one of the men behind me was leaning back with his foot pressed against one of the back wheels of my chair. He was holding my chair in place in an attempt to prevent me from pushing back from the table far enough to get to my feet. I turned and looked at him staring at me with a sneering expression on his pudgy face. Apparently, the bullies behind me had mistaken my lack of response to their brainless remarks as a sign of weakness. But, I knew that I needed to remain a gentleman and exercise some self-control. After all, this was an important group of people and I didn't want to make the wrong impression.

So...I put both my hands on the edge of the large table in front of me and, with one big surge, pushed back with all my might. A daily regimen of push-ups had given me more strength than they might have imagined. When I shoved back my chair, I tipped dumbass over and he fell backwards. As he tilted towards the ground, he tried to catch his balance, but only succeeded in kicking his own chair to the floor and both he and it slammed backwards. His chair landed with a loud, resounding crash and he ended up in the lap of the man sitting behind him. Just like a scene out of some hilarious slap-stick comedy, the domino effect caused both of them and the men sitting next to them to fall back, and they all sprawled out on the floor in a big heap. As the leader untangled himself, he did what all bullies do when they are put in their place – he turned red with embarrassment and began sputtering with rage. I glared at him and the rest of the group who were now all in a pile, gracelessly getting up from the floor. "You should know me well enough by now to know that when you push me, I push back harder. So, do you want to play some more? No comments? I didn't think so." Okay – so my interpretation of 'gentlemanly behavior' and 'self-control' may need some work.

The rest of the room went quiet when I turned back to face the panel, and it was pretty amusing to see the looks on their faces. The expressions seemed to come from all ends of the emotional spectrum, ranging from surprise to confusion to shock and, even, to fear. Apparently, such barbaric behavior was not commonplace at OTA meetings. To the contrary, I did notice two men on the other side of the room who seemed to approve of my actions. One was a full-bird Colonel and the other, a three-star General. Both had grins on their faces, and the General gave me a subtle nod of approval. That small gesture of support encouraged me greatly. Hey, if a General is behind me, screw everyone else. So, I smiled at all the portly, puffed up professors around the table and calmly reached into my briefcase. I pulled out a copy of my manual and copies of *Nightwatch* and *60 Minutes* and placed them on the table in front of me as though nothing at all had happened.

"Mr. Chairman," I began, "unlike all these other gentlemen here assembled, I certainly have no intention of begging for government contracts to study the so-called lie detector simply because it is no more accurate than the art of reading goat entrails in hopes of catching a liar. And, I would thank you for your invitation to be a panel member, but that would not be appropriate since it is now obvious that neither you, nor anyone else associated with this panel actually invited me. I simply have to compare my hand-written nametag to those beautifully engraved nameplates in front of everyone else to get an idea of your opinion of me and to see how welcome I am. It is quite clear that someone with authority over you – and, I suspect it was Congressman Pat Williams – demanded that I be invited. You grudgingly complied, only because you had no other option. Perhaps Representative Williams was motivated by the desire to have at least one member of this panel who would not be a sycophant groveling for a handout from the government."

The Chairman's face began to turn red and I noticed some fidgeting and heard a few fragmented, whispered conversations exchanged between members of the panel. I gave the Chairman a sardonic grin and continued.

"Regardless of who invited me, and in spite of the fact that I'm not exactly an honored guest, I will not waste this opportunity to tell you a few things about the polygraph, things that no one else here has the guts or the honesty to say. I will start by telling you something you already know. Three years ago, in 1983, the Office of Technology Assessment studied the validity of the polygraph as a lie detector."

I paused to retrieve some notes from my briefcase.

"This very organization, the OTA, submitted a report to Congress entitled, Scientific Validity of Polygraph Testing: A Research Review and Evaluation. In this report, this very Body concluded, and I quote,

OTA concluded that there is, at present, only limited scientific evidence for establishing the validity of polygraph testing. Even where the evidence seems to indicate that polygraph testing detects deceptive subjects better than chance (when using the control question technique in specific-incident criminal investigations), significant error rates are possible, and examiner and examinee differences and the use of countermeasures may further affect validity.

"So, we all know two things about the polygraph, assuming you believe the conclusions of your own report: 1) it is not a lie detector; and 2) I can teach anyone how to beat it. That research was done three years ago, and I have here my own research that proves exactly the same things. I will not ask for a grant for thousands of dollars; I will give them to you free of charge."

I held up two VHS tapes.

"These are tapes of *CBS Nightwatch* and *60 Minutes*. I would like to submit them as research, which was conducted after your 1983 report, research that confirms your findings. The first tape proves the statement in the 1983 report which says that the use of countermeasures may affect validity. On this program, I demonstrated how easy it is to train a person in the use of countermeasures. In other words, I proved that I could easily teach anyone how to control every tracing on the polygraph chart at will. It is interesting to note that the person I trained in countermeasures for this program was an attorney from the U.S. Department of Justice, so no one can claim he was one of my people or that he had any hidden agenda. The second tape proves the other point you made in your 1983 report when you stated that even where the evidence seems to indicate that the polygraph test detects deceptive subjects better than chance, significant error rates are possible. In this program, I proved significant error rates are indeed possible. In this research, the results of which were released just last month, I proved that the polygraph is wrong 100% of the time. In this study, three out of three different polygraph examiners called three innocent, truthful people liars about a crime that never happened. This booklet is an instruction manual that I have distributed to thousands of people. It is also part of the Congressional transcript of my testimony in the United States House of Representatives. It details exactly how to pass any polygraph test given by anyone, anytime, anywhere. And, I have taught thousands of people to do just that."

I took a deep breath.

"So, I ask you, why are we here? There should not even be a DOD polygraph program for us to review. The polygraph is worthless. It is, in fact, worse than worthless; it is dangerous – dangerous to the people who are subjected to it, dangerous for the people who use it, and even more dangerous for the people who rely upon it for our national security. As a member of this panel, I am entitled to a report detailing how you plan on wasting taxpayers' money to review a government program which uses an instrument that has been proven to be invalid. So, please send the report, and I will respond to it in a manner that I deem appropriate. But, I will no further dignify nor legitimize this pathetic charade with my continued presence. And, I don't want to hang around any longer in case these bully boys behind me decide to try to whip my ass."

With that, I picked up my polygraph and my briefcase, pushed back my chair, and walked out of the room. Behind me, I heard whispers, gasps, curses – and, to my surprise and amusement – the slight echo of laughter and a smattering of applause.

CHAPTER TWENTY-FOUR

The "Countermeasures" Conspiracy

A few months after I returned to Oklahoma, I did receive a copy of the OTA report detailing their plan for reviewing the DOD's Polygraph Program. I wish I still had a copy of the report, but if I recall correctly, after reading it, I was so disgusted that I tore it up and tossed it into the trash. I did, however, respond to them in a manner that I deemed appropriate, just as I'd promised I would. I wrote a letter addressed to the OTA and sent a courtesy copy to the Chairman of the House Government Operations Committee and to the Chairman of the Senate Armed Services Committee. The text of that letter is as follows:

I am enclosing information I would like to be made a part of the official record for the final OTA report to the Congress and Senate. I hope you emphasize the stupidity of continuing to study a machine that can be controlled, totally and completely, by anyone who can control their bowels. I have taught thousands of people how to manipulate the tracings on the machine – how to out-con those ridiculous con men that call themselves polygraphers. This polygraph scam is the longest running con game in the history of this country!

I cannot believe that we are actually continuing to spend money to study something that is becoming a laughingstock. As I told you in our meeting, I have taught thousands of people to pass their polygraph examinations, and I have never had even one student who was unable after twenty minutes of training to produce a truthful chart. In the past eight years, I have taught thousands of people from all walks of life, and, as I testified to in our meeting, I taught a Justice Department attorney who was kind enough to demonstrate his skill at countermeasures on national television. On pages 7 and 8 of the report you sent me, there is some good evidence - the only credible evidence proving the value of countermeasures in the entire first draft of the OTA report. You state that trained people can beat it 35% of the time using physical countermeasures, and that people using mental countermeasures can also beat it 35% of the time, and that simply educating people about how the polygraph works is also a valid countermeasure. That simply proves that the machine can be totally manipulated by just about anyone, and that the polygraph operator is nothing but a "four flushing con man." My training combines all three: the physical training, the mental training, and education – and it is 100% successful every time in every imaginable situation. Anyone who relies upon the results of this instrument is a fool, and anyone who spends our money to perpetuate this insidious con game is a scoundrel. Page 5 of the OTA report is enough to induce vomiting. I cannot believe that we are spending $590,000.00 to study the modern-day equivalent of walking on a bed of hot coals. And, to devote $100,000.00 to the detection of countermeasures is even more perverted. I'll let you come watch me for free. Better yet, I'll come up to D.C. and teach you all about countermeasures of $200 a day and expenses. It should take me about a week. I am enclosing the VHS tapes from CBS NIGHTWATCH and 60 MINUTES, along with a copy of my manual HOW TO STING THE POLYGRAPH. Please make copies of the tape and enclosed material as part of the final report to Congress, and also make them available to the public. If the government persists in its present course of *expanding the polygraph threat, this information will become even more popular than it already is. Signed, Doug Williams*

Shortly after that meeting at the OTA, I received a call from Dr. Gordon H. Barland, who identified himself as a polygraph examiner and instructor at the Department of Defense Polygraph Institute. (DoDPI). Based upon the information in my manual, he had developed a 40-hour course on polygraph countermeasures and how to detect them.

Dr. Barland actually told me that he was developing a course for the institute that would teach polygraph examiners how to determine if a person was, in fact, using my Sting Technique. He asked if they could use my manual in his countermeasure course, and then asked if he could get a discount for a bulk purchase! I told him that he could distribute copies of my manual for free to all the operators who worked for the government, and to tell them that I dared them to prove to me that they could tell when anyone was using my technique to beat them. I told him that there was no way anyone could determine whether or not a person was using my technique because all I did was teach people how to produce a truthful chart. I continued to try and explain that my intention was not just to teach people how to beat a machine – *it was to prove that the machine was not a lie detector.* However, because telling the truth only worked about 50% of the time in a test, it was often necessary for a person to learn how to use my technique in order to pass. So, I gave Dr. Barland permission to use my manual as his textbook. All I asked in return was that if he were able to detect if someone was using my technique that he would offer me proof. No proof was ever offered. Wow. Imagine that. You can rest assured that the reason was because they were never able to detect anyone ever using my so-called "countermeasures." What follows is an excerpt from a post Dr. Barland made in a public forum concerning this:

I'm here to vouch for Doug's bona fides. I have long believed that his primary motivation in publishing the manual is that he believes the polygraph does more harm than good, and that he is not a Judas selling out his former profession for filthy lucre. I have talked with Doug on the phone many times and, with only one exception, he has always been courteous and helpful. When I was developing a 40-hour countermeasure course, at what was then the DOD Polygraph Institute, I wanted to include Doug's manual in the handout material for the examiners. I called Doug to see if I could negotiate a quantity discount rate, as I wanted to distribute several hundred copies within the Federal polygraph community. As soon as I explained that I wanted to use his manual as part of the curriculum, he immediately and unhesitatingly gave me permission to download the manual, reproduce it, and distribute it to every federal examiner without any fee whatsoever. I sent him a written agreement for that, which he promptly signed and returned. I was deeply impressed. If he were in it for the money, he would never have made that very generous offer. Even a small fee, multiplied by the hundreds of federal examiners, would have been a considerable sum. I am convinced that he is acting primarily out of moral convictions, rather than greed. And, just for the record, although many federal examiners question Doug's loyalty to America, I have never doubted his patriotism. I respect him for serving honorably in a position of great trust. Just thought I'd add my two cents. Peace, Gordon H. Barland.

I had always had a suspicion that Gordon was playing me – acting like he was my friend, when all he wanted to do was to keep tabs on what I was up to and to use my manual as his textbook. I'd played along with him for years because I wanted to prove my points. There was a growing paranoia that I had trained almost every subject they tested, all of whom were now routinely being accused of using my countermeasures. But, if the polygraph community was really so certain about the reliability of their only tool, why worry about me or the content of some manual? Just by virtue of their accusations against the individuals they tested, they were admitting the possibility that the polygraph could easily be manipulated.

In 1999, the Department of Energy held public hearings on its polygraph policy because of a proposal by the Energy Department to give polygraph tests to employees at the Los Alamos National Laboratory. I had given permission for my manual to be distributed to everyone there who was threatened with having to take the test. A speaker at one of these hearings, Dr. Barland attempted to convince his audience of scientists and engineers that, nowadays, polygraph operators were able to detect countermeasures such as those found in my manual. He said, "We are now training our examiners how to detect people who are trying to manipulate their results, and we have learned a lot about how people go about doing that. Earlier this year, we published a case where Doug Williams had given information to a person on how to beat the polygraph, but that person was not successful." What Dr. Barland conveniently omitted saying, however, was that the very reason why the person had not been successful was because he had admitted to having used the countermeasures! Had the subject not made that admission, he would have passed. Dr. Barland had been routinely using my manual and training people to detect countermeasures, but the only proof he could offer was this one example of a subject who had actually *admitted* using my manual to pass his test! Not much proof to show after ten years of study and Lord knows how much taxpayer money.

The fact is that no one at DoDPI has ever come up with a reliable method for detecting these so-called "countermeasures," and Dr. Barland's misleading statement before an audience of top-notch atomic scientists and engineers was proof of the polygraph community's consternation over the fact that they had never been able to catch anyone using my technique. If they had had any proof, they would certainly have offered it by now, wouldn't they? Yes, they sure as hell would have.

CHAPTER TWENTY-FIVE

The British Are Coming...
HOORAY!

During the decade prior to my battles with the industry, the polygraph was used almost exclusively in the United States. However, in 1984, a firm by the name of Polygraph Security Services set up shop in the United Kingdom. By 1987, the British government was beginning to consider its use in criminal cases and for screening personnel within the intelligence and security agencies. In that regard, Margaret Thatcher commissioned a study on the validity of the polygraph prior to implementing its use within the government.

One day, I was in my office at the church when I received a call from a man who identified himself as John Baer. He told me that he was from Scotland Yard, and that he had been sent by the British government to interview me and have me train him in the use of countermeasures. He asked if I would be kind enough to give him an interview in Oklahoma City and train him to use the Sting Technique. Why not? It's not every day you get a call from Scotland Yard, especially if you're a pastor in rural Oklahoma. As our conversation progressed, it became obvious that he had done his homework and had even read the transcript of my testimony in Congress. We met for a couple of hours the following day, during which time

I hooked him up to a polygraph and demonstrated how easy it was to learn how to control the test results.

Mr. Baer explained that his assignment was to assist with an investigation conducted by the British government in discovering what effects countermeasures might have on the validity of the polygraph as a lie detector. Over several hours we discussed in detail the polygraph's functions, uses, and reliabilities. At the end of our discussion, I reminded him to be sure to talk to the 'other side,' as well. He just smiled and said that he already had.

"I want to thank you so much for the time you've allowed me today, Doug," he said with his distinctly British accent.

"No problem," I replied with my distinctly Oklahoma twang.

"I'll be reporting my findings to Dr. Levey – Dr. A. B. Levey is the director of the study."

"Well, I hope you get your report completed soon."

"Actually, the report is a formality. I've already reached a conclusion. The polygraph is not suitable for our purposes in security service screening or in criminal investigations."

"I'm glad we agree," I concurred.

"As you said, Doug, it doesn't work."

The results of the study conducted by Dr. Levey were released in a report in 1988: *It is well established that countermeasures, i.e.: means of producing a misleading result in order to escape detection, can easily be learned and that the capability for escaping detection is extremely high. Indeed, they ae impossibly high given the known limitations on the reliability of psycho-physiological measure. In fact, there is a strong probability that these inflated values represent a mixture of a high proportion of self-deception and a low proportion of simple chicanery.*

The report also found that the polygraph screening was biased against a truthful person resulting in *erroneous exclusion of suitable applicants and the false accusations of those already in employment.*

The report concluded that the polygraph technique had *no*

scientifically acceptable theory at its base and it is applied to the detection of low base rate frequencies in an area such as the identification of honesty which is, itself, ill-understood.

The following is an excerpt from the House of Commons Hansard debates.

December 8, 1988:

Dr. Levey's conclusion from the literature is that the polygraph is probably incapable of achieving a high level of accuracy and reliability when used for screening purposes and, moreover, that individuals trained in the use of countermeasures would have a good chance of escaping detection.

How ironic that the simple demonstration and information I had given to the investigator from Scotland Yard were all that was necessary to prevent the use of the polygraph in the U.K. By merely informing the commission of the facts about its lack of validity and the false premise upon which it was based, I had been able to convince them that the polygraph was not reliable and should not be used. Yet, by contrast in the United States, I had been working for years and was not even close to slowing down the use of the polygraph, let alone, stopping it. As a matter of fact, it was quite the reverse; the use of the polygraph was being expanded in both government and private industry like an out-of-control skin rash.

I had to admit it - I was wearing down. I felt like my very existence was eroding from exhaustion. The years had passed in a blur of phone calls, letters, seminars, visiting politicians, talking to small town store clerks, driving, sleeping in a truck, and demonstrating that ridiculous damn box. Was there any real value in all of this? I wondered.

CHAPTER TWENTY-SIX

A Sign from Above

I was sitting on my couch taking an inventory of my life and wondering what I hadn't done that I should have done and wondering if anyone gave a devil's damn about it besides me. I prayed as I did daily and nightly, thanking the Lord for many things and asking for guidance. Just a sign, I thought, just a little sign. As I sat there alone with my thoughts to ponder, the weariness began to overtake me. Fighting the pained voice of my inner doubt, I took two steps over to my T.V. and turned it on – not to watch it, but to fight the silence of my home. I took off my shoes, lay back down on the couch, and slowly closed my eyes. It was Monday, June 27, 1988.

"Lie Detectors. They've been around for a long time, now – 75 years." In my near-sleep fog, I could hear Tom Brokaw's voice. What the hell is Tom Brokaw doing here? Why is he talking about...?

"But, a majority of states don't allow..."

"...the polygraph." He's on my television! He's talking about the polygraph!

I turned my head to look at the T.V screen and focused. The report wasn't long, but it was good - very good. The news story reported that a new law had just passed which would, in effect, outlaw all polygraph examinations of employees. It was short and simple – but, so are game-winning field goals in the Super Bowl, buzzer-beating 3-point shots in the Final Four, last-number draws in the Lottery. And, this – this, to me and a lot of other people – was a lot bigger.

I had prayed to God for a sign and He had delivered unto me an answered prayer. As the news went to another story, I remained still on the couch. I was just overcome with a feeling, the likes of which I had never experienced before. I felt as though I were being lifted off the couch - almost like I was floating in the air – and I could literally feel waves of relief and joy cascading all throughout me. I wasn't sure what to do; I hadn't really planned on this moment. I mean, I had planned on making it happened, but I had never thought about what to do when it really did happen. I could call someone, or I could jump up and cheer. A few moments before, I would have been too tired to contemplate either one. Now, suddenly, I didn't feel tired. Still, I didn't move. I didn't smile. It was like dreaming while you're wide awake. The faces were there again, the faces from the polygraph tests...but, now they were laughing, crying, expressing their gratitude for all my efforts on their behalf. And, oddly, I felt embarrassed. Had I been doing this for gratitude or a pat on the back? No, I knew that wasn't it. Gently and quietly, the concept that those blurred years hadn't been a waste embraced me, and the word 'success' crept into my consciousness.

That's what it was...success. My mind drifted back to my conversation with Larry Talley when I'd told him I was going to put him out of business. I remembered that moment vividly, and it was only then that I began to grin and congratulate myself. I was suddenly delighted to think about all the headstrong, over-bearing polygraph partisans who would soon be looking for another job.

Moments passed, and I realized that just to lie there in private reflection was the best way for me to celebrate this unbelievable event. I thought of those who had supported me through the years and offered a silent thank you to each one. I made a mental promise to myself to thank as many of them as possible in person when I could. I finished my reflection by giving thanks to God for pushing me and providing for me in my crusade and faded into a peaceful slumber.

CHAPTER TWENTY-SEVEN

Acknowledgement of my CRUSADE

The ramifications of the new law were immediate to both sides. Victor Kaufman, the president of New York Lie Detection Laboratories, was quoted as saying that the new law would "knock-out about 98% of our polygraph business." And, I began to wonder how many polygraph firms would actually shut down. I couldn't deny the need to scratch my nagging curiosity itch and figured there was one sure way to find the answers, at least locally. So, after about a week, I began thumbing through the Oklahoma City Yellow Pages under the 'polygraph section.' Over half the polygraph firms I called that week had already had their phones disconnected. I'll admit, right here and now, that I derived an enormous amount of satisfaction from hearing the little recorded out-going message with the operator saying, "I'm sorry, the number you have reached is no longer in service."

If you were to go back in time and compare the number of polygraph firms listed in the Yellow Pages in 1988 with those listed in 1989, you would see that well over three-fourths of them had disappeared. I know this to be true because I did the research, myself. Back then, the public library had copies of the Yellow Pages from all the major cities in the U.S. And, in 1989, I went to the library and compared the listings between 1987 and 1989. By my calculations, based upon the number of listings of firms that had disappeared in the period of one year, I was able to calculate that I had helped to put over seven thousand polygraph operators out of business! Wow, what a feeling!

A few weeks after the EPPA was signed by President Reagan, I received a call from a producer of a radio talk show on KTOK in Oklahoma City. She asked if I would be a guest on a live broadcast from the Lawn and Garden show at the Oklahoma City Fairgrounds. This might sound like a small deal compared to some of the events I had attended in the past, but it wasn't to me. KTOK had been the first station to interview me when I had begun my crusade long ago, and I was so very proud to return to talk to them about the new law.

When I arrived at the Fairgrounds, I was greeted by the producer and invited onto the small stage where I shook hands with the host. Off to the side, I saw Shirley Berry, my old friend and the head of the Oklahoma ACLU. No one had mentioned that she would be there. That was absolutely fine with me, but she had this big "I've got a secret" smile on her face. There was just something odd about it. She stood there until the producer motioned for her to come up to the stage where we were standing.

"Don't be mad now, Doug. I'm the one who put them up to this," she said, giving me a big hug.

"Put them up to what?" I asked.

"You're getting an award."

"An award. What are you talking about? What kind of award?"

"Well, Doug, you're a little bit old for a Heismann Trophy, but in my world, what you are being honored with is more important than a Heismann."

"And, that is?"

"You are being given the Volunteer Advocate Award."

"What? But, why?"

"Don't be dense, Doug. And, do not act like you don't deserve it. As far as I'm concerned, and as far as the ACLU is concerned, you are the person most responsible for passage of the Employee Polygraph Protection Act."

"But..."

"Don't argue. You're getting the award. Now, sit down and prepare to be thanked for your work."

When the show started, Shirley went on and on about what I had accomplished to get the EPPA passed. She went into detail about all the seminars, the books I'd distributed, the T.V. shows, etc., with particular emphasis on *60 Minutes,* which she said had been the primary piece of evidence that had helped to destroy the credibility of the polygraph industry. I was asked to give a quick run-down of my efforts and then the host opened up the phone lines, which, amazingly to me, were already full. For the next forty-five minutes, person after person was allowed to relate their own private problem with the particular polygraph testing they'd undergone - finally, having a voice.

Each person's thanks humbled me, and I was beginning to become embarrassed. Then, too, I couldn't help but notice that the small crowd that had been there when we started was now growing in size. Rather than milling about the Home and Garden show, people had begun to gather around the stage. They looked different from those who had been there earlier, and I noticed that many of them were dressed in route salesmen's and retail store clerks' uniforms. And, the group grew larger and larger as the broadcast went on.

When the show was finally over, I thanked the host, told the producer and Shirley goodbye, and began making my way to the exit. I barely got off the stage before I was swarmed by people surrounding it. People from all walks of American life were gathering around me, telling me what a relief it was to have the intimidation stopped. I saw tears in the eyes of some, and one woman said, "I won't ever have to go through that humiliation again." It, literally, took me over thirty minutes to go the hundred feet to the exit. It was surreal, and I found myself running out of responses, so I just thanked them for thanking me.

When I finally made it to the exit, though, I stared in disbelief. All the streets surrounding the fairgrounds had been blocked by cars and various kinds of delivery trucks. All of these people had been listening to their radios and gone out of the way to come and offer me thanks. While the crowd inside had been thankful, but serene, this group was vocal. Some honked their horns, others called out to me, and many ran to shake hands. I had made it through the first crowd with my emotions in check, but now, the lump in my throat was swelling.

When I arrived home, I was drained from the experience. I supposed it was kind of like being a rock star for a day - and, for me, a day was plenty. It wasn't that I didn't truly enjoy the thanks and interaction with all the people, I did. Oddly, it was the fact that I had never really thought about how people might actually behave at that moment when their hopes are finally acknowledged. Another realization had set in. I had been focused on defending myself against my opponents for so long that I had nearly forgotten what the fight had been about. My crusade had always been about helping these folks that needed help...the people, and the opportunity for them to be employed without fear of 'the box.' So, at last, I could finally feel relief that I had succeeded in reaching my goal. My Crusade...it had all been worth it.

CHAPTER TWENTY-EIGHT

Beach, Beer, Bikinis

I was tired. Tired of the letters. Tired of the phone calls. Tired of the radio and television interviews. For the first time in ten years, I was gradually feeling my obsession with the polygraph crusade begin to fade. Even though there were exemptions in the EPPA that would allow government contractors, police and fire departments to continue to screen applicants for periodic security clearance, I was certain that the federal, state, and local governments would soon follow the example of those in private industry and take steps to ensure that the polygraph would no longer be used for any purpose.

It was time for a break. Time for a change of scenery. Besides, I was beginning to get wind of predictions of doom about me. I had no fear of a fight, but I had become tired of all the stupid antics and threats. To hell with them.

The road had been long and fraught with peril already. I needed to get away for a while...a long, peaceful while.

Fortunately, I had saved much of the salary I had earned as a local pastor in the Methodist Church and also had a small amount in my retirement account. So, I resigned my position, closed out my account, took some of my savings and bought a very nice used Class C motor home. I rigged it up with a tow bar so that I could pull my little Mazda hatchback behind it and headed to Galveston, Texas.

Galveston was not a random selection spot on the map for me. During my youth, I had spent many happy summers on the Bolivar Peninsula beach across the bay from the city, itself. As I drove south from Oklahoma, I could feel the weight of my obsessive crusade literally fall from my shoulders. I began to breathe easier and was starting to relax a little. I began to feel a sense of freedom that I hadn't felt in a long time. I was singing along with Waylon Jennings on the radio, and it was a good day. When I arrived in Galveston, I parked my motor home in a rundown trailer park right on the Seawall Boulevard, rented space closest to the Gulf of Mexico, and went right to work building a deck on stilts with stairs. I put out a beach chair, a large umbrella, and a nice propane barbecue grill on the deck where I could sit, soak up the sun, feel the sea breeze and gaze at the beach across the street. It was a sweet set-up. My only goal at that moment in my life was to be an unknown beach bum – a goal I soon succeeded in achieving.

Eventually money ran short, so I picked up an odd job or two until I'd saved enough to take time off again. I made sure I paid all my bills, which were few, in cash and always before they were due. A wise man once said, "A single man with no debtors can easily disappear." That's exactly what I did – I disappeared. For a long time, no one on earth knew exactly where I was, and that's how I wanted it. I knew I'd made a lot of enemies, and it was good to be somewhere enemy-free.

Most days, my biggest decisions were whether to sit on my deck and drink beer, watching the tourists on the beach, or whether to exert the effort to walk up to the seawall to a dive called the Poop Deck. Great name for a hang-out. It had an outside deck overlooking the seawall and the beach where I could drink a few beers, talk to Marie, the bartender, and watch the beach bunnies in their bikinis. I discovered that I had a real aptitude as a beach bum, and it was a lifestyle I thoroughly enjoyed for quite some time. I seldom, if ever, thought about the polygraph industry, or anything of importance, for that matter. I went for months without reading a newspaper or watching the news on T.V., or even listening to a radio. As the old song goes, "I had become comfortably numb."

Eventually and probably predictably, I descended into 'oceanside poverty.' I discovered that money is not important unless you have absolutely none, then it becomes very important. I had not maintained my motor home at all, and I was so close to the Gulf that on most mornings the sea breeze would cover it with a salty residue. Often, there was actually sea foam sitting on the hood. It had been almost completely devoured by rust and I hadn't even started the engine in over five years, so it was basically totaled out. I didn't even own a car. I'd traded my little Mazda for a motorcycle that had become my mode of transportation around the island for about four years. Basically, this had been my life.

The problem with a self-inflicted lifestyle like mine was that, over time, you get damn bored. Beach bumming is okay for the short term, but I knew that sooner or later I would need to indulge in some more vigorous activity than drinking beer and breathing. Even though the beer tasted cold and the air was clean, I decided that I needed to catch up on the activities of the human race, if it still existed, which, from my current perspective, was only a presumption. So, periodically, I began to peak at the local newspaper or glance quickly at a news broadcast – just enough to see if the world was still turning, nothing more. No use getting on information overload too soon.

It was early evening. I was seated at my usual spot, third throne from the left of the men's room door, directly in front of the Miller Beer sign. On the way to this location, I had grabbed a newspaper that an earlier patron had left on the bar next to the beer product my lady bartender had put out for me in its proper place. No request from me, of course. Marie had been trained that whenever she saw me, she should put a can of Bud in front of me. It was a sort of Pavlov's dog response. The old scientist had trained his canines that, whenever they heard a bell, they were going to be fed; thus, they automatically salivated. Seeing the beer in front of me automatically made me thirsty. Good for me; good for the bar. Well, at least I wasn't wasting all my time; I was dabbling in psychology.

"So, what's on the agenda today, honey?" Marie asked, turning to watch the T.V. that sat on a corner shelf behind the bar.

"At present, I am in search of the meaning of life. I have been told that it may very well be located in this establishment."

"I cleaned up here this morning, so I probably threw it out," she said, attention still on the television.

"A shame," I said. "Well, in that case, I shall focus my attention on this container of American brew."

"That's what I like about you."

"What would that be?" I asked.

"You are decisive."

"One must be prepared and ever-vigilant."

She remained glued to the T.V and I glanced over at the partially rolled up newspaper on the bar next to my beer. I reached over, picked up the beer, took a long drink from it, and laid it back down. I looked at the newspaper again, reached for it, then grabbed the beer instead and took another drink. Sometimes it's better to deal with one issue at a time. Code of the beach bums.

"It sure is quiet in here tonight," I commented.

"Yeah. Couple of the old-timers were in earlier is all. They borrowed my binoculars and took off down the shore line."

"Spot a stranded whale or a distant squall or some other such spectacle Nature might bestow upon us?"

"College girls sunbathing."

"Mother Nature does provide."

"Anything noteworthy in the paper?"

"Nothing so far," I said, looking at the still-untouched paper, taking a sip of beer and clinking the empty can down on the bar. Marie reached behind her, pulled out another Budweiser and set it out without even breaking her viewing concentration. If Pavlov only knew what his experiment had evolved into.

I was halfway through a near-perfect swig of the world's finest grains and hops when the flashback came to me. Polygraph. Polygraph? What the hell? Where did that come from? Was it a flashback? No, I'd heard it. Just now. Someone had said, "polygraph." I looked at Marie. She was eating a Three Musketeers bar and chasing it with a coke. Shit, am I hearing voices now? "Polygraph." There it was again. The T.V. It was on the T.V. at the bar. A reporter on T.V. was talking about polygraph testing.

What? He was saying something to a man about recent increased use of the polygraph. The man said he was a polygraph operator and that polygraphs were 98% accurate. The reporter said they had tried to contact a leading anti-polygraph spokesman, but no one had been able to locate him. Then, a photo...there's a photo on the screen.

"Hey, Doug," Marie said, pointing at the T.V. "Isn't that you?"

I finally focused completely on the screen. The photo remained momentarily, then faded and the report ended, leading into a commercial.

"Wow!" Marie exclaimed. "That was you! I didn't know you were famous. It's like having Monte Hall in the bar!"

The damn thing was back. I'd known we hadn't completely beaten it, but I'd figured common sense would eventually win out and it would die on its own. I'd hunted it; now, it hunted me. I felt like I was in some black-and-white science fiction movie, fighting some multi-headed serpent. Damn thing's got more lives than a freaking cat.

I got up and tossed some money on the bar. It may have been five bucks or fifty, it didn't matter. I walked out the door to the sound of Marie calling my name. I just walked. I went directly to my run-down residence and stepped into the bathroom. I stood in front of the mirror for a moment. Man, I had a lot of hair. I grabbed all the necessary pruning utensils and began chopping, cutting trimming and shaving. When I was finished, I walked into my living room, such as it was. It was time for a quick inventory of my personal property. Didn't take long. I was flat broke, fifty years old, and had so few possessions that I could easily fit them into a small box. So, I did just that.

Aside from a pair of blue jeans and a couple of shirts, the only things in that box were videotapes and the paperwork that I had generated working on my crusade. I strapped everything onto the back of my motorcycle and headed North. Away from the beach. Away from the bikinis. Away from the peace and anonymity. North... to the world.

CHAPTER TWENTY-NINE

The New Age of Technology

As soon as the front tire hit Okie pavement, I stopped and called my brother, Mike, who was a very successful businessman in Chickasha, Oklahoma. He owned a chemical company, and I asked him if he could use any help. He told me that he could definitely give me a job and, even though I wasn't exactly at home, being around Mike sure made me feel that way.

We went right to work on his business and things were going very well until, one day, Mike mentioned that he would like to develop a website for my crusade and put it up on the internet. I knew I'd been out of the loop for a while, but I didn't think I'd been that far out. When he said, "website on the internet," it sounded so foreign to me that he might as well have said, "I want to make lemon flavored shoelaces for Neptune wombat breeders." Okay, so maybe it wasn't quite that bad, but I realized I had a lot to learn. It was now 1996 and I dove right in and studied this contraption they called the "internet." It was fascinating, and how I wished I'd had such a tool at my disposal all those years before.

We began working with a web designer and Mike asked me if I still had a copy of my manual. Sure, I did. He suggested we sell them on the website. Although it was a great idea to put them on the internet, I preferred to just let people have them for free. Mike looked at me as if I were crazy.

"Give them away? Are you nuts? You gave them away and worked for nothing for over ten years, and I will not allow you to do that again! You will sell them, and you will charge as much as you can possibly get for them. That is the only way I'll help you set up your own website!" Mike could yell a bit and be a little hard-headed, but I knew he was right. We sort of compromised on a price and started to work on a website.

While all this preparation was in progress, I was informing myself more about what the T.V. reporter had been talking about back when I was on the beach. It seemed that polygraph testing was, indeed, alive and well, and actually blossoming. Many people were applying for jobs in federal, state and local positions. The legislation that had been passed had omitted such careers from the guidelines of the EPPA and, as such, they were open to exposure from the polygraph testing procedure. In addition, all those who were already employed by such agencies were still being subjected to polygraph policies. Government contractors, as well, had to be polygraphed if someone up the ladder so determined, and the number of individuals now involved was staggering. The EPPA had significant holes in its structure, and the polygraph operators were rushing through like water through a crack in a dike.

In March 1996, www.polygraph.com was launched. My website finally was up and running, and my manual would now be called an "e-book." My brother, Mike, had loaned me the money to get the process started, which so far amounted to $5,000.00. For that loan and the use of his office to run my business, I gave him 40% of all sales for four years. In the first three weeks, I'd sold enough manuals at $47.95 each to repay the whole loan. I continued to manage the day-to-day operations of Mike's chemical business, while at the same time, attending to calls and emails from people who had purchased the manual. I offered free consultations and began selling more and more every month. This was a whole new experience for me because, for the first time, I was actually getting paid to fight the polygraph industry. And, I was getting paid well. From 1996 to 2000, I had gross sales of close to $200,000.00 a year.

By 1997, things were going well, very well. Then, somehow, things got even better – I met a wonderful woman named Kathy. Kathy was one of those rare combinations of beauty, intelligence, faith, support and...well, I could go on, but I'll simply put it this way. If you have ever been fortunate enough to meet a person like Kathy, then no explanation is necessary. If, however, you've never met anyone like her, no explanation is sufficient. After a time, she and I were married and, for the first time in my adult life, I began to enjoy what you might describe as a normal life. My manuals were selling well, I was refocused on my crusade, and Kathy was a tremendous help and encouragement to me.

All was not sweetness and light when it came to my website, however. Since I had put my phone number on the Web, I was immediately besieged with phone calls from irate polygraph operators who seemed very happy to have a toll-free number they could use to harass and threaten me. On the positive side, though, I also got calls from people wanting to educate themselves on how to pass the polygraph. I asked those who passed their tests to report back to me about what the test had been like. They would tell me what questions had been asked and provided a great deal of information about how tests were now being administered. It was a great way for me to research the changes in the industry since I'd been away from it. I was able to compile a list of the questions that various agencies used in pre-employment exams, as well as questions used by intelligence services in government for what were called lifestyle and security clearance exams. With every bit of information that I received, I continued to update my information on the internet. It was a wonderful tool and made the Education phase of my three-pronged attack easier than it had ever been before. I could reach millions of people and never leave my office. At its peak of popularity, my website received over 30,000 hits per day, a pattern that continued for about four years from 1996 to 2000.

Eventually, however, a few other websites appeared online selling knock-offs of my book and claiming extensive knowledge about the field. As it turned out, none had any expertise in the polygraph world, but they had succeeded in casting doubt about my crusade and my own abilities. Oddly enough, the proliferation of these new websites did help in one small way. I was no longer the only one out there teaching people how to beat the polygraph, so the industry had more than just me to worry about. But, I was – and, still am – the only one stupid enough to have put my phone number on my site. Hence, threats and harassment by angry polygraph operators continued to plague me.

The Litigation Phase

The Litigation Phase of my three-pronged attack was also greatly enhanced by the internet. I put the entire EPPA law on my website, and invited visitors to contact me if their employers violated any of the provisions of this law. Many responded and followed up with individual lawsuits, resulting in substantial monetary awards. I have been asked to serve as an expert witness at many types of hearings, and had attorneys seek my advice as to how to question and cross-examine polygraph operators. I found those endeavors very rewarding.

There was one extremely significant event on the litigation front in 1998. In the case of the United States vs. Edward G. Scheffer, the U.S. Supreme Court ruled that because there was no scientific consensus on the reliability of polygraphs as instruments for establishing the truth, the results of that testing could not be admitted into evidence. Justice Clarence Thomas, writing the majority opinion for the U.S. Supreme Court stated:

...the overall accuracy rate from laboratory studies involving the common "control question technique" polygraph tests assess truthfulness significantly less accurately - that scientific field studies suggest the accuracy rate of the "control question technique"

polygraph is "little better than could be obtained by the toss of a coin, that is, 50 percent.

I was delighted that the U.S. Supreme Court had come to this conclusion and took pride in the fact that, included in their written decision, was the statement that the accuracy rate was "little better than could be obtained by the toss of a coin." Personal pride couldn't be denied...those were the exact same words I had used in my own manual and testimony in many court cases.

Examples of the inaccuracy and ineffectiveness of the polygraph system continued to undercut the argument of its necessity as a means to protect citizens from foreign espionage. It was discovered that in 1994, U.S. CIA Agent Aldrich Ames had passed two polygraph examinations during the time in which he was actively spying on behalf of the Russians. Reports followed substantiating the fact that the polygraph had failed to apprehend any spies or foreign espionage agents embedded in our national security services. More and more, names began to crop up: Karl Koecher, Ana Belen Mantes, Leadro Aragoncillo. They were not familiar names, but names with one thing in common: they were spies, actively working in our country against us - and, each had passed their polygraph examinations without issue. Yet, the CIA stepped up the ferocity of its exams, which became even more abusive, intrusive, and intimidating. Employees were now being forced to take the test at least every five years. The rationale behind such decisions seemed beyond comprehension. What could those conversations have been like?

"Gentlemen, we need to catch some spies."

"How, Sir?"

"We'll use the polygraph."

"But, it doesn't work, Sir."

"Good, good, we'll use it on everyone."

"But, it doesn't work, Sir."

"Yes, but, at least, it's abusive."

Polygraph testing was on the rise, no doubt about it, and the private sex lives of individuals had become fair game. Operators were now asking for information on what kind of sex you liked, how often you had sex, and about your favorite positions. Yeah, that should help catch us some spies. Rather than subject themselves to these tactics, many good employees of the CIA and other government agencies simply resigned. It has been reported that the CIA, alone, lost more than 25% of their case officers during an 18-month period between 1995 and 1996. That total represented more than had resigned over the previous 10-year period. One report noted that a "protest from active officers about lie detector tests are having a marked negative impact, and CIA recruiters are finding it hard to meet their targets." Personnel quality was being forfeited in lieu of bizarre and twisted questions. The FBI and Secret Service, as well as every other intelligence and law enforcement service in the Federal government, reported that over 60% of their applicants were denied employment based solely upon the results of a failed polygraph examination.

By 2000, the demands on my time were such that I realized I could no longer help my brother, Mike, with his business, and Kathy and I moved to Norman, Oklahoma where I set up shop running my website from the comfort of our new home. Now that I had more time, I added a new dimension to my business, offering personal testing preparation training. I rented an office in a building near the University and furnished it with a desk and chair for me, plus a large armchair for my students. I decorated the office with letters from *60 Minutes*, attorneys, professors, and members of Congress. I had my certificate from the National Training Center of Lie Detection and a copy of my diploma from Oklahoma City University framed and placed on the walls.

The testing preparation training consisted of bringing people into my office and administering a polygraph to them – in this case, called a practice test. When I began the project, I was using my old analog machine; but in 2003, I updated my equipment and started using a computerized polygraph machine equipped with a motion sensor pad and the latest scoring software. I was still training people to tighten their anal sphincter muscle in order to produce a reaction in the cardio tracings. However, the companies now manufacturing polygraph instruments had begun selling a motion sensor pad – a pad placed in the seat of the subject's chair - which they advertised was able to detect "countermeasures." I also changed the language in my manual to encourage people to use "mental imagery" rather than to physically manipulate a reaction. The subject was to think calm, relaxing thoughts when answering relevant questions, and to think of a frightening experience when answering the lie control questions.

In another method, I used a form of hypnosis during my one-on-one sessions, which I call the "enhanced mental imagery" training. I had been studying hypnosis for several years and had developed a set of suggestions that I would communicate to my student during hypnosis in order to direct their subconscious mind to bring about the desired effect. I would train them to let their subconscious mind take over and lead them to a peaceful place when they answered a relevant question. Then, all I had to do was to have them imagine a frightening scene or remember a traumatic experience from their past when they answered a control question. The training sounds very simple, and it is. As Albert Einstein once said, "If you can't explain it to a 6-year old, you don't understand it yourself."

CHAPTER THIRTY

If All Else Fails, Try Handcuffs

Enter John. R. Swartz, head of the U.S. Customs and Border Protection Internal Affairs Credibility Assessment Division. Even though the government had been forced to admit that countermeasures could be used effectively, it continued its campaign to enforce use of the polygraph, claiming that operators could be taught to recognize these countermeasures. Of course, that was impossible, but rather than admit it, they turned their attention to "shooting the messenger."

In 2013, Mr. Swartz proclaimed that those who "protest the loudest and longest are the ones I believe we need to focus our attention on." Was protesting a crime an offense, or a responsibility? I considered it the latter. Under our Constitution – supported by our Government and the people of this country – we uphold the First Amendment to the Constitution:

Congress shall make no law respecting an establishment of religion or prohibiting the free exercise thereof; or abridging the freedom of speech, or of the press; or the right of the people to assemble, and to petition the Government for a redress of grievances.

"The right of the people to assemble, and to petition the Government for a redress of grievances." Apparently, Mr. Swartz had decided that this particular part of the Constitution wasn't necessary – he was working to protect the polygraph industry and targeting citizens who complained about it. Since I was complaining the loudest, they decided it was time for me to go. This is how they did it.

At approximately 10:00 AM on February 21st, 2013, I had a personal training session scheduled for a man named "Brian." When he arrived, I remember thinking to myself that his demeanor was markedly different from most of the people who came into my office. Most of time, subjects were uneasy and apprehensive when they arrived for a testing session. It was normal behavior for them to exhibit signs of anticipation and concern, and they would often lock inquisitive eyes on the polygraph machine. This was not the case with Brian.

When Brian came in, he barely acknowledged me and never even once looked at the machine. He had a very large backpack that he immediately took to the corner of the office and placed at an angle facing my desk and the subject's chair. He seemed unduly concerned with its placement, moving it back and forth until he got it at just the right angle. I remember thinking that this guy must have some kind of obsessive-compulsive disorder because of the way he was working so diligently to place his backpack in just the right spot. That accomplished, he looked up at me and seemed to be somewhat confused as to what to do next.

Everyone who comes in has a different story, but they all have one thing in common: they are frightened, and they hope that they'll be able to overcome their nervousness. But, Brian did not show any signs at all of nervousness or anxiety. I considered that he might be on some sort of medication and soon began to suspect that he might have a mental problem. I'd dealt before with individuals suffering psychological issues, and this guy showed definite signs of something. Since he didn't seem dangerous, however, we went on with the process. I would always begin by telling people that the first order of business was to give me my fee – and, I would laughingly say that, as far as I was concerned, it was the most important part. This would usually get a little chuckle and serve as an ice-breaker.

Again, it was different with Brian. He already had the money neatly folded in half in his front pocket. I took the money and told him to sit down. I explained the procedure and while I was hooking him up, he studied the display of letters I had on the wall. He was concentrating on trying to read them from a distance of about three feet away, and still, never even glanced over at the polygraph. You may call it temporary complacency or intermittent ignorance, but no red flag went up or warning bells rang in my head.

As I began my normal introduction to the procedure, Brian interjected that he was taking a pre-employment polygraph exam for Customs and Border Patrol and asked how long the training session would take. I said about an hour and a half to two hours. He mentioned having to catch a plane and that he hoped he would be finished in time to make his flight. I found that a bit unusual, too, because most people were more concerned about whether or not I would spend enough time with them to sufficiently prepare them for their test, rather than how quickly we could finish. But, I'd already concluded that Brian was a different breed of cat, so-to-speak, and told him we'd be finished in plenty of time.

I told Brian to close his eyes and relax and went through the script of enhanced mental imagery training. When I told him to open his eyes, he was like everyone else who experiences the training and was noticeably relaxed. He even let out a big sigh. I explained the difference between relevant and control questions and began to review the standard pre-employment exam questions.

It was then that he did something even stranger than all the strange things he'd been doing since he had entered my office. He blurted out that he was a sheriff's deputy and had once smuggled drugs into the jail – he also said that he'd gotten a blow job from a female juvenile when he was taking her home in his sheriff's cruiser! I was absolutely astounded! This was the first time anyone had ever said anything like that to me during a personal training session. I was also struck by the matter-of-fact, almost rehearsed way in which he'd said it. Before I could even respond, he told me that he was afraid he would lose his job as a deputy sheriff if the CBP told the sheriff about what he had done. He added that a female sheriff's deputy had been denied employment with the CBP as a result of what she had admitted during her polygraph test and was now afraid she was going to lose her job with the sheriff's department. I was at a loss for words. Somehow, I managed to inquire if she had, in fact, lost her job because of anything the CBP had actually said to the sheriff. Brian said that she hadn't, but explained that he was concerned that, if the sheriff knew the details of the things he'd personally done, he would lose his. I didn't know what to say to that, so I mumbled something about the fact that since the CBP had not told the sheriff about what the female deputy had said, they might not say anything about what he would tell them, either.

I didn't inquire into any more details and presumed that, since he was more worried about losing his job than he was about facing criminal charges, what he was telling me was probably bullshit. But, why? I couldn't figure out what could possibly have motivated him to have said such a thing to me, or why his only worry was that when he eventually made these admissions to the CBP, they would tell the sheriff. I couldn't shake the feeling that he was making it up, and I was becoming irritated that he would come in and tell me such a crazy, concocted story. Finally, I concluded that, since there seemed to be no rhyme nor reason to what he was saying or doing, he must be a mental patient. Actually, as I said, so far, he appeared harmless, and I couldn't help grinning when I considered what the CBP polygraph operator would say when Brian admitted to him all the things he'd just told me. I doubted he'd believe them, either.

After I'd run the test, I showed Brian his chart, which wasn't all that good, but I wanted him out of my office as soon as possible. His demeanor was getting more and more bizarre by the second, so I decided to try another tactic by complimenting him on a pretty good reaction he'd had on one of the control questions. His reply?

"Yeah, that's when I was thinking about getting a blow job and smuggling drugs." This crap was getting old quick now. With his attitude and rapidly disintegrating behavior becoming a concern, I decided to go a little bizarre, myself. I pointed to my Walther .380 at my side.

"I don't carry this as a prop, you know." I didn't say it in a threatening voice, but I wanted to see his reaction – and, boy, did he react!

He shouted in a very loud voice, "Don't touch that gun! I am around guns a lot, don't touch that gun!"

What was really weird about his statements was his delivery – and, I call it 'delivery' because it sounded as if he were reading lines in a play and wasn't all that good at it. It was stiff-sounding, very stiff. Then, as though he wanted to make sure I had heard what he'd had to say, he repeated the bullshit admissions he'd made earlier and that he was very worried about it all. Finally, I began to wonder if he might be a polygraph operator. I've often thought that some of my trainees were actually operators. It stood to reason that they would be curious about my training and would want to see for themselves how effective it was. Perhaps that was it, I thought. He was a polygraph operator just pulling my chain and playing head games. But, no matter who this guy was or his reason for being there, I was sick of him and his silly games. It was time to end this charade or whatever the hell he had going on.

I removed all the attachments from him as he carried on his strange monologue.

I thought to myself, you want to act crazy? Okay, let's get crazy. I went around in front of him. He was sitting in the subject's chair and I put my face down within an inch or two of his, almost touching his nose with mine. I licked my finger and made the sign of the cross on his forehead. I then began acting like a crazy priest, giving him absolution for his confession. I began gesturing wildly, jumping up and down, saying something like, "You are absolved of all your sins, my Son." I began chanting gibberish, trying to act like I was speaking Latin and performing some sort of weird exorcism. As I went on like this for two or three minutes with my face very close to his, I watched his eyes grow wider with surprise. To my immense satisfaction, he began to show signs of terror at the sight of this armed man acting like a demented sermonizer, making odd noises, barking strangely, gesturing wildly, and yelling like a crazy man.

I suddenly stopped, leaned even closer, touched my nose to his.

"Are you about ready to stop this nonsense and go catch your damned airplane?"

"Yes," he said in a trembling voice. He nodded his head, quickly grabbed his backpack, and bolted out the door.

As soon as Brian opened the door, the world erupted. A wave of alien life forms crashed into the room, shrieking, pushing and reaching for me. Brian disappeared from sight just as someone grabbed me and held me in a tight grip. Metal restraints were clamped on my wrists. The Government, the unhappy polygraph-supporting government had arrived. They came in numbers. They came with weapons. They came with handcuffs. They came with bulletproof vests. They came with vengeance against my Crusade.

Finally, the one who seemed to be in charge of the raid identified himself as Douglas Robbins, U.S. Customs and Border Protection, Special Agent, Office of Internal Affairs, U.S. Department of Homeland Security. It was a surreal dream…like a movie scene where everything is moving in slow motion. As I tried to focus on the only person speaking, Agent Robbins told me that I was not under arrest, and that if I would just co-operate with him, he would take off the handcuffs.

Click. Click. That's the sound handcuffs make when they are being tightened. Robbins repeated 'co-operate' in a friendly voice, then with his hand on the ring of the handcuffs binding my wrists, *click,* he would tighten the cuffs. They were now so tight that I began to lose feeling in one hand and the other wrist was, literally, screaming out in pain. Keep in mind, he'd said he wanted me to co-operate - but, as yet, I didn't even know why they had crashed in.

"Are you going to co-operate?" he asked again. *Click.*

"You're making this extremely painful," I said.

"All we want to do is have you," *click,* "co-operate."

I told him I had no idea what co-operation he was talking about. "If I'm not under arrest, then why am I handcuffed in the first place?" He said I was handcuffed for their protection but didn't address his controversial handcuff manipulation.

Robbins produced a search warrant listing numerous statutes that he claimed I had violated. I looked at one of the papers he handed me and thought to myself, "so what?" First of all, I had no idea that such laws were still in existence. Secondly, their existence meant absolutely nothing to me. What had I done to violate any of them? Furthermore, if the government believed that I was somehow in violation of any such laws, why had it taken thirty years to pay me a visit? Nothing had changed dramatically since the crusade was launched in 1979 – except for my continued success.

When Robbins told me that he'd been investigating me for over three years and had enough evidence to prosecute me, I had to wonder. What the hell was there to investigate? All they had to do was to call and I would have shown them everything.

Robbins reiterated that I was not under arrest and said that this could all go away if I would just help them out by looking at a few pictures and telling them whether or not I had trained any of the people in those pictures. Oh, now I was beginning to see. What they wanted was to have me tell on people – people who had only wanted to protect themselves. It suddenly became clear to me that if I wasn't willing to throw my other fellow human beings under the prosecution bus, I would become the target. I didn't exactly comprehend it at the time, but the implication was beginning to dawn on me, and instinctively, I knew I'd rather shove needles into my eyes than turn people over to intimidators like these, so I said I would prefer to speak to my attorney. His astounding reply was that *I could not contact my attorney.* He picked up my cell phone from my desk and said, "No. We are confiscating your phone, along with all your equipment and anything else that is of interest in your office." Bear in mind that my office was 8' x 10'. It had two chairs, one desk, one laptop computer, one computerized polygraph instrument with the pneumograph tubes, cardio cuff, motion sensor pad, GSR electrodes, and a few handwritten notes. Confiscating all my items shouldn't be a time-consuming process; however, I had the distinct impression that it was going to be.

Agent Robbins continually insisted that it was in my best interest to co-operate with them, which I know I've mentioned already but he never seemed to quit saying it. Finally, I refused to acknowledge him any longer, other than to repeat my legitimate and legal request to speak to my attorney. Robbins informed me that there was, in fact, a U.S. Attorney present and that I could talk to him, instead. Oh, good, I can't talk to my own attorney, but I can talk to theirs? Enter Anthony J. Phillips, Trial Attorney, U.S. Department of Justice, Public Integrity Section. He introduced himself and said he would be happy to speak with me and get this matter settled right away. Wow, more co-operation.

"You've succeeded in your shock-and-awe routine with your raid and your handcuffs, and all. I am in shock, and I am in awe... but, I am not stupid. I know it is illegal for me to lie to a federal agent, and I am greatly concerned that I might inadvertently say something that is not the truth, since I have no idea how I could have violated any of the laws you have accused me of violating. But, one thing I know for sure, I certainly have no intention of talking to a U.S. Attorney, especially when you will not allow me to contact my own attorney."

Finally, after approximately thirty to forty minutes of their badgering me to co-operate and my continually asking to speak to my attorney, they removed the handcuffs and gave me my phone. I called my lawyer, Chris Eulbert, who told me not to talk to them and asked to speak with the U.S. Attorney who was still present in the room. The attorney talked to Chis for a few moments, and then handed the phone back to me. Chris repeated that I was not to talk about the case and said that he would see me in his office the next day.

I was escorted from the room with the admonishment that I could not be in my office while the search warrant was being executed. A minute ago, they wouldn't let me leave, now I was taken down the hall where he and a few other agents took turns guarding me.

"If I'm not under arrest, then I'm leaving." Robbins kept repeating that I could not leave.

"We are also executing a search warrant at your house and I don't want you going over there and shooting my agents."

Nothing theatrical here, no sir. I assured him that I would never even consider doing such a thing, and that I had spent ten years of my life as a law enforcement officer, myself, and had nothing but the utmost respect for everyone within that community. With that, he handed me my phone and told me to tell my wife not to go home until he gave her permission to do so. I called Kathy and, not wanting to upset her, I told her as little as possible about what was going on. Obviously, though, she was distressed. I mean, what was I supposed to say? "Honey, the Feds kicked in my door, handcuffed me, and are now going through everything we have. Oh, and you can't go home. Other than that, things are fine." Yeah, that should calm her down.

Robbins and his agents detained me for four and a half hours while they searched my small office. Looking back on it, I think that the scene with Brian was an attempt to come up with a reason to arrest me; however, they had been unable to twist anything that I'd said to Brian into any kind of crime at all. Later, I surmised that Brian's oversized backpack had probably been filled with video and recording equipment, a reasonable explanation for why he had been so intent upon getting it placed correctly. Also, Robbins told me that Brian was "singing like a bird." What did that mean? His statement was curious to me for two reasons. First, what would Brian "sing" about? It hardly seemed likely that, if it had been true, he would confess his drug smuggling or inappropriate behavior with a minor to the Feds. Second, I found it hard to believe Robbins had actually said, "singing like a bird." Who the hell says stuff like that? Amazingly, he then took back the fee Brian had paid me, confirming to me that this "Brian" was acting as some sort of undercover agent. It also confirmed my suspicions about the strange and unlikely statements he had made about smuggling drugs and the female juvenile - just as I had thought, nothing but bullshit.

Finally, I was allowed to leave, but was not allowed to go to my residence until Robbins gave his permission. I went to Kathy's office and waited until around 6 o'clock seven hours after they had first started searching my house - before we decided to call Agent Robbins. He said there were more papers than he'd anticipated, and that it would take more time for them to finish their search. We waited another hour and called him again. He finally agreed that we could come home in *three minutes.* When we arrived, we found that they had searched every square inch of our home. They'd taken my computer, all my papers, all my mail receipts, and much more.

Picture yourself walking through your front door and seeing your living room torn apart...your kitchen, dining room, bathrooms all strewn with your personal items tossed about like worthless garbage onto the floor...your bedroom closets and dresser drawers gone through...your most personal possessions poked through, handled and leered at by strangers. Not by burglars. Not by thieves. But, ravaged by government employees - law enforcement employees, no less. Picture seeing your family photos lying all over the floor of your once-Constitutionally secure, protected home.

Adding insult to injury, they had needed to secure a search warrant in order to facilitate this intrusion. The search warrant would require proof of probable cause for the entry into my home and would have had to be based upon information gathered during Mr. Robbins' three-year investigation. If that was the case, consider the fact that I had not changed my work structure or behavior from all the previous years through the three years that Mr. Robbins had investigated me. My work had always included assisting people by instruction through my manual on the Sting Technique and advocating that people protect themselves from polygraph errors by following my instructions. So, if this was somehow sufficient for a search warrant, what about my co-conspirators? What about the people who had mailed out my manuals...the people whom I'd enlisted to help me...the people who had actually paid to get the word out and gone on the record to restrict the use of the polygraph? I am speaking now of the U.S. Congressional Members who had done all these things in order to facilitate the passing of the EPPA. Now, I was in the federal cross-hairs for it all by myself?

The next day, we met at the U.S. Attorney's office in Oklahoma City for a video conference with AUSA Ryan Faulkoner in Washington, D.C. Present were my attorney, Chris Eulber; AUSA Anthony J. Phillips; U.S. Customs and Border Protection, Special Agent Douglas Robbins; myself; and another agent who had been present at the raid. Prior to this, he had not identified himself; however, he now handed my attorney his card which identified him as Fred C. Ball, Jr., Special Agent, Polygraph Examiner, U.S. Customs and Border Protection, Office of Internal Affairs.

Phillips began the conference by informing me that it was illegal to lie to a federal agent. He pointed out, quite needlessly, that Robbins and Hall were both federal agents and said that I would have to be completely truthful when answering their questions. My attorney said, "Why would he talk to you? Are you offering him immunity?" Phillips replied that there would be no immunity; that they had more than enough evidence to prosecute me; that I was being investigated by a Grand Jury; and, that he was certain that he would get an indictment against me. Ah, the Grand Jury, the Prosecution's tool by which the government presents all its evidence without any rebuttal given by the Defense. Hearsay and rumor, which are not allowed in court, are welcomed. Phillips told my attorney that the only thing he could say was that, if I co-operated with them, it would help me when I was sentenced. Chris simply said, "No immunity; no talking." Then, we got up and left.

They had wanted me to name people who had taken my course or read my book or attended one of my seminars - all legal for Americans to do. But, the industry wouldn't stand for it and the Attorney General's office had a vested interest. If I named names, they could go after innocent people for passing their polygraph exams and tell them that I had been the one to turn them in. No deal. But, the Feds didn't give up.

AUSA Phillips called my attorney shortly after the meeting and encouraged him to allow me to talk to them. He implied that it would be in my best interest, and that he would hate for Chris to deprive me of the opportunity to help myself. When he asked what I wanted to do, I told Chris to decline. After having been cuffed, searched, threatened, and having my house ransacked, I sure as hell wasn't in the mood for a group hug. Chris called Phillips back and again told him that I was not prepared to talk to them. Phillips called back at least another three times with requests for me to talk to them, all of which I declined. Eventually, we finally stopped hearing from them and my attorney filed a motion for the return of my property. Two months later, all of it was returned – by Agent Robbins.

CHAPTER THIRTY-ONE

Indictment

The torture of interminable quiet and the inescapable certainty of impending doom is the only way to describe what one endures awaiting the Federal Government to decide one's fate. And, in my opinion, theirs is a systematic, deliberate, calculated way to make a person suffer. At times, the silence was almost unbearable. Then, one day, the silence ended.

The United States of America versus Douglas G. Williams

First Undercover Operation

On or about October 15, 2012, Undercover A placed a telephone call to Williams' telephone number listed on the Williams' website, which connected Williams to his personal cellular telephone.

Actually, I'd received a series of calls over a period of several days, and this caller wouldn't give up. He just kept calling and calling. Extremely persistent. Extremely.

Undercover A told Williams that he was an inspector at the airport and was under investigation for allowing a friend to pass through Customs with contraband. Williams promised to assist

Undercover A to get ready and told Undercover A, "There's not going to be one problem, at all." Undercover A informed Williams that he intended to lie to investigators about his involvement in illegal smuggling.

This guy was the first person to ever come out and say anything like that to me. Nobody else had ever said anything even close to it. And, man, had I gone off on him for it!

Williams chastised Undercover A, saying, "What the fuck do you think you're doing, dumbass? Do you think you have like a lawyer confidentiality with me?" Williams continued, "I haven't lived this long and fucked with the government this long and done such controversial shit and got away with it by being a dumbass." Williams then threatened not to conduct the training for Undercover A, stating "I don't know if you've got sense enough to keep your damn mouth shut."

This guy was pathetic in my eyes. He'd kept calling and pleading with me to help him. He was in a 'world-is-coming-to-an-end' type of mindset. My instinctive, inner objections to assisting him had gradually begun to erode.

After Undercover A asked if there was any way that Williams would train him, Williams stated, "I'm just working on the assumption that you're telling the truth."

I'd asked him, "You're a believer, right?" He'd said, "Yes." So, I said, "Well, I'll tell you what. I'll help you out here just because I don't want to see you have to suffer for one mistake and be accused of a lot of other things that you didn't do."

On or about October 27, 2012, Williams met Undercover A at a hotel in Arlington, Virginia for a private in-person training. Williams stated, *"Now that we're alone in private, tell me what this is all about. But, first things first, you got my money?"*

Up until that point, this guy hadn't told me all the details of his case – as phony as it really was. He'd begged and pleaded with me to help him, and I'd let my guard down. I admit it - I got sucked in. It can happen. It shouldn't, but it did.

During the training, Williams instructed Undercover A: "Do not change your story. Do not tell on yourself. And do not admit to ever seeing me or talking to me or anything else."

When the training session was over, he'd given me a big ol' hug and thanked me for having helped him. I'd even put it up on Twitter that I'd helped another person withstand a traumatic polygraph experience. If I'd thought for one second that helping someone – anyone – was wrong, I surely wouldn't have publicized it.

Second Undercover Operation
On or about February 5, 2013, Undercover B placed a telephone call to Williams' personal cellular telephone. Undercover B told Williams that he was employed as a county sheriff and he was applying for a job with the border patrol. During a conversation, Undercover B told Williams that he was worried about answering questions the CBP might ask relating to sex and drugs. Williams told Undercover B, "I will get you ready. Don't tell me anything that will disqualify you, and I can train you how to pass if you're lying your ass off, so don't worry about that fucking bullshit."

Undercover B tried to further explain his concerns but was interrupted by Williams, saying, "Oh God, please help me. Shut the fuck up. Quit worrying about all that stuff. Listen, I'm fixing to put it all positive, ok?" Williams added, "I don't give a damn if you're the biggest heroin dealer in the fucking United States."

The episode with my subject, "Brian" has been described in a previous chapter exactly as it happened. As I reflect upon it now, I am cognizant of a lack of discernment and poor judgement on my part, which I regret. It's often easy to see things from hindsight, but, when you're in the thick of the moment, although your instincts may be correct, your interpretation of them may be wrong. I had been uncomfortable with Brian without really understanding why. I had not believed that he was telling me the truth with the stories he'd confessed. I'd put them down as ramblings of a would-be tough guy, of a mental patient, or perhaps of someone on medication. I was well aware that when dealing with individuals like that, you must be very careful how you approach the situation. Because of his extremely bizarre behavior, I had discounted any measure of substance or truth in his admissions of either sexual assault of a minor female or drug smuggling. In addition, I knew that Brian was going to be taking a real polygraph exam, and that if he confessed to his examiners the things he'd confessed to me, it would be their job to offer the appropriate punishment. My session with him was a training session, not an actual test for his employment. Looking back on it, though, I probably should have tossed him out on his ear and refused to train him. I should have made some excuse about my machine being on the fritz, or something, but I didn't. Even though he hadn't seemed dangerous, I'd instinctively felt a need to be cautious. So, training him quickly and getting him out of my office as soon as possible had seemed the prudent thing to do at the time. I see now, however, that although my instincts were absolutely correct, my interpretation of them was not. "Brian" turned out to be an undercover agent. That's something I never would have predicted. Lesson learned.

The government also presented evidence of my promise to assist a woman seeking employment as a police officer who claimed she had told me that she planned to lie in her polygraph examination to conceal past conduct. She was not an undercover agent or acting at the government's behest.

After all was said and done, I was charged with three counts of Witness Tampering and two counts of Mail Fraud. Mail Fraud, you may ask – as, did I. According to the government, because payment for two of my training sessions had been sent through the U.S. Mail, that constituted Mail Fraud.

Did I deserve it? That question, now, I leave to you to decide.

CHAPTER THIRTY-TWO

Innocence or Guilt

After I was indicted, the threats of prosecution and persecution reached new heights. If I were to be found guilty, the threat would include a lengthy prison stay and restitution in the millions of dollars. Restitution, you might wonder, for what? Well, according to the Powers-That-Be, because I had helped "Brian" to get a job for which he would be paid $60,000.00 a year, I would owe the government thirty years of salary, just for "Brian," alone. Of course, such employment would never have even been possible because he was already an employee of the Federal Government...but, so what?

I was tired. Extremely tired. I began every morning and finished every evening beaten down by the legal thrashings and ever-increasing intimidation that had thrown me into the abyss of the legal system. Innocence or guilt no longer played any part, and all that mattered now were my financial and mental abilities to battle the lie detection empire that had now enlisted the help of the U.S. Attorney's Office.

Even if one were to consider the possibility that I might be guilty of any one of the crimes that the indictment against me supported, would that change anything, really? Would it change the reality that millions of people were being subjected to improper inquisition at the hand of the polygraph operators? Would it change the fact that people were losing or would lose their jobs because of the polygraph? Would it change the fact that people had been, and would be again, coerced into confessions because of the polygraph? Would it change the fact that many people had spent decades in prison for crimes they'd had nothing to do with because of a polygraph and its operator? Would it change the fact that courts all across this country, including the U.S. Supreme Court, no longer allowed polygraph results to be entered into evidence because they had concluded that the polygraph was no more accurate than the flip of a coin? Would it change the reality that no one – positively, no one – could provide scientific proof that the polygraph could detect an actual lie? It certainly didn't seem so to me. I knew that I was innocent. But, my guilt or innocence changed nothing. The polygraph didn't work, and never would. In the eyes of the government, the polygraph industry, and others whom I didn't even know, I'd been deemed unpatriotic by my actions. Were those actions unpatriotic? I thought not. On the contrary, I had believed it my patriotic duty to right a wrong that I knew for a fact was hurting innocent people. I'd wanted to stop the corruption and greed. Patriotism comes in different forms, I guess.

The legal siege was finally too much for me. The mere idea of possibly pleading guilty was abhorrent to me. It made me feel as though I would be turning on myself, my crusade, and everything that I had come to believe in. I thought I would be letting down the many people who had turned to me for help. But, with more torturous assaults on the horizon from an assembly line of prosecutors who had access to endless resources and all the money they needed to eventually get what they wanted from me, I realized that there was little hope, if any. I knew I had to stop the bleeding. So, I decided to give them some of what they wanted.

Lost in a crisis of conscience and succumbing to endless and insurmountable fatigue, I searched my soul. I would not give the government any specific person's name whom I had helped or had even talked to...no, I would not give them anyone else. I would give them me. After I'd decided that this was the only course I could follow, my mind became more at ease.

I had been charged with three counts of Witness Tampering and two counts of Mail Fraud. On the second day of trial, I plead *Guilty* to all five counts and was sentenced to twenty-four months of imprisonment, followed by three years of supervised release.

The conditions of the supervised release would require me to refrain from participation in any form of polygraph-related activity during the period of that supervision.

I consoled myself with the reminder that this was only a lost battle – not a lost war. I would regroup. Somehow. Somewhere.

CHAPTER THIRTY-THREE

The Valley of Evil

I was told to report to the United States Federal Prison Camp in El Reno, Oklahoma to serve a two-year sentence. Not great news, but at least it would be close to home. But, then, at the last minute, even that was taken away. I was instructed instead to turn myself in at a prison camp in Florence, Colorado. Rules provide "camps" for shorter sentenced and non-violent inmates, and if you qualify under these guidelines, you are considered a low-level offender. I'd heard that the camp had very low security and the most freedom of any of the prisons, and that its inmates were charged with maintaining all the buildings on the compound. The "camp" is where I was sent.

When I first arrived at Florence and saw the prison, I thought to myself, "Oh, man, what kind of place is this?" At first glance, it was obvious that it was a prison system that had expanded and industrialized itself. It's an expansive compound that consists of four main facilities. The Administrative Maximum-Security Prison – called the ADX for short – is the perpetual home to high-profile and extremely dangerous inmates, such as the Unabomber and Boston Marathon Bomber, who are never allowed to mix with the general population. It is an under-ground facility, where each inmate is kept in solitary confinement, and is thought of as Supermax, the Crown Jewel of the Federal Prison System, the "Alcatraz of the Rockies." Down the road is the PEN, a high-security facility for extremely violent or long-term inmates who are allowed to mingle to some extent. After that and close to the main road is the facility called the FCI, the Federal Correctional Institution. "Correctional" is a misnomer, that's for sure. This set of buildings houses lower-security level inmates than either the ADX or the PEN. And, finally, the only group of structures not surrounded by fences is the FPC, the Federal Prison Camp. The inmates incarcerated at the camp are allowed more freedom – if that were an appropriate word, which it's not. I guess it would be a better description to say that, due to the fact that the "campers" work all over the compound, they are allowed to move about in a less-restricted manner. Essentially, the camp is like a small city.

But, at second glance, the valley – the little valley of Florence, Colorado seemed alive with evil...you could feel it. The despicable deeds committed by the most hardened of criminals incarcerated there seemed to have brought a darkness to the spirit of the place. You couldn't mistake it. And, you couldn't escape from it. They were all there – the worst of the worst at the largest prison facility in the country. At 6,500 feet with nothing but dry desert surrounding you, it seemed forlorn and lonely. For all the 30,000 occupants of this small city, it felt like a wasteland of humanity – of anything good or safe. It would be a long two years...very long, and very lonely.

I didn't really socialize with most of the men I met in prison. But, there were a few that I spent some time with from the diverse mix of wayward lawyers, street-level drug dealers, and accountants that apparently couldn't count or put numbers into the correct columns. Shake those guys up in a bag with doctors who had overcharged Uncle Sam, higher-level drug dealers who had told on their friends and family members in order to get a shorter sentence, and some Native Americans who'd gotten into drinking trouble on their Reservations (because all crimes committed on Reservations are considered federal crimes), and you'd pretty well covered the social possibilities in the camp. Of course, there were others: tax cheats, unauthorized distributors of cigarettes (no kidding), and a guy who illegally shot an animal on a game preserve. Desperate criminals. Don't get me wrong, crimes had been committed, but to spend the hundreds of millions of dollars we spend on camps to corral people like this? It seemed to me that common sense seemed to have gone out the window.

I have to admit that there were some interesting characters there; however, my meeting with one particular man became a prophetic event for us both.

"Well, I finally found one," the inmate said.

"Found one what?" I asked.

"Innocent guy in prison," he responded, tossing my case paperwork that he'd been perusing onto a desk between us.

"You've been looking?" I asked.

"Hobby. As a mandatory guest in the Bureau of Prisons for six or seven years, everyone I have met here claims he's innocent. But, when you flick on the legal lights, they're standing in illicit shit clear up to their armpits."

The man's name was Jack Straw. We were sitting in the Education Office, which was one of the offices that Jack worked out of as the inmate in charge of Education and Recreation at the camp.

"So, you believe I'm not guilty?" I asked.

"Read your case a half dozen times. Only thing you're guilty of is being a little thick-skulled. Being guilty has nothing to do with you being here." Jack took a drink out of a can of Diet Cherry Coke, then pointed the can towards me. "You're here because of shin-kicking."

"Shin-kicking?"

"Call it what you want, but the fact is you've been barking, biting, and kicking at these polygraphers so long they're starting to have visions of your face in their morning oatmeal. They might even see your lovely mug if they closed their eyes during sex."

"That would be a mood killer."

"WOULD it! But in all your exuberance, you overlooked one thing."

"That is?" I asked.

"Those people whose foreheads you've been tapdancing on? Well, they're friends with the keyholders. And now you, as I'm sure you can tell by your surroundings, are in the possession of the keyholders."

"As you are."

"No question."

"So, we both made mistakes."

"No."

"No?"

"No. You made a mistake, my friend. I committed a crime. I deserve to be here. You do not."

"You seem very certain about both of us," I said.

I am. Listen, Doug, everyone has some reservations or disbelief, or maybe even complete internal denial about their guilt. I don't. Self-admission might be hard to swallow, but once you gag it down, you can find ways to make life a lot better."

Suddenly, the door opened and a long-bearded face poked in.

"Jack, I've been looking all over for you," the visitor said.

"Congratulations, C.B., your work is done," Jack replied.

"Huh? Oh, uh, yeah. Well, anyways, don't forget you're going to help me write that letter tonight."

"It has become my sole purpose in life."

"Uh...okay. So, I'll see you in a bit," C.B. said.

"Wings on my feet."

C.B. smiled at me, raised and lowered his eyebrows, and left.

"Legal issues?"

"Nope. He's proposing to his pen-pal."

"So, they've met?"

"No."

"No? But, he's proposing?"

"Sure. She's a voluptuous model from a famous modeling agency in New York and he's a wealthy oil baron and Texas ranch owner."

"Really?"

"No and no. But, who am I to stand in the way of the fiction-kindled flames of love?"

"Seems a bit..."

"And, it is. But, back to my point, Doug. People need to face what they have done and then realize one thing: You are not your crime. That was an event. The incident is not the person. The person perpetrated an act, but that person is still himself – and, that fact is the first step in repairing life."

"Makes sense."

"Actually, it doesn't have to make sense to you. You, Doug Williams, are not of the guilty world."

And, that's how it was with Jack. He would lend other men a sympathetic ear and the benefit of the doubt, if that's what they wanted. But, for himself, there was no gray. It was black or white. He had taken money he shouldn't have, and he was now serving time for it. But instead of sitting still, he was on a mission - a mission to make up for what he had done, and to get back to what he had been before he became an idiot. "Idiot" is his term, by the way. Jack was a writer – songs, books, children's stories - and after sending 162 letters to publishers and people in the literary world, he was finally getting some very serious interest. He was in good physical shape, too, especially for a man near sixty. He ran daily, played the guitar and performed in bands at the camp. He helped inmates with legal problems and court issues to love letters and girlfriends, from GED testing to music lessons. Anyone who had a problem went to Jack. They called him, "Mayor."

But, Jack's finest moments were when he spoke of his four daughters and their families back in Iowa. Even though distance and circumstance separated them from him, they were, and are, the driving force in his life.

"I'm going to continue my crusade," I said to him one day.

"I hope the hell you do," he answered. "Just because you're here doesn't mean that you stop. It just means that you regroup and reload."

"What do you suggest? I mean, what can I do from this place?" I asked.

"First of all, it's *we*, not just you."

"You're on board?"

"Nothing pressing on my schedule for a few years. So, let's ride this horse all the way to the saloon. Now, what we need to do is this," he said, holding up a copy of my book, *FROM COP TO CRUSADER*. This is a two-hundred-page police report you wrote."

"Okay..."

"No one wants to read a two-hundred-page police report."

"Okay..."

"Even the cops don't want to read a 200-page police report."

"Got it," I smiled.

"This is a hell of a story. People need to know about it. They need to know the story of the polygraph. You need to tell it, and I need to write it."

I nodded at the man sitting across from me. I felt a strong bond forming. I had wanted someone to be able to tell my story and had read some of Jack's writings. Suddenly, I knew he was the guy. And, now, Jack knew it, too.

"When do we start?" I asked.

Jack pulled a pen from his pocket and grabbed a nearby notebook and put it on the table in front of him.

"Now." Just that simple...we were off and writing.

In prison, time passed like it passed everywhere — just not as pleasantly. But, writing with Jack made days and nights bearable, and even enjoyable. I was reliving my life, so-to-speak, and he was setting it to literary music. For some time, we struggled with how to end the book. But eventually, we realized that we were struggling with an ending that didn't yet exist. There had been no ending to the crusade. There was no hero sweeping a good-looking gal off her feet or a cop closing a case or a cowboy saddling his horse and riding off into the sunset. Although somewhat curtailed, the polygraph machine was still plugged in. The lie detection industry still continued to creep through the night – like a thief in your house, trying to steal the very breath from your future. As yet, there was no ending to either my book or my crusade, but I had a strong feeling that if America would stand up against this machine, someday – and, someday soon – we'd be saddling up that horse.

CHAPTER THIRTY-FOUR

Freedom and My Future

Prison changes a man. It can break you, if you let it...or, it can strengthen your resolve. I had walked the halls of the West Wing of the White House alongside Henry Kissinger and shared morning coffee with Alexander Haig. Now, I walked the cold halls of Federal Prison alongside criminals. I'd served with distinction and the highest security clearance under two Presidents during my time in the Situation Room. I'd lived as a beach bum in a trailer overlooking the ocean. I'd met with Congressmen and Senators, and citizens from all walks of life. I'd been a police officer and a Methodist Minister. And, now – with two years ahead of me to contemplate the avenues and choices of my life, so many questions kept coming into my mind.

How does a Communications Director of the White House Situation Room end up confined to a prison with murderers and terrorists? And, make no mistake, they were all here...sleeping just a few buildings away from me, all of us confined to a desperate valley inhabited by lost and tormented souls. Ramzi Yousef, the mastermind of the World Trade Center terrorist attack; Terry Nichols, the Oklahoma City bomber; Ted Kaczynsniki, the Unabomber; Harold Nicholson and Robert Hanssen, former CIA and FBI Agents who had passed classified information to the Russians...and so many more.

Men who had *wanted* to kill, had raped and murdered with conscious intent many innocent people...men who had plotted to overthrow our government and to destroy our democracy...men who had planned and executed terrorist plots and willingly killed thousands of our citizens in the process - these men were here, and I can only tell you that they brought with them a darkness that permeated the entire valley. If a person has ever contemplated whether or not true evil does exist, he need only visit Florence, Colorado. It always seemed to me that with every breath these vicious criminals exhaled, their desire to kill and to destroy rose up from their lungs and out from their jail cells, rising farther still into the air and the atmosphere around the camp, filling it with their dark spirits whose rancid stench dominated and oppressed even the very desert land we walked upon. Living underground and alone could only have enlivened their rage and fantasies, giving way to their frustration born of hatred to grow and seethe beneath the surface until the most dangerous of their thoughts obliterated reason and left unintelligible horror in its wake.

We had a softball field surrounded by a tarmac track that some of the inmates could use for exercise. If you walked West along the North side of the track and looked through the razor wire, you could see Pikes Peak in the distance. What a beautiful site! At first, I enjoyed that view, but, after a while, I concluded that it would probably be far easier to be locked up with no windows at all than to be out on the grounds and able to see those beautiful sunsets and know you could not go there. That was a specific torture I found difficult to bear. Those amazing sunsets – so unattainable, so far out of reach. Though beautiful, the terrible loneliness left in the aftermath of a vibrant sunset was terrible and made a man feel bitter. The eyes beheld all the colors and a smile might come to your heart, but it was immediately replaced by growing loneliness on the long walk back to the two-story concrete block building with the solid steel windowless doors leading into your drab concrete block 8' x 10' cubicle...two bunks, two lockers, an elementary school sized desk mounted to the wall, the sound of keys jangling...and, more loneliness. Yes, it is very lonely in prison despite the fact that you are constantly surrounded by other men. It is a phenomenon only men in prison can understand. Better it would have been not to know that those magnificent sunsets over Pikes Peak were ever there, at all. And, at times, I even envied the men locked up in solitary confinement over at the ADX Supermax dungeon. One of the things I missed most, besides my family, was privacy.

I found the nights impossible, too. In fact, I did not sleep one whole night through during the entire two years I was in prison. The guards would come through every three hours at night to do a count of the inmates to make sure no one had escaped, and you'd just have fallen into some peaceful dream when the hall lights would go on full-blast. Sometimes, a few of the guards would just use flashlights that they'd shine over the sleeping bodies, which was a welcome surprise. But, even then, you couldn't fall back to sleep. Most of the time, though, the guards would turn on all the bright lights in the hall just a couple of feet from your bunk, so that it was impossible not to be awakened from whatever slumber you'd escaped into. Every three hours...

But, even though prisons ooze with monotony, sometimes things do change. One memorable change happened in January of 2017. That day after lunch, I was walking out of the chow hall and saw Jack surrounded by a group of men who were taking turns shaking his hand. Jack was being relocated to another prison to finish his term. This would be our goodbye, but our long adventure of writing this book would continue, as would the friendship we'd forged and the plans we'd made. Jack was leaving and, soon, I would be, too. I walked up to him, he offered his hand and I gripped it hard, as though trying to hold onto him long enough to lock this moment into my memory bank. I don't make friends easily - nor, I suspect, does Jack. We'd had conversations about friendship and both agreed that friendship carried with it a responsibility for the men involved, a responsibility to be loyal and trustworthy - and we had entered into our friendship with full knowledge of what that meant. This would not be the end for us, we both knew that. Yet, it was hard to know that, since he had quite a lot of time left to serve in his sentence, it would probably be many years before we met again. Goodbyes are hard...this one, especially so.

Finally, on the morning of July 5th, 2017, I awoke and looked at the calendar I had taped to the side of my locker and saw it: Three weeks to go, I told myself. Just three more weeks. I'd seen other men go home and it often seemed like their last few weeks made some of them uneasy, some irritable, some nervous. Pending freedom brought with it the perils of a changed world - a world that you hoped would accept you, and yet, with no assurances that it would. Finally, those three weeks passed, and suddenly, it was my turn to believe - if even I could - that freedom was on the horizon. Freedom. What would that feel like?

That day finally arrived, and with all the relief that expectation brought, it also brought the drive over to the ADX for the formality of a prisoner's release. The prison driver took me over to where I'd have to fill out the proper paperwork in order that I might be "returned" to society, but as we approached that Supermax high-security facility, the evil that permeated the place once again struck me with such force that I could barely breathe. "Hold tight," I told myself, "it's almost over."

On July 26th, 2017, I signed the required papers and was "processed out" of prison. Beyond the front gate, my wife, Kathy and my grandson, Christian, were waiting for me. What a sight! As I looked at them standing over by the car, I almost felt shy, as though I wasn't quite sure what to do. Then, it occurred to me. My friend who ran a blog from Antipolygraph.org, George Maschke, had told me that he wanted a photo of me with the fence of prison wire behind me in the background. "Okay," I decided to myself. "Behind me is better than in front of me." So, I asked Christian to take me down the road a bit where we could pull over and he could take my picture with that miserable prison in the background. After the photo was taken, the only thing I could say was, "Let's get the hell out of here."

Then, the three of us began to drive...and drive. We didn't say much else, as I recall, but after a bit, something came over me that, even today, is practically indescribable. It hit me with the shocking force of a hurricane and began to envelop my whole being. At first, I started to giggle, and then the boil of hysteria that was rising from the center of my being just burst into life - like a musical show when the drums start to go wild and you can't stop yourself from singing along. I started to LAUGH, and LAUGH, and LAUGH. I could NOT STOP! It came through my toes to my legs to my stomach through my lungs and throat to the top of my being...I laughed and laughed and laughed. Everything struck me as funny, even just the landscape whizzing by. Sometimes, the breath would stick in my throat and barely little sound came out. At others, I suffered fits of giggles as if I were being tickled, or my body would begin to shake with overwhelmingly deep belly-laughs until my chest hurt. *Why I was I laughing?* I truly didn't know; I still don't know. I suspect it was the immense relief of knowing that I was going home... that it was over...that I would never set foot in Colorado again... that I'd served my time...that I was still alive, and that my wife and grandson loved me. Oh, it was so many things. Too many to understand...maybe it felt silly that I'd ended up in a place like that, and what it could all mean. Still the laughter came - for a full thirty minutes, I simply could not stop myself. And, it was physical, organic. I couldn't stop until my very soul was spent. Gratitude to God, relief...I'm a Christian, and all the good was filling up my entire being, once again...away from evil; away from darkness. And, now, I needed a steak!

As soon as we crossed the border into Texas, we stopped for the biggest steak we could find. A baked potato, a salad...food that tasted better than I'd eaten in two years. Christian said that the meat really wasn't all that good - but, are you kidding? I've never tasted and will never taste any steak as good as that again as long as I live!

We made the twelve-hour drive to Norman, Oklahoma, and amazingly, for so many reasons, I was home again. I had trouble sleeping for a long time. I kept waiting for someone to burst through the door and send me back to prison or ransack my home...something, anything. But, nothing happened - at least, not yet.

But, I know very well how despised I am by those in the government polygraph industry, so I'm still waiting for the other shoe to drop. As I stare at these final pages, there is a part of me that wants to verbally lash out at those who attacked me. After all, they are true enemies of civil rights and human progress. But, to name them individually here could possibly give them some measure of evil satisfaction for the pain they've caused so many people, including my family and me. Make no mistake, they are extremists. As an illustration of that point, many of their group have actually said they hoped I would die in prison. Sounds pretty extreme to me.

Those who have so adamantly opposed me have hoped that by attempting to demonize my crusade, they have halted my efforts. In order to try and stop me, they have managed to weaponize a publicly-funded legal department of the U.S. Government. They have prosecuted and imprisoned me, simply because it was I who "protested the loudest and the longest against the polygraph." I'm sure they are confident that they have won the battle.

On the other hand, it has been documented by historians that the Confederacy won many battles during the course of the Civil War. Some say that the South even won more battles than the North. But, despite those victories in battle, the Confederacy lost the war. The North would not settle for less than abolishment of a malicious practice. If it was destiny that the North should *win*, it was because slavery was *wrong*. To me, the comparisons to my crusade are striking. I believe that we, too, will settle for no less than abolishment and are destined to *win*. And, why? Because the polygraph is *wrong*.

What will come of this? Only time will tell. A lot has been accomplished, but there is, as yet, more to do. The crusade's mission still festers within me, and I still believe in all the things it stands for. I'm a different man all these years later, but my heart still beats with one hope. The dreams I dream at night are still the same. I'm a man of faith, and so I believe that the Lord will guide my path, and, hopefully, a more wizened Doug Williams will follow. I am grateful for my life, my family, and the path I have chosen. Whatever may come, I embrace it all. This is not to say that I am not frightened, because I am. I am very frightened. I have experienced the full weight of the Federal Government coming down on me, and I can tell you that it is a terrifying experience. But, just because I'm frightened does not mean that I am going to abandon my crusade. I cannot in good conscience stand by while millions of people are abused by the perpetrators of the fraud of "lie detection."

Yes, I'm scared, but as John Wayne once said, "Courage is being scared to death, but saddling up anyway." I am saddling up, and I am going to stay in the saddle and ride this horse all the way to the finish line. And, if there is any justice in this world - and I pray to God there still is — then, my Crusade will prevail, and this insidious Orwellian polygraph industry will be banned forever.

THE END

AFTERWORD

By Doug Williams

"How people treat you is their karma; how you react is yours."

"With everything that has happened to you, you can either feel sorry for yourself or treat what has happened as a gift. Everything is either an opportunity to grow or an obstacle to keep you from growing. You get to choose."
                    Dr. Wayne W. Dyer, Author of *Living an Inspired Life*

As I reflect upon the journey of my life's adventures, I can't help but to marvel at the huge disparity of ups and downs. And, I wonder, do other people experience such extremes in their lives, or has mine been an exception to the rule? I think of my humble beginnings as the son of a beloved Methodist Minister, and the values instilled in me that enabled me to become worthy of a high-level security position on the White House Staff under two Presidents with whom I interacted on a personal basis. I consider the myriad of personalities I encountered there, the lessons learned during my subsequent years in law enforcement, the praise lauded over me from the polygraph world, and then, its disdain. And, I remember all-too-well the call within me to right what I believed a terrible wrong being forced upon an unsuspecting public, and the force of my conscience to embrace that call. But, I also consider the terrible toll it took on my life...the lies, the destruction of truth...the betrayals...the years in prison.

But, through it all, I've tried to learn the lessons that God has intended for me to learn. The highs of my life – the accolades and support, the notoriety and acceptance - were tremendous, and my downfall under the wrath of government bureaucracy was a treacherous blow not only to my self-esteem, but also to my crusade. Yet, I have not been felled and my enthusiasm remains. The bitterness, anger and resentment I feel at times is a reminder to me that I do have an option. I can either react to all that has happened with spite or maintain my dignity and persevere. As Wayne Dyer reminds all of us: we do have a choice.

> *"It's not important what happens to you –*
> *it's how you react to it that's important."*
> My dad, the Reverend Ed Williams
> Director of the United Methodist Foundation,
> Oklahoma Conference

> *"And we know that God causes all things to work together for good to those who love God, to those who are called according to his purpose."*
> Romans 8:28, *The Bible*

The kindness of the Methodist church in sheltering me, supporting me, and giving me livelihood and a moment's peace at a time when I desperately needed them, is not only a Grace I received, but also a reminder of the meaning of Charity. I could be bitter about the travesty of justice that has been visited upon me – or I could understand that God does indeed cause all things to work together for good. I choose to believe God -and I am seeing how He is causing even the most difficult challenges I've faced to work together for my good – and for the good of others.

You have just finished reading about my crusade against the oppressive, Orwellian polygraph industry. I have paid a heavy personal price for "protesting the loudest and the longest" against them. Professor Alan M. Dershowitz, one of the nation's most distinguished defenders of individual rights, Professor of Law, Emeritus at Harvard University Law School, and author of 25 works spoke out against this criminalization of differences when he said:

Let's not go down the road of criminalizing differences. This idea of throwing around criminal charges against anyone you don't like... We have to reserve the criminal law only for the most extreme deliberate violations of existing statutes.

Representative John Radcliffe of the House Judiciary Committee said:

The fundamental premise of our criminal justice system is that we investigate crime or suspicious activity, we don't investigate people with the intent of uncovering criminality.

To that I might add:

It should be unlawful for the criminal justice system to manufacture a crime and, then, charge a person with that crime –as they did with me - simply because that person voices informed, fact-based protest against what he believes to be an oppressive government activity.

I have often been asked about the details of the trauma I suffered at the hands of the government polygraph supporters who not only prosecuted, but also persecuted me. I respectfully decline to do that, however, because it is still too painful. I will simply say that my wife became physically ill as a result of the unrelenting attack against me by the Federal Government, which lasted for many years prior to my incarceration, and, that I personally suffered greatly, as well – physically, mentally, spiritually and financially. But, our Christian faith has sustained us both and we are emerging from this ordeal stronger than ever. I see God's hand in the opportunities I now have to speak out about my cause and in the world-wide support that grows all the time in opposition to undisciplined use of the polygraph. And, I am thankful that my family and I have weathered the raging storm.

My father always said that if a man was still walking on this earth, then God's purpose for him was not yet finished. So, be it. "Lie Detection" is a dangerous myth. I hope that I have made my case succinctly against the polygraph industry. If you agree, please help me in my quest to have this abusive procedure banned forever.

Thank you,
Doug Williams
For more information please go to my website: POLYGRAPH.com
Or, follow me on Twitter: @DougWilliams_PG

How To Sting The Polygraph

BY DOUG WILLIAMS

WWW.POLYGRAPH.COM
PO BOX 720568
NORMAN, OK
73070
405-226-4856
doug@polygraph.com

HOW TO STING THE POLYGRAPH

My name is Douglas Gene Williams. I was a detective sergeant with the Oklahoma City Police Department and ran the polygraph section of the Internal Affairs Unit for seven years. I administered thousands of tests for the Oklahoma City Police Department, and for many other agencies including the Secret Service and the FBI. I have also administered hundreds of tests as a private polygraphist.

I have the dubious distinction of being the only licensed polygraphist to ever tell the truth about the so called "lie detector". And the truth is, the polygraph is no more accurate than the toss of a coin in determining whether a person is telling the truth or lying – and I am proud to say, that is the exact same phrase the US Supreme Court used when they refused to allow the results of the polygraph into evidence.

While on the police department, I discovered that what I did for a living was a fraud, and in 1979 I resigned and embarked upon what turned out to be a crusade to outlaw the polygraph. I set about to prove three things about the polygraph that I knew to be true: (1) The polygraph test has a built-in bias against a truthful person, (2) It is certainly not capable of determining truth or deception, (3) Anyone can learn to control the test results so as to ALWAYS produce a "truthful" chart.

For example, regarding facts one and two, I offer this evidence. Some time back I was invited to prove these statements on CBS 60 Minutes. I spent about five weeks in New York City setting up a sting operation to prove that the polygraph has a built-in bias against a truthful person, and that it is certainly not capable of determining truth or deception. For this investigation, we set up a mock situation in a business setting. The setting was the offices of the magazine Popular Photography located in New York City. We cut holes in the walls of an office in the magazine's corporate headquarters and put our video cameras next door to secretly document the polygraph examinations, and we had our microphones in what appeared to be an overhead sprinkler system. We then picked three polygraph operators at random out of the yellow pages in New York City and hired them to test the employees of the magazine regarding the alleged theft of a camera. No camera had been stolen, but all three polygraph operators called honest, truthful people liars and thieves, and each one picked a different person! Talk about a sick joke, those guys showed what they were on national television with millions of people watching! Unfortunately there continues to be literally millions of private stories about innocent people who have been branded as criminals by this machine. I rest my case on facts one and two.

Concerning fact number three, that anyone can learn to control the test results so as to ALWAYS produce a "truthful" chart, I have demonstrated this on every major network on national television over 20 times. For more information on this check out the media clips on my website www.polygraph.com. I have taught thousands of people how to control every tracing on the polygraph chart at will. It is ridiculously simple to master the skills necessary to pass the "lie detector" and produce what the polygraph operator should call a "truthful chart". I rest my case on fact number three.

Something that will be of interest to anyone taking a polygraph test is my new book which I have recently finished writing about my crusade against the polygraph; it is entitled: *"FROM COP TO CRUSADER: The story of my fight against the dangerous myth of "lie detection"*. This book will answer many of the questions that I have been asked over the years, such as: Why do you do what you do? What made you start a crusade against the polygraph? Why do you teach people how to "beat" the polygraph? Why did you quit the police department and quit running polygraph tests? What is wrong with the polygraph test? The book answers these, and many more questions that have been asked of me over the years. You can purchase a copy of this book from my website http://www.polygraph.com/ It tells all about my crusade and some of the behind the scenes details about the CBS 60 MINUTES program, my testimony in the US CONGRESS, and many of the other things I have done over the past decades in my fight against the polygraph industry. It is a very exciting and informative book, and I hope you get a copy. Now back to HOW TO STING THE POLYGRAPH.

I'm sure you already know the polygraph is a joke, but you don't want the joke to be on you. This manual is designed to teach you how to protect yourself by teaching you how the machine works and to show you how to control your reactions so that you will be able to produce a "truthful" chart.

Due to the fact that parts of this manual are somewhat technical, and you must read it at least four times in order to fully comprehend the information it contains, I have condensed it to as few pages a possible.

The word polygraph is derived from two Greek words: poly, which means many, and graphos, which means writings - many writings. The "many writings" which the polygraph records on its charts are you blood pressure, pulse rate, respiration and galvanic skin response. Your blood pressure and pulse rate is recorded by the cardio pen which traces your heartbeat; this is referred to as the cardio tracing. Your breathing is recorded by the pneumo pens. This is referred to as the pneumo tracing. Your Galvanic Skin Response, which is basically the sweat or perspiration activity on your hand, is recorded and is referred to as the GSR tracing. (See Exhibit A)

Changes in your blood pressure, pulse rate, breathing, and sweat activity are referred to as reactions. These reactions appear on the polygraph chart as follows. (1) A pneumo reaction, which is simply a pen tracing up and down on the chart as you inhale and exhale. (2) A cardio reaction, which is the pen tracing your heart beat, and showing an increase or decrease in your blood pressure and pulse rate. (3) A GSR reaction which is nothing but a pen tracing of the increase or decrease of the sweat activity on your hand. In other words the polygraph operator can watch you breathe, watch your blood pressure and pulse rate go up and down, and watch your hand sweat. And on the basis of this, he presumes to be able to say whether or not you are a liar. How absurdly ridiculous!

The validity of the polygraph as a lie detector rests on the theory that physical changes, or reactions, are caused by the emotional stress of lying and cannot be manipulated. There is only one thing wrong with this theory, and that is it is just not true. In fact you can learn to control every tracing on the chart at will.

The problem with the polygraph is that the reaction the polygraph operators call a "lying reaction" can be and is caused by many things other than a lie. As a matter of fact any number of innocent stimuli can and do cause this exact same reaction. Fear, rage, embarrassment at having been asked a personal question, pain from the cardio cuff, even the tone of the examiner's voice can all cause the exact same reaction that the polygraph examiner would brand as a lie.

The polygraph is not a lie detector, and it is not a truth verifier, it is simply a crude reaction recorder, and the so called reactions it records can be caused by many things other than deception. I can even teach you how to duplicate this reaction by a simple breathing and muscle exercise. In fact, when you finish reading this manual, you will be able to control every tracing on the polygraph chart at will.

What is involved in a polygraph test? Polygraph tests are divided into three phases: (1) The "pre-test" interview and "stim test", (2) The "test" phase, and, (3) The "post-test" interrogation. I will explain each of these in detail.

The "Pre-Test" Interview

In this phase, the polygrapher will tell you he just wants to get to know you, to get you to get everything off your mind. He may even tell you that all this is "just between you and me". Don't be fooled the polygrapher will report all admissions you make.

The pre-employment polygraph examination is the setting for some of the worst cases of polygraph abuse because, unlike the criminal suspect, the job applicant cannot refuse the test without suffering as a result of the refusal. It is unfortunate and ironic that applicants for government agencies requiring security clearances, and law enforcement applicants are about the only ones who still have to take a pre-employment polygraph. These polygraph ex-aminations are simply interrogations, the only part the polygraph plays is to scare you sufficiently to insure the full disclosure of all the sordid details of past indiscretions. Do not tell the polygrapher anything that isn't already a matter or record and certainly do not admit to anything that could disqualify you. During the pre-test interview for pre-employment polygraph tests, the polygraph operator will ask you a series of questions, some of which are listed below. The whole point is to get you to make damaging admissions – so be careful how you answer.

* (These pre-employment pre-test questions are listed in the back of the manual)

The polygrapher may tell you the reason he is asking so many questions is to get to know you better so he can administer a good test. He may also tell you that passing the test is more important than any admissions you make, and that it will be to your advantage to tell the complete truth in order to pass the exam. He will exhort you to "get everything off your mind, discuss anything that is worrying you, so that nothing interferes with your polygraph test". Do not be deceived, these are merely interrogation tricks designed to try to get you to change your goal. What is your goal in taking a pre-employment polygraph examination? Your original goal is to get a job; you are trying to sell yourself to a prospective employer so you naturally put emphasis on your most positive attributes, your ability, training, education, energy, attitude, etc. The polygraph con man will try to change your goal by telling you that in order to get the job you must pass his test, and in order to pass, you must tell the complete truth to all the questions he asks. Your goal then will be to spill your guts in front of the hidden video camera while he sits back and prods you into disclosing information you would never tell another person. Do not allow the interrogator to turn the polygraph room into a confessional! Perhaps you cannot refuse to answer these questions, but you can control the amount of information you give. Do not buy into the polygraph operator's lie that he will respect the confidentiality of what you tell him, every word you say is being recorded and will be played back to the person paying for the test. Audio and video recorders and cameras, as well as the ever-present see-through mirrors on the wall, with the adjacent observation room to witness the proceedings, is all a part of the well-equipped polygraph suite.

The polygrapher will then explain "how the polygraph works" - it is all B.S. and they all memorize some version of this little speech. This is the textbook explanation that Department of Defense Polygraph Institute-trained polygraphers provide.

"You may be a little nervous, especially if you have not had a PDD ["psychophysiological detection of deception," a more scientific- sounding term for "lie detection"] examination before. This is expected and is quite normal. To help put you at ease, I will explain what the instrument is and how it works. The polygraph is a diagnostic tool that is used to de-termine if a person is telling the truth. It simply records phys-iological changes that take place in your body when you are asked questions. Today, changes in your respiration, sweat gland activity, and blood pressure will be recorded. Please notice the two rubber tubes on the desk. One will be placed across your chest and the other will be placed around your abdominal area. They will be used to record your breath-ing. There are two metal finger plates next to the rubber tubes. These plates will be attached to two of your fingers and will record your sweat gland activity. Finally, there is a blood pressure cuff on the desk. It is the same type of cuff a doctor uses to measure blood pressure. It will be placed on your arm and will monitor changes in your cardiovascular activity. These physiological changes are a result of an au-tomatic response system in your body. It is a response sys-tem over which you have no control. For example, visualize yourself walking down a dark alley late at night. Suddenly you hear a loud noise. You will instantaneously decide ei-ther to remain where you are and investigate the source of the noise, or to flee the area, sensing danger to your well being. Regardless of the choice you make, your body auto-matically adjusts itself to meet the needs of the situation; your heart may beat faster, your breathing may change and you may break out in a cold sweat. When you were grow-ing up, if you are like most people, you were raised to know the difference between right and wrong. Quite probably, all of the adults you came in contact with--your parents, grandparents, relatives, teachers, church officials--taught you that lying, cheating, and stealing were wrong. Ever since you were a young child, you have been programmed to know that lying is wrong. Think about the first time you lied and got caught. Remember how your body felt during that confrontation. Your heart may have been racing or you may have been sweating. However, the responses were au-tomatic; your body adjusted to the stress of the situation. People are not always 100% honest. Sometimes it is kinder and more socially acceptable to lie than to be honest - such as telling someone you like their clothes when you really think the clothes are awful. It is important for you to under-stand that even though a lie might be socially acceptable or only a small lie, or a lie by omission, your body still re-sponds. The recording on the polygraph will show only the physiological responses. It cannot know what kind of lie you are telling. Therefore, it is extremely important that you be totally honest..."

This whole speech is designed to scare and intimidate you. The polygrapher's explanation is deliberately false and he is trying to mislead you - telling a lie may or may not result in physiological changes measurable by the polygraph. When the polygrapher says, "It is important for you to understand that even though a lie might be socially acceptable or only a small lie, or a lie by omission, your body still responds," he really means, "It is important for me that you believe this to be true." Fear is an essential element of all poly-graph "tests." In its 1994 assessment of the Ames case, the U.S. Senate Select Committee on Intelligence reports, "A former polyg-rapher noted that without proper preparation, a subject has no fear of detection and, without fear of detection, the subject will not necessarily demonstrate the proper physiological response." (U.S. Senate Select Committee on Intelligence, 1994) But the problem is that this fear of being falsely accused may also cause you to have a reaction that would result in truthful persons being accused of deception.

If you are taking a specific issue polygraph test. (criminal, fidelity, probationary, etc), the pre-test is more of an interrogation about the specific incident that you are accused of. Again, don't admit anything they don't already know. Keep insisting that you are telling the truth and that you look forward to taking the polygraph test in order to prove it.

Sometime during the pre-test interview phase, the polygrapher will conduct what is commonly referred to as a "stimulation test" or "stim test," - DoDPI calls it an "acquaintance test." He may tell you that the purpose is to allow him to "adjust the instrument" and to make certain that you are "capable" of physiologically responding if you were to intentionally tell a lie. This explanation is also B.S. – it is just another way to try to "psyche you out". The real purpose of the "stim test" is to fool you into believing that your polygrapher can read your mind and that your deception will be detected. The most common "stim test" is to let you pick a card out of a deck of supposedly randomly numbered cards. The polygraph operator will then instruct you to answer "no" to all the questions, even to the question about the card number you actually picked. He will then ask, "Did you pick card number fifteen?", "Did you pick card number seven?", and so on down the list of all the numbers on the cards. At the conclusion of the test, he will tell you, based on his analysis of the chart, which card you picked and therefore, which question you lied to. This is simply a trick. He has used two decks of cards. He makes a big deal of shuffling one deck in front of you, he will then divert your attention and change decks using one whose "random" numbers are in order. He has memorized the sequence of numbers, i.e. 15, 8, 3, 5, 7, 10, and

13, and he knows which card you have picked as soon as you pull it from the deck. Sometimes, the "stim test" is done with a deck of cards. The polygrapher will ask you to pick a card and not show it to him. Then, while you are connected to the polygraph, he will ask you to answer "no" to each question he asked. Suppose you draw the jack of diamonds. Your "stim test" might go like this: Did you pick a face card? (No.) Did you pick a number card? (No.) Your polygrapher nonchalantly tells you, "It's obvious you picked a face card." He then proceeds to ask: Did you pick a king? (No.) Did you pick a queen? (No.) Did you pick a jack? (No.) He then informs you, "The polygraph shows me you have drawn a jack." He continues: Did you pick a spade? (No.) Did you pick a club? (No.) Did you pick a diamond? (No.) Did you pick a heart? (No.) The polygrapher "analyzes" the charts and tells you, "It's clear you picked the jack of diamonds. No doubt about it. You're are an excellent candidate for the polygraph. You can't tell a lie without your body showing a reaction." But what your polygrapher wouldn't tell you is that you drew your card from a trick deck, in which every card is the jack of diamonds. Some polygraphers use a "known-solution" numbers "test," in which the polygrapher will ask you to pick a number, say, from one to nine, and to write the number you picked on a sheet of paper. The polygrapher will tell you to answer "no" each time as he asks, "Did you write 1? Did you write 2?," etc. And he will tell you that when you answer "no" to the number that you wrote - to deliberately lie and say "no." Did you write 1? (No.) Did you write 2? (No.) Did you write 3? (No.) Did you write 4? (No.) Did you write 5? (No.) Did you write 6? (No.) Did you write number 7? (No) Did you write 8? (No) Did you write 9 (No). Regardless of whether or not you showed any reaction when you lied about the number you picked, the polygrapher will attempt to convince you that you are not capable of lying without the polygraph instrument detecting it. This is how DoDPI instructed examiners to explain the "stim test" to volunteers in a recent research project:

"Administer a standard known solution numbers test-- using the rationale below. DO NOT show the test to the examinee, but convince the examinee that deception was indicated. NOTE: be sure to use the word acquaintance or demonstration test when discussing this with the examinee. I'm now going to demonstrate the physiological responses we have been discussing. This test is intended to give you the opportunity to become accustomed to the recording components and to give me the opportunity to adjust the instrument to you before proceeding to the actual test. In addition, this test will demonstrate to me that you are capable of responding and that your body reacts when you knowingly and willfully lie. The standard four components (two pneumograph tubes, electrodermal plates, and cardiovascular cuff) are attached at this time, followed by the acquaintance test. The acquaintance test should be conducted in the manner taught at DoDPI.... The results will be discussed with the examinee as follows: That was excellent. It is obvious that you know lying is wrong. You're not capable of lying without your body reacting. You reacted strongly when you lied about that number. Even though I asked you to lie and it was an insignificant lie, you still responded. That will make this examination very easy to complete as long as you follow my directions."

Play along with the polygrapher's silly game and do not try to subvert this test. When the polygrapher picks your card, you may turn it to your advantage by congratulating him on his expertise and telling him that you are now more confident than ever that the polygraph test will show you are telling the truth. NOTE: A secondary purpose of this "test" is to show the polygraph operator what type of a reaction you will have on the real test. Therefore, let us assume you picked card number five, or number five; you should manipulate a reaction when you answer "no" to this question. This will accomplish two things; first it will show him you are a "good subject", that you have the ability to react, and, second it will cause him to look for that specific type of reaction on the real test which is to follow.

The polygraph operator is confident of his technique, and you must be equally confident of yours. Don't be the polygrapher's punk. Don't let him "play" you. Learn how to "play" him. The polygraph cannot detect lies (it only records physiological data) and you can learn how to control every tracing on the chart.

Next, the polygrapher will tell you the questions that he is going to ask on the test. There are two types of questions - RELEVANT & CONTROL.

It is important that you recognize the difference between relevant and control questions in order to know when to manipulate or cause a reaction and when to control or stop a reaction. A relevant question is obviously one that pertains to the issue at hand, for example, if the polygraph test is about a specific theft, and then the relevant questions have to do with the specific item that was stolen and whether you stole it. The relevant questions are those that are relevant to why you are taking the test. If you are taking a pre-employment test, the relevant questions are those that decided whether you get the job.

The polygraph test is simply a comparison of your reactions. The polygraph operator will compare your reaction to the relevant question with your reaction to the control questions. If your reaction to the relevant question is greater than your reaction to the control question he will assume you are lying, if your reaction to the control question is larger, he will assume you are truthful. Obviously you should show the correct reaction to the control questions, and show no reaction whatsoever to the relevant questions. And you must PRACTICE until you can do it properly!

There are three types of control questions. We will start with the KNOWN-LIE CONTROL QUESTIONS since they are the most commonly used.

KNOWN-LIE control questions are those which the polygraph operator assumes you will respond to with a lie, for example, "Have you ever stolen anything?" The stress involved in your lying answer to this question will theoretically result in a reaction which is then compared to your reaction to the relevant question.

These known-lie control questions are matched to the situation, for example if you are a sex crimes suspect, or if you are taking a marital fidelity test, one of the known-lie control question may be, "Have you ever engaged in any unusual sex acts?" Known-lie control questions are different from the relevant questions because they are general in nature and nonspecific in terms of time. Another example of a commonly used known-lie control question is, "Have you ever stolen anything?". The polygraph operator will insist that you make some admissions to this question during the pre-test interview, and some will go to great lengths to "stimulate" you with this question. The polygraph operator will ask the basic question in the pretest interview, and you will make some minor admissions, admit a few minor childhood thefts, but do not say anything incriminating. The questions will then be reworded to, "Besides what you've told me, have you ever stolen anything else?" That will be the way the question is worded on the test. On the test itself, you will answer no and manipulate a reaction. Here are more examples of the known-lie control question:

Have you ever engaged in any unusual sex acts? You will make some minor admissions, then the question will be reworded, and on the test itself he will ask, "Besides what you've told me have you ever engaged in any unusual sex acts?" When this revised known-lie control question is asked on the test, you will answer "no" and manipulate a reaction.

Have you ever deliberately hurt another person? You will make some minor admissions, then the question will be reworded, and on the test itself he will ask, "Besides what you've told me have you ever deliberately hurt another person?" When this revised known-lie control question is asked on the test, you will answer "no" and manipulate a reaction.

Have you ever stolen anything? You will make some minor admissions, then the question will be reworded, and on the test itself he will ask, "Besides what you've told me have you ever stolen anything?" When this revised known-lie control question is asked on the test, you will answer "no" and manipulate a reaction.

Have you ever done anything that if discovered you would be ashamed of? You will make some minor admissions, then the question will be reworded, and on the test itself he will ask, "Besides what you've told me have you ever done anything that if discovered you would be ashamed of?" When this revised known-lie control question is asked on the test, you will answer "no" and manipulate a reaction.

These questions may start with the phrase, before the age of 21, before this incident, between the ages of 20 to 30, or something similar. The known-lie control questions on your test may be worded somewhat differently but they will be similar to the examples listed above so you will be able to recognize them.

Here are some more examples of this type of known-lie control question.

Did you ever bring shame upon yourself or your family?
Are you the type of person who would lie to get out of trouble?
Did you ever cheat anyone out of anything?
Did you every lie to anyone in a position of authority?
Did you ever blame someone for something you did?
Did you ever cheat anyone out of anything?
Did you every lie to anyone in authority?
Did you ever tell a lie to someone who trusted you?
Did you ever lie to cover up something?
Have you ever told a lie that would get another person get into trouble?
Have you ever told a lie about a person, even if the person is telling the truth?

Have you ever lied to a loved one?

Have you ever taken something that does not belong to you?"

Since the age of 18, have you ever considered hitting someone in anger?

Have you ever lied to a supervisor?

Have you ever lied to loved ones?

Have you ever lied to parents, teachers, or the police?

Have you ever lied to get out of trouble?

Did you ever reveal anything told to you in confidence?

Did you ever cheat in school?

Did you ever cheat in college?

Did you ever betray the trust of a friend or relative?

Do you sometimes intentionally mislead or deceive your friends?

Are you a really honest person?

Are you absolutely trustworthy?

Do you think you are smarter than most people?

Are you an untrustworthy person?

Are you a dishonest person?

Have you ever done anything that would embarrass you if your parents found out?

Have you ever done anything you would be embarrassed to tell me about?

Have you ever lied about anything serious?

Memorize these questions so you can recognize them quickly. AND REMEMBER: IF THE POLYGRAPH OPERATOR IS USING KNOWN-LIE CONTROL QUESTIONS YOU ONLY REACT TO THE KNOWN-LIE CONTROLS. And you will know he is using the known-lie control questions because he will review them with you before the test.

When answering these questions, don't tell the polygraph operator anything he doesn't already know or can't find out on his own. Remember,, the polygraph test is the most important test any of you will ever take. Until you take one, you have no idea how traumatic and grueling it can be - it is that way for a reason. The polygraphers want you to be so frightened that you "spill your guts". Some federal agencies even give bonuses to the polygraph operators who get the most damaging admissions! In fact, many people are so intimidated that they make statements that the polygrapher will use to disqualify or incriminate them - some people are so frightened that they confess to things they haven't even done! DON'T DO THAT! If you have anything to admit, put it on your application, or if you have anything to confess, tell it to the investigator. Please don't give the polygraph operator the satisfaction of bragging about what you told him that they could not have known without him and his magical machine! That is how these polygraph con men justify their existence - by getting you to make admissions to them that you haven't told anyone else!

The polygraph operator may ask you why you reacted to the control question, you need to make up some reason like, "I remember the look in my daddy's eyes when he found out I had stolen the harmonica.", or "I'm still embarrassed to talk about it.", or something such as that – use your imagination. Remember when he asks you about a control question rather than a relevant question you have already stung him. Most people flunk their polygraph tests because they say too much. You are being forced to take the test so it is up to you to be in charge of the amount of information you disclose. The polygraph operator is lying about the validity of the test, and you are under no obligation to take the test seriously. Most of the juicy information I gleaned during polygraph sessions was in response to illegal questions. Do not tell these perverse purveyors of purloined personal information anything more than is necessary to get through their 'trial by ordeal'! Do not believe anything they say about this being "off the record" or "just between us" – they will report every scrap of information they get from you!

In my humble opinion, everything about the "lie detector" is totally irrelevant, but the next category of control questions is even labeled as such. The irrelevant control questions are easily recognized because they are usually absurdly irrelevant. Some of the irrelevant control questions asked during the test may be:

Can you drive a car?
Do you smoke?
Is today Thursday?
Are you setting down?
Are the lights on in this room?

DO NOT REACT TO THE IRRELEVANT CONTROL QUESTIONS. IF THEY ARE THE ONLY CONTROL QUESTIONS BEING USED – DON'T REACT TO ANY OF THEM. IF THE POLYGRAPH OPERATOR IS USING BOTH KNOWN-LIE CONTROLS AND IRRELEVANT CONTROLS YOU ONLY REACT TO THE KNOWN-LIE CONTROLS.

The third category of control questions deal with the surprise stimulus or embarrassing personal questions. These are even more absurd than the irrelevant question, and may include some of the following: "What is the tenth letter in the alphabet?", or What does fourteen time three hundred sixty nine equal?" Some examiners may ask an embarrassing personal question, such as, "Did you masturbate this morning?" Others merely threaten by saying, "OK now Karen, I'm going to ask you a very personal and embarrassing question, in your entire life have you ever...?" The polygraph operator never finishes the question; he just records you reacting away in anticipation. Fortunately, only the worst of the verbal voyeurs in the polygraph profession still use this type of control question, so you shouldn't be confronted with it very often.

Here's an update regarding the questions on the LAPD's pre-employment polygraph examination. A recent applicant was asked the following questions (categorized here by type):

Relevant Questions:

Have you stolen more than $400 in cash or property from an employer?

Are you withholding information regarding your illegal drug history?

Are you withholding information regarding a serious undisclosed crime?

Have you physically harmed a significant other during a domestic dispute?

Regarding your background package, do you intend to answer each question truthfully?

Known-Lie Control questions:

Before applying with LAPD, did you ever cheat on a test?

Prior to applying with LAPD, did you ever tell a lie to someone who trusted you?

Prior to applying for this position, did you ever do anything that would cause anyone to question your integrity?

Before applying for this position, did you ever violate any official rules or regulations?

Prior to applying with LAPD, did you ever do anything bad in your life?

Irrelevant Questions:

Are you now sitting down?

Are you now in the State of California?

Before applying with LAPD, did you attend High School?

Is this the month of April?

Is this the year of 2009?

The (Polygraph) Test Phase

The polygrapher will put a blood pressure cuff around your arm, metal contact bars on your ring and index fingers, and pneumo-graph tubes around your chest and stomach. (See Exhibit C) The po-lygrapher tell you the test is about to begin, pump up the pressure in the cuff, and then he will usually ask about ten questions – seven or eight relevant and two or three controls. He will tell you to set up straight, keep your eyes open, (some may say to keep your eyes closed), remain still, and answer "yes" or "no" to each question. The polygrapher will ask the questions at intervals of about 15 to 20 seconds – and he will repeat the question series three times. In other words, he will ask you all the questions, stop and release the pressure in the cuff – then he will start again and ask you all the same questions again two or three more times.

You must learn how to manipulate and control every tracing on the chart during the polygraph test – both the breathing or pneumo tracing and the blood pressure or cardio tracing.

I WILL DESCRIBE HOW TO PHYSICALLY MANIPULATE ALL THE TRACINGS ON THE POLYGRAPH CHART, BUT AFTER MUCH TESTING IN MY PRIVATE POLYGRAPH PREPARTION TRAINING, I HAVE CHANGED MY TECHNIQUE, AND NOW RECOMMEND THAT YOU JUST USE THE MENTAL IMAGERY INSTEAD OF PHYSICALLY MANIPULATING THE REACTIONS. YOU WILL SEE ON THE ONLINE

VIDEO/DVD THAT THE MENTAL IMAGERY LOOKS MUCH MORE NORMAL AND NATURAL THAN THE PHYSICALLY MANPULATED REACTIONS.

Your breathing, or pneumo tracing, is recorded by the pneumograph tubes which are placed around your chest and stomach. (See exhibit C) When you inhale or breathe in, these tubes expand and the pneumo pens on the chart go up, when you exhale or breathe out, the tubes deflate and the pneumo pens go down.

The polygraph operator is constantly alert of a person who is controlling his breathing. (See Exhibit D) You will notice the difference between the normal and controlled breathing pattern. The controlled breather shows his attempt to control by consciously thinking of his breathing only to the point that he inhales and exhales, he breathes in and immediately breathes out, showing a jagged edged tracing. You should show a normal breathing pattern on all the questions except the control questions. I don't want you to be obvious about this, I simply want you to breathe the way you normally do - whatever is normal for you

After you answer the RELEVANT questions, your breathing should appear even and restful. You have a pattern for a normal breathing if you simply breathe as though you are asleep and you are not aware of your breathing – picture yourself on a beach watching the waves gently rolling into the shore – just relax. This normal breathing pattern is what the polygraph operator would expect to see from a cooperative, truthful person. Remember: (1) your breathing is recorded on the polygraph chart by the pneumo pens; (2) you must avoid a jagged edged breathing pattern, and (3) breathe as though you are breathing in a normal relaxed manner. The best way to do this is when you hear a relevant question, just think about the most relaxing thing you can imagine and picture yourself doing it. I don't want you to try to make your breathing look "normal" - I just want you to let it be normal. Just relax. Do not internalize the questions – don't think about what the polygrapher is asking. You are to listen to the questions only to determine whether they are relevant or control and if they are relevant, your only job is to keep your mind in a calm, relaxed state. This is just a game - relax and play your part.

After you answer a CONTROL question, you must show a breathing or pneumo reaction. Exhibit E shows the five common pneumo reactions. These are easily produced by simply using the mental imagery – thinking of something frightening – don't try to memorize these reactions just know that they will be produced by mental imagery as easily as trying to duplicate them. You don't have to be perfect – just show a slight change in your breathing pattern after you answer the control question – even a slight change looks big on the polygrapher's chart. PRACTICE until you can do it without being obvious – subtlety is the key! Study the explanation of the reactions shown in Exhibit E, watch the video/DVD, and practice until you can do it without making it obvious that you are manipulating the reaction.

Figure 1 depicts the most common reaction seen in the pneumo tracing. This reaction is manipulated by duplicating the pattern shown. Breathe by the numbers again. (1) Inhale about one-third the normal amount of air, hold slightly, and exhale slowly, showing no jagged edges, (2) inhale again, this time inhaling about two-thirds the normal amount of air, exhale slowly, (3) inhale and exhale the normal amount of air, (4) inhale again, this time inhaling just a little more air than normal, and exhale slowly. You now take two deep breaths, and resume your normal breathing pattern.

The pneumo reaction in figure 2 is manipulated by inhaling more than you exhale each time in a series of five small breaths until, with your last breath; you fill your lungs with slightly more than the normal amount of air, just like you are frightened and gasping for breath. You then take two deep breaths and resume normal breathing.

Figure 3 is too obvious so don't use it. It is true that it is the easiest, but it is also the least desirable.

Figure 4 illustrates still another pneumo reaction which is

manipulated by simply inhaling a normal amount of air and then taking a series of five to seven shallow breaths with your lungs partially full.

Figure 5 is a variation of 4 except that you take five to seven shallow breaths with your lungs almost empty.

That is all there is to controlling your pneumo tracing on the polygraph chart. It doesn't have to be perfect; you are basically just showing a departure from your normal breathing pattern after you answer a control question. You are showing the polygraph operator that the control questions bother you and the relevant questions don't.

NOTE: WHILE I HAVE EXPLAINED HOW TO PHYSICALLY MANIPULATE THE BREATHING, IT IS MUCH BETTER TO JUST USE THE MENTAL IMAGERY – THINK OF SOMETHING FRIGHTENING AND YOU WILL PRODUCE THIS VERY SAME BREATHING REACTION WITHOUT ANY PHYSICAL MANIPULATION AND IT WILL LOOK MUCH MORE NATURAL.

Now that you have mastered the manipulation and control of the pneumo tracing, believe it or not, you have mastered the most difficult part of the "Sting Technique". I told you the polygraph exam was a joke!

OK, so you can now manage to show a "normal" breathing pattern and a breathing "reaction", but what about your blood pressure? Please don't take drugs, they will only make you easier prey for a skilled interrogator, and don't put a tack in your shoe, you will only hurt your foot. Just beating the operator is not enough, you have to "sting" him - and remember, a sting is when you con a con man and he never knows he has been conned. If you are going to sting, you must use your stinger. Please turn to Exhibit F as we discuss a well-known phenomenon associated with your stinger or more correctly your anal sphincter muscle. The anal sphincter muscle is the ring-like muscle that surrounds the lower bowel opening. I became well acquainted with the phenomenon known as the "pucker factor" during my military and police careers. The pucker factor is simply a physiological reaction to fear. For example, every time a gun was fired at me, the pucker factor got very high, and anal sphincter started pinching holes in my underwear.

What happens if you are not really frightened, but you "pucker up" just like you do when you really are? Does it look like a blood pressure increase on the polygraph chart, or as polygraph operators say, a cardio reaction? Yes, if you tighten up your anal sphincter muscle, like you are trying to stop a bowel movement, you can cause a magnificent increase in the cardio tracing immediately. The anal sphincter muscle, when tightened or puckered up, causes a rise in the cardio tracing which leads the polygraph operator to believe you have had a really significant cardio reaction. The anal sphincter muscle when tightened or tensed, manipulates a rise in the cardio tracing that duplicates a cardio reaction. A cardio rise, or reaction, can be controlled by relaxing the tension. You simply tighten your anal sphincter muscle and the cardio pen goes up (manipulated reaction), or relax your anal sphincter and the cardio pen goes down (controlled reaction). This muscle is not only capable of manipulating and controlling the cardio tracing, it has the added advantage of being concealed from the polygraph operator.

CAUTION, a few years ago the polygraph industry came up with a "sensor pad" that you sit on while taking the test. I have this "motion sensor pad" attachment on my own computerized polygraph instrument - this is the polygraph instrument I use to train people when they come to me for personal polygraph test preparation training. It really doesn't detect anything, but often people overdo it with the anal sphincter and it looks too obvious. *That is why I now teach people to just use the mental imagery – think of something frightening and it will cause a subtle increase in blood pressure and pulse rate that is just as effective as the tightening of the anal sphincter muscle, AND IT IS MUCH MORE NATURAL LOOKING - see the mental imagery reactions on the online video or DVD.*

The GSR (Galvanic Skin Response), or sweat activity is relatively unimportant and will be both manipulated and controlled to some degree by the manipulation and control of the breathing and blood pressure. If you manipulate and control the pneumo and cardio tracings, the GSR will mirror these responses.

Timing is very important in the manipulation and control of your chart tracings; you must know when to show a manipulated reaction and when not to show a reaction. Your reaction should last about 7 to 9 seconds, and the cardio rise should peak at about 4 to 5 seconds. In other words when you are duplicating your pneumo reaction you should also duplicate a cardio rise by tightening your anal sphincter muscle gradually until you are about halfway through the breathing pattern and then gradually relax it so that the peak blood pressure increase is in the middle of the breathing pattern. You must do this after you have answered the control question. You are to react to the control questions, and your best bet is to mix up the pneumo reactions, using different ones each time.

All I am teaching you to do is to duplicate the physiological response to fear, but you must be able to do it on demand and at the appropriate time. When you are frightened you breathe in shallow, erratic, panting gasps, your anal sphincter muscle puckers up, your blood pressure increases, and you start to sweat. You will also show all these things on the chart when you think of something frightening.

This brings us to our primary method of manipulating reaction – the mental imagery reaction. This is the one I recommend most because it is foolproof and looks like a natural reaction on the polygraph chart. This reaction is manipulated by simply thinking about a math question such as, "What is 278 divided by 13?" Or you can count backwards from 700 by 3s. Most people think about the thing they fear the most or the most frightening thing that has ever happened to them - and they put that image in their mind after they answer the control questions. That frightening mental image causes a great reaction to the control question!

CAUTION!!! It is important that you fine-tune the "sting". The polygraph operator will usually ask the same questions over 2 or 3 times. And I want you to manipulate a reaction to the controls using only the mental reactions.

NOTE: I suggest using the mental imagery to cause a reaction to a control question on all the control questions because it works the best and all the polygrapher will see is a perfect natural reaction. I have given personal instruction to many people, and everyone has been able to manipulate a very good reaction to the controls by simply using the mental imagery. Most people think about the thing they fear the most or the most frightening thing that has ever happened to them - and they put that image in their mind after they answer the control questions. That frightening mental image causes a great reaction to the control question! And, of course, on the relevant questions, you simply concentrate on the most relaxing thing you can think of. As a matter of fact, the mental imagery works best, and it is absolutely natural.

IF YOU ARE NOT SURE IF A QUESTION IS RELEVANT OR CONTROL, DON'T REACT TO IT. IT IS BETTER TO REACT TO ALL THE CONTROLS - ESPECIALLY THE KNOWN-LIE CONTROLS BUT, AS LONG AS YOU REACT TO ONE OR TWO OF THE CONTROLS YOU ARE GOING TO BE IN GOOD SHAPE.

TIMING IS IMPORTANT! You must show both a breathing and blood pressure reaction simultaneously when you answer the CONTROL questions, and you must appear calm, relaxed, and breathing normally when you answer the RELEVANT questions.

When you are employing the Sting Technique, your polygraph examination is in fact your examination. Your interests alone dictate whether the questions are relevant or control. Always bear in mind that the purpose of the test is to elicit information from you. The purpose of the Sting Technique is to allow you to control the amount of information you give, and to teach you to manip-ulate and control your reactions so the polygraph will verify your truthfulness.

THE VSA, AND CVSA

The VSA, (VOICE STRESS ANALYZER), or the CVSA, (COMPUTER VOICE STRESS ANALYZER), as the name im-plies simply tries to detect deception by the tremor in your voice. It is even more of a joke than the polygraph. It is easily manipulated and controlled. They use the same type of rel-evant and control questions as the polygraph. You just answer the relevant questions in a monotone and you give your an-swer after you have INHALED a normal breath. In other words you answer the relevant question and then exhale. And when you answer the control questions you tighten the anal sphinc-ter muscle and answer the question after you have EXHALED your breath. In other words you answer the control questions after you have exhaled all your breath.

RELEVANT QUESTIONS - answer in MONOTONE AFTER YOU INHALE a normal breath. CONTROL QUESTIONS-tighten up your anal sphincter and answer after you have expelled all the air from your lungs. Don't be obvious about it - and spend some time practicing so you can do it right.

The "Post-Test" Interrogation

Your mastery of the Sting Technique is almost complete; the only area left unexplored is how to conduct yourself during the in-terrogation. Remember, the whole test is nothing but an interroga-tion. The sole purpose of the polygraph test is to get incriminating information from the subject. The polygraph operator is usually an expert interrogator, and, like most interrogators, he relies on his ability to con you or scare you. Do not allow him to do either, concentrate on what you are saying, and what you are doing. Stay alert, remember the polygraph is a joke, and the polygraph operator is playing a con game, a game you will win if you use the Sting Technique correctly. If the polygrapher suspects you of deception (and sometimes even if he doesn't), he will tell you the polygraph indicates deception and try to get some admissions from you. Interrogation techniques vary, but typically, the polygrapher will ask you to explain why you reacted to a certain question. Here are some examples of "tried and true" interrogation techniques.

These interrogation approach phrases are taken from are from the DoDPI "Interview and Interrogation"handbook

- They didn't bring me here to ignore my report. The test confirms that you haven't been completely truthful. Your situation will only get worse if we don't get this cleared up.
- The only thing that will help you now is to be completely truthful. When a person hides something or lies they usually regret it later on when the truth comes out... like it will in this situation.
- We've all been in situations when we withheld or told a lie about something that didn't seem too bad. But then, we had to tell another lie and another lie and another until the whole story fell apart.
- It is no longer an issue as to whether you did this or not. The only things left to discuss are why and how you got involved in this matter. In fact it is really an insult to my intelligence for you to tell me that you have been completely truthful here today.
- I promised that I would be honest with you here today [!] and you promised me the same thing. You and I both know that you haven't been truthful now. I could respect

you more if you just told me that you don't know how to deal with this... that you don't want to confess.

- If you were to show me a picture of someone close to you, I could never persuade you that it was someone else. These charts are like a picture of truth or deception and we can't change them no matter what we say.

- A lie is like a cancer inside of you that eats away at you and never goes away until it is taken out. Then the body can get well. Raymond J. Weir, Jr., former head of the NSA polygraph program and past president of the American Polygraph Association, has described a favorite NSA "post-test" interrogation approach (Weir, 1974): "We have a standard interrogation procedure where the examiner looks at the charts, looks at the subject, shakes his head, and says sadly, "I'd like to believe you, Mr. Jones. You do sound sincere to me. But how can I believe you, when you don't believe yourself? You can lie to me, and I don't know you well enough to tell. But you can't lie to yourself—and that's what I'm getting on these charts." (pp. 154-55) Veteran polygrapher Leonard H. Harrelson, president of the Keeler Polygraph Institute in Chicago since 1955, suggests this outrageous ploy in describing what he terms the "unexpected" or "shock" approach (Harrelson, 1998): ..."the imagination and the role-playing ability of the examiner is given free reign. This approach would include such tactics as suddenly shutting off the instrument in the middle of a test, removing the attachments from the subject and requesting that he get down on his knees to join you in praying for his soul and courage to tell the truth. This approach, if used with sincerity and conviction, can carry a tremendous psychological impact on certain subject types".

When a person is lying, they use many different body signals.

A liar is worried about being found out (unless they are psychopaths or good actors), they demonstrated this tension by sweating, sudden movements, minor twitches of muscles (especially around the mouth and eyes), changes in voice tone and speed.

Liars try to avoid detection by over-control. For example, there may be signs of attempted friendly body language, such as forced smiles (mouth smiles but eyes do not), jerky or clumsy movements. The person may also try to hold their body still, to avoid tell-tale signals. For example they may hold their arms in or put their hands in their pockets.

A liar has to think more about what they are doing, so they may drift off or pause as they think about what to say or hesitate during speech.

They may also be distracted by the need to cover up. Thus their natural timing may go astray and they may over- or under-react to events.

Anxiety may be displayed by actions such as fidgeting, looking around the place or paying attention to unusual places.

Deceptive people are worried about being detected - this may be seen in what they do:

Deceptive people:	Do these things:
... are tense because they are worried about being caught or are feeling guilty.	...speak in a high pitched voice ...hesitate. ...stutter. ...have jerky movements.
...can't remember.	...story is inconsistent. ...leave out irrelevant details. ...are vague, or leave out information about times, places and feelings.

...manufacture information.	...often hesitate so they have time to think about what to say. ...or they forget and have to take time to try to remember what they have said.
...don't want to answer the questions.	...cover their mouths. ... press lips together when difficult topics are mentioned.
...try to avoid answering some important questions.	...so they wander away or try to change the subject.
...try to confuse the interrogator.	... they try to give complex answers. ...question the minor details of the question.
...try to appear truthful by acting innocent.	...eyes wide open, with raised eyebrows. ...carefully enunciate speech. ... pout. ...start to cry.
...are worried about what might be asked.	...ramble on to try to use up time. ...try to get emotional to get you off the subject.
...are worried about making admissions that would incriminate them.	...choose their words carefully. ...pause before answering. ...give short answers.
...fear making eye contact because they feel it will give them away.	...avoid eye contact, turn their eyes or head down or away. ...glance away when they start to lie. ...blink and/or rub eyes.

...the fear being detected.	...so they try to say as little as possible.
	...try to get away from or change the subject.
	...repeat back your words with a denial.
	...make exaggerated statements about being truthful.
...use controlled language.	...try to be very precise. e.
	...generalize, using words like "always", "nobody", etc.).
	...do not use contractions (saying 'do not', vs. 'don't').
...try to control their body language.	...hold the body still and rigid.
	...smile with the mouth but not the eyes.
	...try to act innocent by using exaggerated movements.
...when they can't control their body language.	... eye pupil dilation.
	...briefly shrug and grimace
	...fidgeting movements with hands and feet.
...become nervous and speed up.	...talk faster.
	...blink more.
	...swallow more.
	...move faster.
...think they are threatened.	...attack, defend or deflect.
	...place barriers in front of them, from arms to books to tables.
...liars need time to think.	...stall, by repeating the question back to the interrogator
	...talk very slowly and deliberately.

...try to remain neutral and tell a story.	...they look up and/or up and right as if they are remembering and describe things as if they are looking at a picture.
...try to distance themselves from what is being asked.	...don't use "I" in their answers. ...say, "believe it or not" or "you probably won't believe this, but...". ...flatly deny any involvement at all.
...Start to sweat.	...their skin gets redder or damper. ... they rub their palms and head, or the neck and nose.

These things are important to keep in mind during your interview/interrogation so you don't give yourself away.

Always appear cooperative, act sincere, use plenty of eye contact, stay alert, concentrate on what you are doing, and never exhibit any hostility, arrogance, or fear, and you can counter any interrogation technique the examiner can throw at you. Just continue to maintain that you have told the complete truth. Volunteer to take the test again if that would help to prove your truthfulness. Now, if you can add one more finishing touch, it is to look the examiner in the eyes when you talk to him. If you can't do that, focus on the bridge of his nose, right between his eyes, it will have the same effect, which is to prove to him you are truthful. Do not tolerate physical violence, but do not confuse noise with violence. Hang in there unless he gets physical. The polygraph operator who is not well versed in the fine art of interrogation, (or those who have gone crackers from too much hog killin'), relies more on noise and threats than on intelligence, and may try to intimidate you with loud yelling, hostile accusations, and threatening gestures. He is easily manipulated, do not respond to him in the same manner, remain calm, appear cooperative, and act like you are confused by his anger. He will wear out and leave you alone if you refuse to respond. Stick to your story; let him rant and rave, while you think about cartoons or something pleasant. Remember that the entire polygraph examination must be manipulated and controlled if your sting is to be complete. That includes the pre-test interview, the test itself, and any post-test interrogation you may encounter.

Practice Examinations

Please practice before you go one-on-one against a professional! To successfully duplicate a "truthful" polygraph chart tracing, you must be prepared to deal with any polygraph technique you may encounter. The following are three practice examinations; each employing one of the three different techniques previously discussed. You will be told how to manipulate and control your reactions as we examine each of these tests. If you are prepared to handle these, you can handle any type of polygraph test, but please practice.

The first test is called a specific issue test. As the name implies it deals with a specific issue, such as theft, murder, rape, etc. You simply change the relevant questions to suit your situation. This one deals with a "leak" of information. Other specific issue tests are called by other names but they will have this same structure they are sometimes called CI-, or counterintelligence-scope polygraph examinations deal which with whether or not you have disclosed classified information to unauthorized persons, had unauthorized contacts with representatives of a foreign government, or been directed by someone to seek employment with a U.S. agency, or "lifestyle" polygraph examinations which deal with more than the subject matter of CI-scope polygraph examinations and will probably include questions about drug use, undetected felony crimes, and, in some cases, sexual conduct.

1. Do you live in the United States?
2. Is your name Harry Jones?

® 3. Do you know for sure who gave that information to the New York Times?

® 4. Did you give that information to the New York Times?

© 5. Besides what you've told me, have you ever stolen anything else?

® 6. Can you name the "informed sources" quoted by the New York Times?

® 7. Have you lied to me about leaking classified information?

® 8. Have you lied to me on any of these questions?

© 9. Besides what you've told me, have you ever lied to anyone else who trusted you?

® 10. Are you now concealing any information whatsoever about the leaks of classified material?

With questions one and two, (IF THE FIRST TWO QUESTIONS ARE THE SAME OR SIMILAR TO THOSE LISTED ABOVE, THEY ARE CALLED INTRODUCTORY QUESTIONS – YOU DO NOT MANIPULATE A REACTION TO INTRODUCTORY QUESTIONS), the polygraph operator is allowing you time to become accustomed to the sound of his voice, this gives you time to relax and just breathe calmly. Question three is your first relevant question. You should listen to the questions only to determine whether they are relevant or control, don't let the polygraph operator "psyche you out", remember this is just a game, and all you have to do is breathe normally. Question four is the most relevant question. Simply picture the most relaxing thing you can imagine in your mind and you will automatically produce normal breathing pattern on the polygraph chart.

REMEMBER, KNOWN-LIE CONTROL QUESTIONS ARE THE MOST COMMONLY USED, IF THE POLYGRAPH OPERATOR IS USING KNOWN-LIE CONTROL QUESTIONS YOU ONLY REACT TO THE KNOWN-LIE CONTROLS.

Question five and nine are your prime control questions. When you use the frightening image in your mind, the reaction will look just like Exhibit B.

The scenario for the second polygraph exam is as follows: You have applied for a job, one of the few that still are legally allowed to require polygraphs - most police and federal agencies still require a pre-employment exam.

1. Is your first name Janine?
2. Do you live in Dallas?
® 3. Did you tell the complete truth on you job application?
® 4. Have you ever been arrested?
® 5. Do you drink?
© 6. Besides what you've told me, have you ever stolen anything else?
® 7. Have you ever used or sold narcotic drugs?
® 8. Are you now concealing any information about your previous work record?
® 9. Are you behind on any of your bills?
® 10. Have you told me the complete truth about how much you owe?
© 11. Besides what you've told me, have you ever told any other lies?
® 12. Have you told me the complete truth about your physical condition?
® 13. Is there anything in your background that would disqualify you from getting this job?
© 14. Besides what you've told me, have you ever lied to get out of trouble?
® 15. Have you lied to me about what you have stolen from previous places of employment?
® 16. Is there anything in your personal life that might interfere with your employment?
® 17. Do you gamble?
® 18. Have you lied to me on any of these questions?
© 19. Are you absolutely trustworthy?
    REMEMBER, KNOWN-LIE CONTROL QUESTIONS ARE THE

MOST COMMONLY USED, IF THE POLYGRAPH OPERATOR IS USING KNOWN-LIE CONTROL QUESTIONS YOU ONLY REACT TO THE KNOWN-LIE CONTROLS.

NOTICE!!! SOME PRE-EMPLOYMENT TESTS NOW HAVE ONLY RELEVANT QUESTIONS WITH NO CONTROLS AT ALL; (But this is very unusual and most will have some sort of control question to which you can manipulate a reaction.)

1) Do you live in California?
2) Do you intend to lie on any of these questions?
3) Have you lied about your qualifications to do this job?
4) Have you lied about your driving record?
5) Have you lied about your criminal or arrest record?
6) Have you lied about your drug use?
7) Have you ever struck a significant other?
8) Have you ever stolen something from an employer?
9) Have you shoplifted anything since age 18?
10) Have you committed any sexual crimes?
11) Have you placed any false information on your application?
12) Have you omitted any information from your application?
13) Have you committed any serious crime?
14) Have you lied about your involvement in any alcohol related crimes?
15) Have you omitted anything that if discovered would prevent you from being hired by this department?
16) Have you lied on any question I have asked you?

IF YOU ENCOUNTER ONE OF THESE, YOU ARE TO SIMPLY BREATHE IN A CALM EVEN MANNER WHEN YOU ANSWER THESE QUESTIONS. (I have only heard of a few of these, and it is absurd that they do it but if they do, it is very simply, just relax and think of a relaxing image in your mind and you will have no problem).

A good way to practice your Sting Technique is to have a friend read the questions to you, or records them on a tape recorder, allowing an interval of about fifteen to twenty seconds between questions. You should answer the questions aloud with a yes or no, while at the same time manipulating or controlling your reactions to these questions. It is very important to spend as much time as is necessary to feel comfortable before you take the test. The more often you hear the questions, the less likely you are to react to them on the test. So get the tape recorder and get busy! PRACTICE MAKES PERFECT, SO PRACTICE!!!!!!!

The third practice test is a periodic polygraph examination. This Gestapo-type test is usually given every six months to employees "picked at random" from the work force.

1. Is your last name Jones?
2. Were you born in Oklahoma?
® 3. Can you name anyone in the company who is stealing?
® 4. Have you stolen anything from the company in the past six months?
© 5. Besides what you've told me, have you ever lied to a supervisor?
® 6. Have you violated any of the company's rules and regulations?
® 7. Are you working with anyone to steal from this company?
® 8. Have you devised a plan to steal from this company?
© 9. Besides what you've told me, did you ever lie to cover something up?
® 10. Do you use or sell drugs?
® 11. Have you ever used drugs or alcohol on company time?
® 12. Are you covering up for anyone who is stealing from this company?
© 13. Besides what you've told me, did you ever reveal anything told to you in confidence?
® 14. Have you lied to me on any of these questions?

You should have no difficulty recognizing these control questions! REMEMBER : IF THE FIRST TWO QUESTIONS ARE THE SAME OR SIMILAR TO THOSE LISTED ABOVE, THEY ARE CALLED INTRODUCTORY QUESTIONS – YOU DO NOT MANIPULATE A REACTION TO INTRODUCTORY QUESTIONS.

Remember to manipulate a reaction to the control questions, and show no reaction whatsoever to the relevant questions. The examiner will ask probably ask all of the questions over again 3 or 4 times, each time the questions may be in a different order.

REMEMBER, KNOWN-LIE CONTROL QUESTIONS ARE THE MOST COMMONLY USED, IF THE POLYGRAPH OPERATOR IS USING KNOWN-LIE CONTROL QUESTIONS YOU ONLY REACT TO THE KNOWN-LIE CONTROLS.

NOTE: I suggest using the mental imagery to cause a reaction to a control question on all the control questions because it works the best and all the polygrapher will see is a perfect natural reaction. I have given personal instruction to many people, and everyone has been able to manipulate a very good reaction to the controls by simply using the mental imagery. Most people think about the thing they fear the most or the most frightening thing that has ever happened to them - and they put that image in their mind after they answer the control questions. That frightening mental image causes a great reaction to the control question! And, of course, on the relevant questions, you simply concentrate on the most relaxing thing you can think of. As a matter of fact, the mental imagery works best, and it is absolutely natural.

Often, the polygraph operator will tell you not to answer the questions aloud but to remain silent, (some will ask you to nod or shake your head yes or no). You are to manipulate a reaction to the control questions and remain calm on the relevant questions just like you would if you were answering aloud.

Also he may ask you to deliberately lie on all the relevant questions - DO NOT manipulate a reaction to ANY of the questions when he tells you to do this - DO NOT react to the relevant questions or the control questions.

If you are not sure if a question is relevant or control - don't react to it! There will be at least one or two that you will recognize and that will be sufficient to pass the test. One more quick tip, the polygraph operator may ask you which question you remember out of them all, always say you remember the control question, because that indicates to him it troubles you the most. Never indicate by words or actions that the relevant questions caused you any trouble at all, and never ask him how you did on the test, just assume you have passed, thank him for his time and leave the room.

I have one more bit of instruction for you to remember. Often, especially in pre-employment tests, the polygraph operator will tell you that you had a problem with one or two questions. Usually your "problem" was with the drug questions. He will tell you to tell him what you are withholding or to go home and write it all down. He will schedule you for another test later that will concentrate on this issue. Don't panic!!! The sky is NOT falling. This is just another interrogation trick. Stick to your story and go back and do the "sting" on the next test.

The polygraph profession has accused me of having a myriad of sordid motives for writing this little manual, perhaps their anger stems from the fact that the only power they have is derived from the fear and ignorance of their victims. I only hope I have been successful in tipping the balance of power from the terrorists to the victims by telling some of the tricks of this terrible trade. I have done a great deal to outlaw the use of this insidious Orwellian instrument of torture in the private sector, but much more needs to be done. I look forward to the day when the polygraph test will just be a bad memory. As to my ex-colleagues' criticism, I would offer this thought for consideration. It would, after all, be the ultimate irony for a "lie detector" operator to object to the truth.

By the way, I have made polygraph operators so paranoid that they are now asking everyone they test whether they have looked at my website and read my manual, (some will even hold up their personal copy and show it to you to try to convince you they know all about me). The question about whether you have prepared for the test or are trying to beat it is often asked on the polygraph test itself! The mere fact that they accuse everyone proves they don't see anything but a truthful chart tracing - they are just fishing, trying to bluff you into making an admission. Don't admit anything, just stick to your story, keep telling the polygraph operator that you have told the truth, and tell him that if he needs to run another test to see that to go right ahead!

What a joke these guys are - over 100,000 people have used my technique to pass their polygraph tests and there are literally hundreds who use the "sting" technique daily and they haven't caught even one of them. The only ones they "catch" are those that use some of the other crap put out by guys whose only experience with the polygraph is that they once flunked a test.

One more reminder, PLEASE PRACTICE!!! That is the only way to be properly prepared and also the only way to overcome nervousness. Get your tape recorder, record the questions and practice answering aloud yes or no. Practice until you are able to show your normal breathing patterns on the relevant questions and your manipulated reaction on the control questions. The more you hear the questions, the less likely you are to have a reaction on the relevant questions and the more you practice your mental imagery the easier it gets. And before you answer the questions, label them in your mind as either relevant or control and then just think of the most relaxing thing you can imagine on the relevant and the most frightening thing you can imagine on the controls – that is the perfect way to produce a perfect chart. So PRACTICE, PRACTICE, PRACTICE!!!

If you have any questions at all about the "Sting" technique, call or e-mail me. I WILL get you ready and I WILL be your very own personal DRILL INSTRUCTOR. I want you to be prepared. I want you to succeed. I do require that you read the manual over again at least 4 times so that you have a thorough understanding of the information before you call or email me with any questions. You are wise to prepare yourself because just telling the truth is no guarantee of passing the test.

One last word of advice: It is up to you to make sure you are PROPERLY PREPARED! What does it mean to be PROPERLY PREPARED? It means you are able to do exactly what the manual and dvd tell you to do, and do it the right way! You must study the manual, you must practice, and you must do everything the manual and dvd tell you to do – nothing more and nothing less! As a matter of fact, it is entirely your responsibility and yours alone to make sure you are PROPERLY PREPARED. I can give you the information, but it is up to YOU to do it PROPERLY!!!

Review:
Remember, there are two types of questions on the polygraph test – RELEVANT & CONTROL

You are to listen to the questions only to determine what they are and what you are to do in response to them.

RELEVANT QUESTIONS – Answer them and just RELAX – think of the most relaxing place you have ever been and go there in your mind after you answer the relevant questions.

CONTROL QUESTIONS – Answer them and manipulate a reaction after your answer. And just do the mental imagery after you answer them. Think of the most frightening thing that has ever happened to you and relive that experience in your mind after you answer the control questions.

Review the KNOWN-LIE CONTROL QUESTIONS – and memorize them so you can recognize them immediately – they are the most commonly used control questions.

LABEL THE QUESTIONS IN YOUR MIND BEFORE YOU ANSWER THEM! LABEL THEM AS RELAVANT OR CONTROL AND DO THE APPROPRIATE MENTAL IMAGERY.

It really is that simple! And you will pass if you just follow these simple instructions!

DO YOU WANT TO BE ABSOLUTELY SURE YOU WILL PASS YOUR POLYGRAPH TEST?

In addition to his excellent manual and training video/ DVD, Doug Williams also offers personal polygraph test preparation training.

This unique, confidential training consists of;

1) Special training in an "enhanced mental imagery technique" developed by Doug Williams. A review of the material in the manual & training video/ DVD.
2) A comprehensive, realistic, practice polygraph test - with questions individually designed to match the test you are going to take. The test will be administered by Police Polygraph Expert Doug Williams - utilizing a state of the art Computerized Polygraph System. With this new digital computer controlled polygraph, you will be trained on the most up-to-date polygraph equipment available.
3) An evaluation of your test results, a critique of your performance, and instructions on how to improve your technique.

"I GUARANTEE YOU WILL PRODUCE A TRUTHFUL CHART BEFORE YOU LEAVE MY OFFICE!" Doug Williams

Administered in Doug Williams' Polygraph Test Preparation Training Room, Norman, OK. (Located in Norman, OK - 20 minutes from the Oklahoma City Airport) $1000

A $750 non-refundable retainer is required in advance - the

balance of $250 is due upon your arrival.

Administered at your location - $5000 plus expenses (first class airline tickets and hotel)

A $4000 non-refundable retainer is required in advance - the balance of $1000 is due upon my arrival at your location.

Here is an email I received recently:

Doug: I am writing to thank you for your personal instruction. I came to your office to prepare for my polygraph test, and wow, did I get prepared! You gave me three practice exams and I aced all three of them on your computerized polygraph instrument with the computer score showing NO DECEPTION INDICATED. Your skillful use of hypnosis in the "enhanced mental imagery" training was a stroke of genius, it really calmed me down and, as you promised, it made it impossible for me to fail my polygraph test. This test was very important to me, and thanks to you, I passed with no trouble at all. Thanks again.

If you need an expert witness to testify in a case involving the polygraph, contact Doug Williams. Fee - $5000 (in advance, non refundable) plus expenses (first class airline tickets & deluxe hotel)

405/226-4856 doug@polygraph.com

* PRE-EMPLOYMENT PRE-TEST QUESTIONS:

1. Is the above name your true legal name?
2. Have you ever used any other name?
3. How many times have you been married?
4. What us your true date of birth?
5. Do you have a legal right to work in this country?
6. Are you skilled or trained in any field in which you could make more money than this job pays?
7. If offered this position, will you accept it?
8. If you accept this position, will you stay with this agency for at least 2 years?
9. Have you had any conflicts with your family because you want this job?
10. Have you ever before been asked to take a polygraph examination?
11. Have you ever failed a polygraph examination?
12. Have you placed any false information on your employment application or personal history background forms?
13. Have you omitted any information requested on your employment application or personal background forms?

14. When you left high school did you receive a graduation diploma?
15. Have you completed a law enforcement academy?
16. Have you ever failed or dropped out of a law enforcement academy?
17. Would you have any reason to be concerned about an investigation into your past work record?
18. Were you ever fired from a job?
19. Were you ever asked to resign from a job?
20. Did you ever leave a job to avoid being fired?
21. Have you ever left a job without giving proper notice?
22. Have you ever been accused of misconduct at a place of employment?
23. Have you shown the true and complete reasons for leaving each of your previous jobs?
24. Did you ever leave any job with hard feelings toward the management or coworkers?
25. Do you think you could return to work for all your former employers?
26. In the past year, how many times have you been late to work?
27. Have you ever received a written or verbal reprimand?
28. In the past year, how many unauthorized days of work have you missed?
29. Have you ever worked at any law enforcement agency in any capacity?
30. Have you ever before applied at any law enforcement agency for any type of job?
31. Have you ever been rejected by any law enforcement agency for any type of job?
32. Were you turned down as unacceptable by the military or draft board?
33. Are you currently registered for the draft?
34. Have you ever served in any branch of the Armed Forces?

35. Would you have any reason to be concerned about an investigation into your arrest record?
36. As a juvenile or adult, have you ever been arrested?
37. Have you ever been held, detained, questioned, or taken into custody for any reason?
38. Have you ever had a warrant issued for your arrest?
39. Are you now wanted for any reason by any law enforcement agency?
40. Have you ever been a suspect in any criminal investigation?
41. Have you ever been charged with a crime?
42. Have you ever been present when anyone else committed a crime?
43. Other than minor traffic matters, have you ever been fined by a court?
44. Have you spent any time, either as a juvenile or an adult, locked up in a jail?
45. Have you ever falsified an income tax form?
46. Have you ever falsified an insurance claim?
47. Have you ever collected unemployment or welfare benefits when you were not entitled to it
48. Have you ever stolen a motor vehicle?
49. Have you ever shoplifted anything from a store?
50. Have you ever been sent to jail over anything involving a motor vehicle?
51. Have you ever deliberately damaged or destroyed any property or committed an act of malicious mischief?
52. Other than from an employer have you ever stolen anything?
53. Have you committed any serious undetected crime?
54. Have you ever made serious plans to commit: A. Burglary, B. Rape, C. Robbery, D. Murder, E. Arson, F. Theft
55. Have you within the past 5 years done anything at all that you could have been arrested for doing?

56. Would you have any reason to be concerned about an investigation into your moral background?
57. Have you committed any type of sexual crime?
58. Since you were 18 years old, have you thought about committing some type of sexual crime?
59. Have you ever paid for sex?
60. Have you ever received payment for sex?
61. Have you ever sexually molested a child?
62. Have you ever committed a sexual act in public or an act of indecent exposure?
63. Would you have any reason to be concerned about an investigation of any illegal drug use by you?
64. Have you ever smoked marijuana in your life?
65. Have you ever used: A. cocaine, B. LSD, C. PCP, D. Magic mushrooms, E. Hash, F. Meth, G. Uppers, H. Downers, I. Any illegal drugs?
66. Have you ever worked under the influence of illegal drugs?
67. Have you ever ingested a substance you thought was an illegal drug and then found out it wasn't?
68. Have you ever illegally misused or abused any prescription?
69. Of your own knowledge, do your present circle of friends and acquaintances use any type of illegal narcotics, pills or drugs?
70. Within the past 3 years, have you been in the presence of anyone else using illegal drugs?
71. Have you ever illegally purchased any type of narcotic, pill, or drug?
72. Have you ever sold any type of illegal narcotics, pill, or drug?
73. Have you ever cultivated marijuana?
74. Have you ever been involved in the manufacture of any drug?

75. Have you ever been the "middle man" for a drug deal?
76. Has anyone other than a medical person injected anything into your body?
77. Do you object to others using narcotics?
78. If employed as a peace officer, would you arrest a friend, if you came upon that friend using narcotics or any drugs?
79. Would you have any reason to be concerned about an investigation concerning your honesty?
80. Have you ever stolen any money from a place where you worked?
81. Have you ever borrowed money from an employer and not paid it back?
82. Have you ever embezzled any money from an employer?
83. Have you ever stolen any merchandise or property by false representation?
84. Have you ever taken any property that didn't belong to you from a place where you worked?
85. What is your total indebtedness?
86. Could you successfully manage your financial affairs on the salary this job offers?
87. Have you ever had a debt turned over to a collection agency?
88. Have you ever been late in paying rent?
89. Has your salary ever been garnished?
90. Have you ever had purchased goods repossessed?
91. Have you ever filed bankruptcy?
92. Have you ever avoided paying any lawful debt by moving away?
93. Have you ever been late paying your taxes?
94. Have you ever failed to support any child of yours?
95. Have you ever been late in making child support payments?
96. Have you ever been late in repaying a student loan?
97. Have you ever had a check "bounce"?

98. Have you ever borrowed money to gamble with?
99. Have you ever borrowed money to pay a gambling debt?
100. Do you feel you now have a problem with gambling?
101. Have you ever been the plaintiff or defendant in any civil court action?
102. Do you presently have any civil actions pending in court?
103. Have you had any judgments filed against you?
104. Have you ever been arrested or convicted for any alcohol related crimes?
105. Have you ever worked under the influence of alcohol in violation of company policy?
106. Would you have any reason to be concerned about an investigation into your driving habits?
107. How many traffic citations have you received in your life?
108. Have you ever had a ticket go to warrant?
109. Have you ever had a traffic citation that did not show on your DMV printout?
110. Have you ever been the driver in any traffic accident?
111. Has your driver's license ever been suspended or revoked?
112. Has your auto insurance been placed in the assigned risk pool?
113. Has your auto insurance ever been canceled for cause?
114. Do you now have auto insurance as required by the State?
115. Since being licensed to drive, has there ever been a time when you did not have insurance as required by law?
116. Have you ever caused anyone serious injury by your operation of a motor vehicle?
117. Have you ever caused the death of anyone by your operation of a motor vehicle?
118. Have you ever fled the scene of a hit and run accident?

119. Have you ever driven a motor vehicle while under the influence of: A) Some type of drug? B) Alcohol? C) Combination of above?
120. In the past month have you driven a motor vehicle while under the influence of A) Some type of drug? B) Alcohol C) Combination of above?
121. Have you ever been arrested for driving while under the influence of alcohol or drugs?
122. Would you have any reason to be concerned about an investigation into your personal background?
123. In the past year, have you been in any fight? If so, did you start it?
124. Have you ever struck or injured any person?
125. Have you ever struck someone you were living with?
126. Other than in warfare, have you ever caused serious injury to a human being?
127. Other than in warfare, have you ever been involved in a shooting, knifing or fight, where someone was killed or seriously injured?
128. Other than in warfare, have you ever used any weapon against someone?
129. Other than in warfare, have you ever caused the death of a human being?
130. If it became necessary in the course of your duties to take a human life, would you have any reluctance to do so because of religious or other beliefs?
131. Do you frequently lose your temper?
132. Are you afraid of physical combat?
133. Have you ever fired a firearm?
134. Are you afraid of firearms?
135. Have you ever applied for a permit to carry a concealed weapon?
136. If employed here, would you fear physical resistance by someone you might arrest?

137. Do you feel you can take orders from your superior officers without resentment?
138. Do you have any prejudices relating to race, religion, gender, national origin, or ethnic background?
139. Do you feel your prejudices might affect your ability to perform this job?
140. Have you ever maliciously burned any property?
141. Have you ever turned in a false fire alarm?
142. Have you ever made an obscene or threatening phone call?
143. Have you ever in your entire lifetime done anything at all that you are ashamed of?
144. Is there some undisclosed reason why you want to be a peace officer?
145. Do you know of any reason why you should not be hired by this department for the position you have applied?
146. Is there anything at all in your background that you have not been asked about that might eliminate you from consideration for this job if it were found out?
147. Can you say in complete honesty that you have answered each of these questions truthfully?

Legal Notice: Disclaimer –

The information in this manual is provided for informational purposes only, and is not intended to serve as a source of legal or professional advice. This manual contains the opinions of the author and it in no way guarantees that you will pass a polygraph examination – it is simply the author's opinion that what you have been taught to do here represents the author's best efforts at preparing you for your test. The author and publisher of this manual make no representation or warranties, (expressed or implied) with respect to its accuracy, applicability, fitness, merchantability or completeness. The author and publisher shall in no event be held liable for loss or other damages, including, but not limited to special, incidental or consequential damages.

CPSIA information can be obtained
at www.ICGtesting.com
Printed in the USA
BVHW032357140123
656344BV00004B/237